ABR-NAHRAIN
SUPPLEMENT 6

To Prof. Dr. J. HOFTIJZER
with esteem and affection
for his initiative and imagination

ABR-NAHRAIN
SUPPLEMENT SERIES

Volume 6

AN ANNUAL PUBLISHED BY THE
SCHOOL OF FINE ARTS
CLASSICAL STUDIES
AND ARCHAEOLOGY
UNIVERSITY OF MELBOURNE

SEMANTICS OF ANCIENT HEBREW

EDITED BY

T. MURAOKA

PEETERS
LOUVAIN
1998

ISBN 90-429-0592-1
D. 1998/0602/270

PRINTED IN BELGIUM

Orientaliste, Klein Dalenstraat 42, B-3020 Herent

CONTENTS

LEXICAL ENTRIES

FOREWORD

These are the first-fruits of an international, currently European, joint research project, Semantics of Ancient Hebrew Database (abbreviated SAHD). Though the ultimate aim of the project is to make the contents of its research efforts electronically available, it has been thought meaningful to present some of the results obtained so far in this traditional format and to seek some input and reaction from a wider circle of scholars and students for whom the project is intended.

As editor of the volume I am indebted to the co-workers of three centres who have done the basic research on the entries presented here: Dr Stefan Bindi of Florence, Dr James K. Aitken of Cambridge, and Dr Alison Salvesen of Oxford. The entries submitted by each of these three had been seen by the leader of their respective centre: Prof. I. Zatelli (Florence), Dr G.I. Davies (Cambridge), and Prof. H.G.M. Williamson (Oxford). Dr. P. Williams of Cambridge assisted in translating a manuscript submitted by Dr Bindi in Italian. All this intensive research would have been impossible without generous financial support provided by the Leverhulme Trust in respect of Dr Aitken and Dr Salvesen, the Jerusalem Trust and the Humanities Research Board of the British Academy in respect of Dr Williams. The Cambridge team is also grateful to their Faculty of Divinity's Centre for Advanced Religious and Theological Studies for the provision of facilities there.

We are grateful to Dr G. Bunnens, editor of *Abr-Nahrain*, who graciously agreed, as in the case of *Studies in Ancient Hebrew Semantics* (1995), to include this volume as another title in the supplement series of the annual. Thanks are also due to the publisher Peeters of Leuven and Dr Kristin de Troyer, an editor of Peeters, for their attention to some technical aspects involved.

10 April, 1998
Leiden

T. Muraoka
Chairman
Executive Committee of SAHD

INTRODUCTION

Semantics is an engaging scholarly discipline, for it is concerned at the deepest level with the meaning of words and phrases and thus with interpretation of a linguistic utterance, whether oral or written. In the case of an ancient language the discipline of semantics becomes an intellectually demanding pursuit because of the limited amount of preserved texts and the absence of native speakers. Furthermore, semantics is not a self-contained compartment of linguistic science, as phonetics or phonology can be. It often needs to itneract with, and draw upon, other branches of scholarship concerned with interpretation of linguistic message such as history, archaeology, theology, textual criticism, art, botany, zoology and many others as well as traditional, straight grammar with phonology, morphology, syntax. This is illustrated in some of the entries included in this volume.

The recent upsurge of interest in Biblical semantics and lexicography may partly stem from the general background as sketched above. In the case of Biblical Hebrew, in addition to old, but still much used dictionaries of BDB, Gesenius (17th ed.), Zorell, we have witnessed completion of Koehler-Baumgartner's third edition as *Hebräisches und aramäisches Lexikon zum Alten Testament*, 6 vols. (1996) and Alonso Schoekel's *Diccionario bíblico hebreo-español* (1994). In addition, there are four on-going dictionary projects: the historical dictionary being prepared by the Academy of the Hebrew Language, the 18th edition of Gesenius, *The Dictionary of Classical Hebrew* (ed. D.J.A. Clines) of Sheffield Academic Press, with a borader corpus and a lexicographical approach of its own,[1] and an English translation, with occasional revision, by M.E.J. Richardson of *HAL*.

Whereas the Sheffield project is a storehouse of raw data which one may make use of in order to undertake one's own lexicographical, semantic research, all the remaining conventional bilingual dictionaries present translation equivalents with varying degrees of lexicographical data such as data on syntagmatics and paradigmatics of Hebrew lexemes. *HAL* also provides the most extensive up-to-date bibliographical information, though the earlier volumes are getting fast outdated in this regard. Obviously all these dictionaries are based on a critical assessment of past Hebrew lexicographical works. Dictionaries, however, by their nature, do not offer a forum for presenting arguments and reasonings lyhing behind the results offered in the form of translation equivalents. The need for such information is met to a certain extent by two existing theological dictionaries, namely *Theologisches Handwörterbuch zum Alten Testament* ed. by Jenni and virtually complete *Theologisches Wörterbuch zum Alten Testament* by Botterweck, Ringgren, and Fabry. In spite of their widely acknowledged

---

[1] See a review article by T. Muraoka, "A new dictionary of Classical Hebrew," in T. Muraoka (ed.), *Studies in Ancient Hebrew Semantics* [*Abr-Nahrain* Supplement Series, 4] (Leuven: Peeters, 1995), pp. 87-101.

value they have a couple of important limitations. Firstly, their orientation is, as already apparent from their respective title, theological by design. Thus lexemes which have no theological import or significance are excluded. Secondly, their scope is confined to the Hebrew Bible. Whereas the first limitation may be justifiable, the second is problematic in that the vocabulary of the Hebrew Bible is investigated in blessed isolation, when vigorous efforts have been made, and are still being made, to place the Jewish Bible in its wider Near Eastern context in terms of archaeology, literature, religion, history, technology, and even comparative Semitic linguistics! This is a truly remarkable situation. According to the Sheffield dictionary, non-biblical Hebrew texts as percentage of all Classical Hebrew texts amount to 13.6%, which is hardly a negligible figure.[2] Even leaving the obvious political aspect out of consideration, this specialisation is hardly justifiable. Even if one's principal concern is with the Hebrew Bible, one cannot possibly turn a blind eye to contemporary literary remains in basically same langauge. With our steadily improving understanding of the Hebrew of the early post-biblical period, say up to Qumran Hebrew, we cannot be content in this respect with studying early epigraphic materials. The Hebrew of Ben Sira, epigraphic materials up to the mid second century C.E. and, last but by no means last, Qumran Hebrew or Hebrew of documents emanating from Qumran and its environs, must be regarded as testifying to the use of Hebrew as a linving language, albeit not uniform in every respect. In this respect, the broadening of the text corpus as in the Sheffield dictionary is fully justified. To go for the mid second century C.E. as a cut-off point as against the design and scope adopted by Ben Yehuda, the Historical Dictionary of the Hebrew Language Academy, Even Shoshan and Kenaani is defendable for more than one reason.

The inability or difficulty in critically and independently assessing and evaluating arguments which resulted in translation equivalents proposed and presented in current (Biblical) Hebrew lexica was one important consideration which originally led to the formation of a group of Hebraists cum Old Testament scholars around my predecessor at Leiden, J. Hoftijzer, who helped to lay the foundation for our SAHD project.[3] Following a phase of exploration headed by Hoftijzer and funded by the European Science Foundation, the project got off the ground in early 1995. Currently five centres are actively taking part in this joint effort. Each centre has selected a group of semantically related lexemes to investigate. Below is a list of those five centres with the name of their leader(s) and chosen field(s) of lexemes:

Cambridge: G.I. Davies—roads and ways, cursing, particles, weapons
Florence: I. Zatelli—purity, knowledge, justice
Leuven: Schoors and Vervenne—covenant
Oxford: H.G.M. Williamson—kingship and royal appurtenances

---

[2] D.J.A. Clines, *The Dictionary of Classical Hebrew*, vol. I א (Sheffield: Sheffield Academic Press, 1993), p. 28. This figure does not take into acocunt texts published since around 1990.

[3] For a prehistory of the project, see J. Hoftijzer, "The history of the data-base project," in T. Muraoka (ed.), op. cit. [n. 1 above], pp. 65-85.

Rome: Amadasi Guzzo—metal, domestic animals, fragrant plants

The project is being directed by an executive committee (with the present editor as chair) and advisory committee. Dr David Reimer of Edinburgh serves as the secretary of both committees. It is hoped that more centres will join hands, not only in Europe, but also outside of it. Participation by individuals is also an option available. Given the nature of the project and the size of the vocabulary of the chosen corpus and the inherent difficulties it is highly desirable to have more centres participating in it. Moreover, it is also our intention to maintain this project as an on-going one with its database being updated at regular intervals.

By studying the ensuing entries selected for this volume the discerning reader would be able to gain a pretty good idea of the nature and scope of the project. It may, however, be found helpful to present a brief overview of the structure of entries and the general considerations lying behind it.

The project is first and foremost a bibliographical survey of lexicographical and semantic studies published on Ancient Hebrew since around 1950. Items published prior to 1950 may also be taken into account when they are made to play a significant role in publications thereafter. We do not, however, intend to produce a mere bibliographical listing, even an annotated bibliography, but rather to go through publications as systematically as practicable, critically to assess and evaluate views expressed, arguments advanced and conclusions arrived at, and to suggest, as appropriate, gaps in the current research and point to possible new ways of looking at the data. Individual coworkers have an option of undertaking a certain amount of independent research as appropriate.

The structure of entry is standardised and uniform. It has seven sections:

1. Root and comparative material
2. Formal characteristics
3. Syntagmatics[4]
4. Versions
5. Lexical/semantic fields
6. Exegesis
7. Conclusions.

Each entry is prefaced by a sub-section called "Introduction" where the grammatical category of the lexeme in question—noun, verb, gender etc.—is indicated, the number of occurrences per corpus—Old Testament, inscriptions, Ben Sira and Qumran documents—is given, and textually doubtful cases, including Qere/Ketiv, are mentioned.

At this point we would mention the parameter of functional languages, on the importance of which for our project a member of our group, I. Zatelli, presented her conviction a couple of times.[5] The group has yet to decide how to integrate this aspect into its work.

---

[4] The aspect of paradigmatics is subsumed under Semantic/lexical fields.

[5] See for the time being I. Zatelli, "Functional languages and their importance for the semantics of Ancient Hebrew," in T. Muraoka (ed.), op. cit. [n. 1 above], pp. 55-64.

Within each section results of our assessment and our own independent research are presented in the form of a series of numbered subsections, each subsection dealing with one aspect. We further make a distinction between views we positively evaluate and those which we consider implausible or rather unlikely. The former are presented as **A.1**, **A.2** etc., and the latter as **B.1**, **B.2** etc.

As regards the text editions used for the database, the Old Testament is that of BHS, whereas for old inscriptions H. Donner and W. Röllig's *KAI*, Davies, *Ancient Hebrew Inscriptions: Corpus and Concordance* (Cambridge, 1991) and J. Renz - W. Röllig, *Handbuch der althebräischen Epigraphik* (1995-) have been used. For the book of Ben Sira we have used the edition put out by the Academy of the Hebrew Language (1973) and a recent edition by P.C. Beentjes (1997). For the Dead Sea Scrolls the ongoing DJD series has been used. All these standard editions have been supplemented, as appropriate, by editions of individual texts or studies on them. For the ancient versions, see below under ABBREVIATIONS.

The bibliography appended to each entry lists all authors mentioned in the body of the article. Select standard reference works such as dictionaries, grammars, bible dictionaries are mentioned without the year of their publication, as full bibliographical details are given under ABBREVIATIONS.

Whereas the format of entry as described is stnadardised and uniform, coworkers are allowed to exercise a certain amount of freedom in the way certain aspects are accorded particular attention.

Coworkers are further encouraged, and even required, to consult specialists when they feel they are on unsure ground. The phrase "personal communication" occurring in a couple of entries in the present volume attest to such consultation.

T. Muraoka

ABBREVIATIONS

Abbreviations Used in the Body of Entries

abs	absolute
adj	adjective
AH	Ancient Hebrew
AHw	von Soden, W. *Akkadisches Handwörterbuch*. (Wiesbaden, 1965-81).
Akk	Akkadian
Alonso Schoekel	Schoekel, Luis Alonso. *Diccionario Bíblico Hebreo-Español*. Valencia, 1990-93.
ANEP	Pritchard, J.B. *The Ancient Near East in Pictures Relating to the Old Testament* (Princeton, ²1969).
ANET	Pritchard, J.B. (ed.), *Ancient Near Eastern Texts Relating to the Old Testament* (Princeton, ³1969).
Aq	Aquila
Arb	Arabic
Arm	Aramaic
Bab	Babylonian
BCE	before the Common Era (= B.C.)
BDB	Brown, F., S.R. Driver & C.A. Briggs. *A Hebrew and English Lexicon of the Old Testament with an Appendix Containing the Biblical Aramaic based on the Lexicon of William Gesenius as translated by E. Robinson* (Oxford, 1907).
BH	Biblical Hebrew
BHS	Biblia Hebraica Stuttgartensia
BibArm	Biblical Aramaic
BL	Bauer, H. and Leander, P. *Historische Grammatik der hebräischen Sprache des Alten Testamentes*. (Halle, 1922). {287 p = page 287, subparagraph p.}
BRL	Galling, K. *Biblisches Reallexikon* (Tübingen, ²1977).
Brockelmann	Brockelmann, C. *Lexicon Syriacum* (Halle, ²1928).
CAD	*The Assyrian Dictionary of the Oriental Institute of the University of Chicago*. (Chicago: 1956-).
Can	Canaanite
CE	the Common Era (= A.D.)
CIS	*Corpus Inscriptionum Semiticarum* (Paris, 1881-).
Clines	Clines, D.J.A. (ed.). *The Dictionary of Classical Hebrew* (Sheffield, 1993-).
Cohen	Cohen, D., F. Bron, and A. Lonnet, *Dictionnaire des racines sémitiques ou attestées dans les langues sémitiques. Comprenant un fichier comparatif de Jean Cantineau* (Paris, The Hague, and Leuven, 1970-).

Copt	Coptic
CPA	Christian Palestinian Aramaic
cstr	construct (state)
CT	Cuneiform Texts Babylonian Tablets in the British Museum
Dem	Demotic
DJD	Discoveries in the Judaean Desert (Oxford, 1955-).
DLU	Del Olmo Lete, G. and J. Sanmartín, *Diccionario de la lengua ugarítica* (Barcelona, 1996-).
DNWSI	Hoftijzer, J. and Jongeling, K. *Dictionary of North-West Semitic Inscriptions*. 2 vols. (Leiden, 1995).
EBH	Early Biblical Hebrew
Eg	Egyptian
EgArm	Egyptian Aramaic
Ep	epigraphic materials
ESArab	Epigraphic South Arabian
ET	English translation
Eth	Ethiopic
f	feminine
Ges.	Gesenius, W. *Wilhelm Gesenius' Hebräisches und Aramäisches Handwörterbuch über das Alte Testament in Verbindung mit H. Zimmern, W.Max Müller und O. Weber, bearbeitet von F. Buhl*. Leipzig, [17]1915.
Ges.-18	Gesenius, W. *Hebräisches und Aramäisches Handwörterbuch über das Alte Testament. Unter verantwortlicher Mitarbeit von Dr Udo Rüterswörden bearbeitet und herausgegeben von D. Rudolf Meyer und Dr.Dr. H. Donner* (Berlin, Heidelberg, New York, London, Paris and Tokyo, [18]1987-).
GK	Gesenius, W. and Kautzsch, E. *Gesenius' Hebrew Grammar as Edited and Enlarged by the Late E. Kautzsch. Second English Edition revised in Accordance with the Twenty-Eighth German Edition (1909) by A.E. Cowley* (Oxford, [2]1910).
Gr	Greek
HAL	Koehler, L., W. Baumgartner, B. Hartmann, E.Y. Kutscher, P.H. Reymond, J.J. Stamm, Z.B. Hiayyim, *Hebräisches und Aramäisches Lexikon zum Alten Testament*. 5 vols. (Leiden, [3]1967-95).
Hatr	Hatran
Heb	Hebrew
ImpArm	Imperial Aramaic
impv	imperative
inf	infinitive
inscr	inscription
JArm	Jewish Aramaic
Jastrow	Jastrow, M.M. *A Dictionary of the Targumim, the Talmud Babli and Yerushalmi, and the Midrashic Literature* (New

	York, 1886-1903).
JM	Joüon, P. and Muraoka, T. *A Grammar of Biblical Hebrew*. 2 vols. Rome, 1991 [corrected ed., 1993]. { § 113 *p*}
KAI	Donner, H. and W. Röllig, *Kanaanäische und aramäische Inschriften* (Wiesbaden, vol. I [3]1971, vol. II, [2]1968, vol. III, [2]1969).
KB[2]	Koehler, L. and W. Baumgartner, *Lexicon in veteris testamenti libros* (Leiden, [2]1958).
KTU[2]	Dietrich, M., O. Loretz and J. Sanmartín, *The Cuneiform Alphabetic Texts from Ugarit, Ras Ibn Hani and Other Places* (Münster, [2]1995).
LBH	Late Biblical Hebrew
LSJ	Liddell, H.G., R. Scott and H.S. Jones, *A Greek-English Lexicon* (Oxford, [9]1940) with a Supplement by E.A. Barber (Oxford, 1968) and by P. Glare (Oxford, 1996).
Luc	Lucianic
LXX	Septuagint (Göttingen ed. and ed. Rahlfs)
m	masculine
Mand	Mandaic
Mg	Margin
MT	Massoretic Text
n	noun; note
NEB	New English Bible
Nf	Targum Neophyti
NJB	New Jerusalem Bible
NRSV	New Revised Standard Version
NWSem	Northwest Semitic
OAkk	Old Akkadian
OArm	Old Aramaic
OAss	Old Assyrian
OBab	Old Babylonian
obj	object
OT	Old Testament
p	(grammatical) person
pass	passive
Payne Smith	Payne Smith, R. *Thesaurus syriacus* (Oxford, 1901).
Pers	Persian
Pesh	Peshitta (Leiden, 1966-, Urmia and Mossul editions)
Ph	Phoenician
pl	plural
PN	personal name
pred	predicate
ptc	participle
PS	Proto-Semitic
Pun	Punic
Q	Qumran
Qum	Qumran

RH	Rabbinic Hebrew
RV	Revised Version
s	singular
SaArm	Samaritan Aramaic
Sab	Sabaean
SAHD	Semantics of Ancient Hebrew Database
Sam	Samaritan
SArb	South Arabian
Sem	Semitic
sg	singular
Socr	Socotori
Sokoloff	Sokoloff, M. *A Dictionary of Jewish Palestinian Aramaic of the Byzantine Period* (Ramat Gan, 1990).
st	status, state
STT	Sultanteppe Tablets
subj	subject
suf	suffix
Sum	Sumerian
Syh	Syrohexapla
Sym	Symmachus
Syr	Syriac
Tg	Targum
TgFrg	Fragment Targum (ed. M. Klein [Rome, 1980])
TgNeo	Targum Neophyti (ed. A. Díez Macho [Madrid-Barcelona, 1968-79])
TgO	Targum Onkelos (ed. A. Sperber [Leiden, 1959])
TgPsJ	Targum Pseudo-Jonathan (ed. E.G. Clarke [Hoboken, NJ, 1984])
Thd	Theodotion
Ug	Ugaritic
UT	Gordon, C.H. *Ugaritic Textbook*. Rome, 1965. {Refer to a lexeme number in Glossary}
v	verse
var	variant
vb	verb
Vg	Vulgate (ed. R. Weber [Stuttgart, [2]1975)
Zorell	Zorell, F. *Lexicon hebraicum et aramaicum veteris testamenti* (Rome, 1968).

ABBREVIATIONS USED IN BIBLIOGRAPHY

PERIODICALS

AbrN	*Abr-Nahrain*
AfO	*Archiv für Orientforschung*
AION	*Annali dell'Istituto Orientale di Napoli*
AJBI	*Annual of the Japanese Biblical Institute*
AJSL	*American Journal of Semitic Languages and Literatures*
AMI	*Archäeologische Mitteilungen aus Iran*
ArOr	*Archiv Orientální*
ASTI	*Annual of the Swedish Theological Institute in Jerusalem*
AusBR	*Australian Biblical Review*
BASOR	*Bulletin of the American Schools of Oriental Research*
Beit Mikra.	
Bib	*Biblica*
BN	*Biblische Notizen*
BO	*Bibliotheca orientalis*
BSOAS	*Bulletin of the School of Oriental and African Studies, London University*
BZ	*Biblische Zeitschrift*
CBQ	*Catholic Biblical Quarterly*
DSD	*Dead Sea Discoveries.* Leiden
ErIs	*Eretz-Israel*
EstBíb	*Estudios bíblicos*
ETL	*Ephemerides Theologicae Lovanienses*
HAR	*Hebrew Annual Review*
Hen	*Henoch*
HS	*Hebrew Studies*
HTR	*Harvard Theological Review*
HUCA	*Hebrew Union College Annual*
IEJ	*Israel Exploration Journal*
Int	*Interpretation*
JANES	*J. of the Ancient Near Eastern Society. Columbia U. and Jewish Theol. Seminary*
JAOS	*J. of the American Oriental Society*
JBL	*J. of Biblical Literature*
JCS	*J. of Cuneiform Studies*
JJS	*J. of Jewish Studies*
JNES	*J. of Near Eastern Studies*
JNWSL	*J. of Northwest Semitic Languages*
JPOS	*J. of the Palestine Oriental Society*
JQR	*Jewish Quarterly Review*
JS	*Journal for Semitics, Tydskrif vir Semitistiek*
JSS	*J. of Semitic Studies*
JSOT	*J. for the Study of the Old Testament*
JSJ	*J. for the Study of Judaism*
JTS	*J. of Theological Studies*

Leš	*Lešonénu*
Ma	*Maarav*
OLZ	*Orientalistische Literaturzeitung*
Or	*Orientalia*
OrAnt	*Oriens Antiquus*
OTS	*Oudtestamentische Studiën*
PEQ	*Palestine Exploration Quarterly*
RB	*Revie Biblique*
RBI	*Rivista Biblical Italiana*
ReQ	*Revue de Qumran*
RevSém	*Revue sémitique*
RSO	*Rivista degli Studi Orientali*
Sef	*Sefarad*
Sem	*Semitica*
SJOT	*Scandinavian Journal of the Old Testament*
ST	*Studia Theologica*
StOr	*Studia Orientalia*, Helsinki
Tarbiz	
TB	*Tyndale Bulletin*
Text	*Textus*
TLZ	*Theologische Literaturzeitung*
TQ	*Theologische Quartalschrift*
TRu	*Theologische Rundschau*
TS	*Theological Studies*
TZ	*Theologische Zeitschrift*
UF	*Ugarit-Forschungen*
VD	*Verbum Domini*
VT	*Vetus Testamentum*
WO	*Die Welt des Orients*
WZKM	*Wiener Z. für die Kunde des Morgenlandes*
ZA	*Z. für Assyriologie und vorderasiatische Archäologie*
ZAH	*Z. für Althebraistik*
ZAW	*Z. für alttestamentliche Wissenschaft*
ZDMG	*Z. der deutschen morgenländischen Gesellschaft*
ZDPV	*Z. des deutschen Palästina-Vereins*
ZK	*Z. für Kirche*

COMMENTARIES AND OTHER SERIAL OR MULTI-VOLUME PUBLICATIONS

AB	Anchor Bible
ABD	Freedman, D.N. (ed.), *The Anchor Bible Dictionary* (Garden City, NY, 1992).
AnAcScFen	Annales Academiae Scientiarum Fennicae
AOAT	Alter Orient und Altes Testament
ATD	Alt Testament Deutsch

BHH	Reicke, B. and L. Rost (eds), *Biblisch-historisches Handwörterbuch* (Göttingen, 1962-79)
BK	Biblischer Kommentar
*BRL*²	Galling, K. (ed.), *Biblisches Reallexicon* (Tübingen, 1977).
BZAW	Beihefte zur Zeitschrift zum Alten Testament
CAT	Commentaire de l'Ancien Testament
CBC	Cambridge Bible Commentary
CBOT	Coniectanea biblica. Old Testament series.
DJD	Discoveries in the Judaean Desert (Oxford, 1955-).
EHAT	Exegetisches Handbuch zum Alten Testament
EM	Sukenik, E.L. et al. (eds), *Encyclopaedia Biblica* (אנציקלפדיה מקראית) (Jerusalem, 1965-82)
Herm	Hermeneia
HzAT	Handbuch zum Alten Testament
ICC	International Critical Commentary
IDB	Buttrick, G.A. (ed.), *Interpreter's Dictionary of the Bible* (Abingdon, 1962-76).
JSOTSS	Journal for the Study of the Old Testament Supplement Series
KAT	Kommentar zum Alten Testament
KHC	Kurzer Handkommentar zum Alten Testament
NCBC	New Century Bible Commentary
NTC	New Torah Commentary
OBO	Orbis Biblicus et Orientalis
OTL	Old Testament Library
OTS	Oudtestamentische Studiën
SANT	Studien zum Alten und Neuen Testament
SBLSCS	Society of Biblical Literature. Septuagint and Cognate Studies
SBLDS	Society of Biblical Literature. Dissertation Series.
TBü	Theologische Bücherei
THAT	Jenni, E. and C. Westermann (eds) , *Theologisches Handwörterbuch zum Alten Testament* (München-Zürich, ²1975-76)
TWAT	Botterweck, G.J., H. Ringgren, and H.-J. Fabry (eds), *Theologisches Wörterbuch zum Alten Testament* (Stuttgart-Berlin-Köln-Mainz, 1970-)
TWNT	Kittel, G. and G. Friedrich (eds), *Theologisches Wörterbuch zum Neuen Testament* (Stuttgart, 1933-54).
VTS	Vetus Testamentum Supplement
WBC	Word Biblical Commentary
WMANT	Wissenschaftliche Monographien zum Alten und Neuen Testament
WUNT	Wissenschaftliche Untersuchungen zum Neuen Testament

LEXICAL ENTRIES

בְּרִיאָה

Introduction
Grammatical Type: n f.
Occurrences: Total 1x OT, 1x Sir, 14x Qum, 0x inscr.

Text Doubtful:
A.1 4Q382 105.7 presents the form בריה with the addition of a supralinear
א as a scribal correction. The state of the text does not allow us to exclude the
possibility that in fact this is an occurrence of the term בריה 'fat' which has
suffered hypercorrection (cf. DJD XIII:402). The same orthography occurs in
4Q216 v 1, although here the text permits the identification of our lexeme. In
6QD i 3 the extremely uncertain text is reconstructed under the guidance of CD
iv 21, and therefore the two occurrences are identical.

B.1 [nil]
Qere/Ketiv: none.

1. Root and Comparative Material
A.1 בריאה is derived from the root ברא (I labial, II liquid, III laryngeal)
from which the verb בָּרָא 'create' derives (BDB:135, Ges.:156, Ges.-18:150,
HAL 146-47). The term is formed as a deverbal noun. The lexeme is not
attested in the most ancient Semitic languages, but occurs in SaArm (*birya*),
JAram (*bryʾ*), RH (*bryh*), with the meanings "creature" or "creation" (cf. BDB,
Ges., Ges.-18, *HAL* loc. cit.; Foerster 1933:1015).

B.1 According to Humbert (1958:147) the term בריאה in Nu 16.30 is to be
connected with the root ברא with the meaning "cut". The author presents two
arguments in support of this thesis: 1) the fact that the source J, to which the
verse seems to belong, does not know ברא in the meaning "create"; 2) the
parallelism of the verb ברא in Nu 16.30 with the verb בקע 'open up' of v. 31.
However, Humbert refrains from advancing any convincing proposal for the
translation of the syntagm בריאה יברא in v. 30.

2. Formal Characteristics
A.1 *qati:l-h* form.
This is a noun of a verbal noun pattern quite common in RH (Barth
1894:137; Segal § 228). Spelling variation between forms of the etymological
בריאה and the secondary בריה is also widely attested in RH (Segal § 58). Cf. also
Kutscher 1974:515 and Qimron 1986:26.

B.1 [nil]

3. Syntagmatics

A.1 The lexeme, in its occurrence in Nu 16.30, fulfils the function of internal object of the verb ברא in the conditional clause: וְאִם־בְּרִיאָה יִבְרָא יהוה. As in all its other occurrences, the verb ברא 'create' indicates here too an action of which the subject is YHWH. Schmidt (1971:337), who translates the formula בְּרִיאָה בָרָא as "Neues, Wundervolles bewirken", defines the syntagm as a "blassere Wendung", foreign to the vocabulary of the Yahwist, and probably the result of a later redactional insertion. The lack of further attestations of the syntagm allows neither confirmation of this hypothesis, nor, still less, the exclusion of the possibility that this is a sign of an individual linguistic rule which, capable of playing with the opportunities offered in the system, coins, on the basis of the verb, a substantive to which to transfer part of the semantic content of the verb itself. Since ברא 'create' always expresses the exclusive action of God, the substantive that is derived from it (בריאה), when used as its internal object, cannot but express the result of this action with all the exclusive characteristics that belong to the verb.

A.2 In Sir 16.16 the lexeme fulfils the function of a dative, governed by the preposition ל, within the syntagm: רחמיו יראו לכל בריותיו "his mercies are revealed to all his creatures". The 3psm suf ו refers to YHWH, the subject of the action.

A.3 In 4Q216 v 1 הבריה is a nomen rectum in the genitive phrase כל דב]רי הבריה. The syntagm is the object of the restored verb כתב 'write'. It is the beginning of a direct discourse in which the angel of the Presence commands Moses to write "the entire account of the creation". There follows a lengthy quotation from Gn 1.

A.4 In 4Q216 v 9 בריותו is a nomen rectum in the genitive phrase רוחות בריותו. This syntagm is followed by two restored relative clauses: [אשר עשה בשמים ואשר עשה בארץ] and is object of the restored verb ברא 'create' (line 4). The 3psm suf refers to YHWH.

A.5 In 4Q217 ii 2 הבריאה takes מן in the temporal sense, *terminus a quo*: לכל שני העולם מן הבריאה. The state of the text does not permit a deeper analysis.

A.6 In 4Q225 i 7 הבריאה עד יום הבריאה the state of the text only allows us to recognize the function of nomen rectum of the lexeme in the עד-phrase cited above. In DJD XIII (145) the hypothesis is advanced that the adjective חדשה 'new' should be added after הבריאה (second time).

A.7 In 4Q253 ii 3 the lexeme is preceded by the preposition מן. The state of the text does not allow further analysis.

A.8 In 4Q504 1-2 vii 9, according to the reconstruction proposed in DJD VII (150), the lexeme, with the suf ו, referring to YHWH and preceded by כול, is the subject (vocative) of the verb ברך 'bless'.

A.9 In CD iv 21 הבריאה is the second member of the genitival syntagm ויסוד הבריאה. This phrase is followed by the citation of Gn 1.27c זכר ונקבה ברא אותם "male and female he created them".

A.10 In CD xii 15 בריאתם is governed by the term משפט cst in the כי-clause כי הוא משפט בריאתם. The suf refers to כל החגבים "all the locusts". For the first time the lexeme בריאה is not connected by a personal pronoun to YHWH.

A.11 In 4Q266 10 ii 10 הבריאות is governed by the adverbial לפני in the ptc-phr: הבריאות [הלך ערום לפני]. The text continues, establishing the penalty of six months' exclusion for those who, precisely, walk "naked" לפני הבריאות.

A.12 In 4Q267 i 8 the text does not allow syntagmatic analysis. It is, however, able to show the occurrence of the term בריאה in parallellism with the syntagm כל בשר.

B.1 [nil]

4. Versions

This section is only relevant to Nu 16.30.
  a. LXX: φάσμα
  b. Pesh: *briṯāʾ*
  c. Tg: בְּרִיאָה
  d. Vg: *nova res*
  e. Aq, Sym, Thd: χάσμα

A.1 The different translations attested in the LXX, and in Aq, Sym, and Thd depend on diverse, but in both cases erroneous interpretations of the lexeme בריאה as the syntagmatic form *b* + *rʾy*, rendered by the LXX as ἐν φάσματι "in a manifestation", and by Aq, Sym, Thd as ἐν χάσματι "in a cleft".

B.1 [nil]

5. Lexical/Semantic Field(s)

A.1 In the passage around Nu 16.30 there is no term clearly in paradigmatic opposition to the lexeme בריאה. In fact, there are no antonyms present, either belonging to its own pole, or to the opposite pole. To define successfully the meaning of the lexeme it is therefore necessary to consider the meaning of the verb ברא, of which it is the internal object, and to consider the context in which the lexeme is used and from which there emerges an opposition at the level of sense, and not, as stated, of the paradigm. From the analysis of these data it seems possible to confirm the meaning "extraordinary event", "miracle", as attested by BDB, Ges., Ges.-18, *HAL* (loc. cit.).

In this connection the views of Böhl (1913:45) and Van der Ploeg (1946:145) appear illuminating and convincing, though they refer only to ברא, and not to the noun בריאה. According to them the verb ברא expresses the idea of a novelty, and is particularly suitable to indicate an extraordinary action such as a miracle or the creation of the Universe.

A.2 In Sir 16.16 the syntagm לכל בריותיו is in paradigmatic relationship to the syntagm לבני אדם. There is a semantic opposition within the same pole, as a result of which it is possible to assign to the lexeme בריאה (here in pl) the meaning "creatures". Such a meaning seems to display a development in the technical sense of the lexeme, by which it has come to indicate (and thus will also do so in later Hebrew) the products of the act of creation, with particular reference to human beings (cf. Foerster 1933:1015). The possibility cannot be excluded that such a development is also a sign of evolution in the concept of creation.

In the passages belonging to exegetical and biblical texts, terms in paradigmatic opposition to our lexeme are either not present or the state of the text does not permit their identification. The consideration is worth stressing that, in all the occurrences for which it is possible to conduct an analysis, the lexeme, when used in the singular form, presents a clear reference to the act of creation.

A.3 In this connection the occurrence at 4Q216 v 1 is significant: [כתוב כל דב[רי הבריאה "write the entire account of the creation" (as restored in DJD XIII:14 and followed by García Martínez 1996:397). The lexeme is used here as a technical term to express the work of God narrated in Gn 1, a lengthy quotation of which follows.

A.4 The same meaning "creation" seems appropriate for the occurrence in 4Q217 ii 2: לכל שני העולם מן הבריאה "for all the years of eternity, from the creation" (thus DJD XIII:26), where a temporal aspect seems to be inherent in the meaning of the lexeme, though this is purely as a contextual feature.

A.5 The same consideration seems to hold for 4Q253 ii 3: טהורים מן הבריאה "those pure from creation" (thus DJD XXII:211 and García Martínez 1996:361). However, the state of the text cannot guarantee any firm conclusions. However, taking account of the absolute non-existence of the lexeme in the biblical account of creation, it is particularly interesting to observe the presence here of בריאה with the meaning "creation" precisely in a text which is a commentary on Genesis.

A.6 4Q225 i 7 הבריאה עד יום הבריאה [החדשה] "the creation until the day of the [new] creation" (thus DJD XIII:144 and García Martínez 1996:406). The hypothesis advanced by scholars to fill the textual lacuna with the adjective חדשה, with predicative function, allows us to take בריאה as referring not only to the primordial creation, but also to the eschatological creation. Such a reference does not have any value at the level of meaning, but at least confirms the use of our lexeme in the singular as a term specifically for "creation".

A.7 4Q216 v 9 רוחות בריותו [אשר עשה בשמים ואשר עשה בארץ] "the spirits of his creatures which he made in the heavens, and which he made on the earth..." (thus DJD XIII:14 and García Martínez 1996:397). In this case also terms in paradigmatic opposition with our lexeme do not occur. The occurrence confirms the meaning "creatures" for the pl form בריאות, as already in Sir 16.16 (see **A.2** above). However, here the term does not refer solely to the human race but, it seems possible, to all animate beings. The presence of the pronominal suffix referring to YHWH leads us to recognize, among the semantic traits that constitute the meaning of the lexeme, the trait "work of God".

A.8 The only occurrence in the language of poetry is that of 4Q504 1-2 vii 9: כול בריאותיו תמיד לעולמ[י עד אמן אמן] "all his creatures continually for the eternal [ages. Amen, amen]". (Thus DJD VII:151 and García Martínez 1996:416.) In the preceding lines the fragment lists the syntagms כול מלאכים "all the angels" and כול מחשביה "all rational beings". Given the state of the text, however, it is not possible to establish the role of כול בריאותיו in relation to these phrases. The possibility that our lexeme fulfils the function of an unmarked, inclusive term with regard to מלאכי and מחשביה is purely hypothetical and, in any case, may be due to contextual reasons. Also in this occurrence the lexeme בריאות in the plural does not seem to indicate only human creatures. There remains also in poetic texts the semantic trait <work of God> for the lexeme in the plural form.

In the language of legal texts, only two of the four occurrences of the lexeme present terms in clear parallelism with our lexeme: 4Q266 10 ii 10 and 4Q267 i 8. The overall state of these texts is, however, very uncertain. The other two, CD iv 21, xii 15, which do not present paradigmatic oppositions, are, however, able to be subjected to a substantial analysis.

A.9 CD iv 21 שתי נשים בחייהם ויסוד הבריאה זכר ונקבה ברא אותם "zwei Weiber zu ihren Lebzeiten nahmen; aber die Grundlage der Schöpfung ist: Als Mann und Weib hat er sie erschaffen" (thus Lohse 1986:75; cf. also García Martínez 1996:119). This is a legal text which confirms, under the guidance of Gn 1.27, the prohibition of polygamy. The presence in the midst of the text of the lexeme בריאה in the singular, with the meaning "creation", confirms also for the language of juridical-cultic texts the employment of the lexeme as a technical term, specific to the vocabulary of creation.

A.10 CD xii 15 עד הם חיים כי הוא משפט בריאתם "während sie noch le[ben]; denn das ist die Bestimmung ihrer Natur" (thus Lohse 1986:93; cf. also García Martínez 1996:129). The text, which contains various rules of purity, refers here to the necessity of throwing locusts, still alive, into water or fire. In the preceding line, referring still to חגבים 'locusts', we meet the syntagm במיניהם "according to their kinds", which has clear reminiscences of the Bible (cf. Gn 1.11, 12), though with a different modification of the BH idiom, which is always with ל. The consideration that for the first time the lexeme בריאה appears, via a pronominal suffix, in conjunction with an entity other than God may be taken as proof of a new meaning. However, when dealing with an exceptional datum, it is not possible to establish whether such a meaning constitutes a stable fact of the system, or merely a phenomenon of personal linguistic norm determined by the context. Given the paucity of data available, the nature of the relationship between בריאתם and מיניהם also remains uncertain, even in the light of the fact that the latter is highly stereotyped. However, though our term has appeared up till now with rather fixed semantic characteristics, the evidence should not be undervalued that here it is assigned an unexpected vitality.

A.11 4Q266 10 ii 9-10 ואשר יהלך לפני רע[הו ערום בבית או בשדה הלך ערום הבריאות [חודשים לפני] והובדל ששה "He who goes about [naked in the house] in the presence of his fel[low, or out in the field in presence] of p[eo]ple, shall be excluded for six [months." (Thus DJD XVIII:74-75.) García Martínez (1996:146) provides a translation identical with the one just given, but translates הבריאות "i bambini". Even though the condition of the text makes any evaluation of the parallelism between רעהו and הבריאות uncertain, it could be intended as a case of antonymy between terms belonging to opposite poles of meaning, as in fact seems to have been decided by DJD. The two lexemes would turn out to be in opposition by the semantic features: private + near / public + foreign, the former pair belonging to רעהו, and the latter to בריאות. The law would therefore impose the same penalty on those who walk naked in private in front of neighbours ("fellow"), as on those who do it in public in front of strangers ("people"). The proposal advanced by García Martínez of attributing the meaning "i bambini" to הבריאות does not find confirmation in any other occurrence of the lexeme. The data in our possession are not therefore sufficient to establish the validity of this hypothesis. However, appeal to a metaphorical use of the term בריאות

'creatures' in the sense of "children, sons" cannot be ruled out a priori.

This occurrence reveals in Qumran legal texts an employment of the lexeme in the plural outside the rigid framework of a technical term of the vocabulary of creation. This is, however, a feature shared by Ben Sira (16:16).

A.12 4Q267 i 8: from this very corrupt text it is not possible to gain any secure indication concerning our lexeme. We merely register the recurrence in juxtaposition of כל בשר "all flesh" and ובר]יאה "and crea[ture" (DJD XVIII:97). The lack of other comparable occurrences does not permit us to evaluate the real paradigmatic nature of the opposition בריאה/בשר. Moreover, we cannot exclude the possibility that the opposition is not at the level of the lexemes, but rather between the whole syntagm כל בשר and the lexeme בריאה. In that case it could no longer be considered a paradigmatic opposition, though the כל may relate to בשר ובריאה as a whole. At any rate, it is interesting to note that in this occurrence too the lexeme בריאה does not carry out the function of a technical term of creation, but acquires the features of an unmarked term indicating living beings. If it is intended here to refer solely to human beings, the data provided by the text are insufficient to demonstrate this. There is also here a lack of any specific reference to the work of creation.

B.1 [nil]

6. Exegesis

It should be stated at the outset that bibliographical items specific to this lexeme are virtually non-existent.

A.1 BDB (135), Ges. (156), Ges.-18 (150) and *HAL* (150) agree in attributing to בריאה in Nu 16.30 the meaning "something new", "Neugeschaffenes", just as Gray (1903:206) and Levine (1993:417), who, by translating, respectively "creation" and "new creation", seem to recognize the feature of "extraordinariness" as belonging to the meaning of the lexeme—"something new and marvellous" (Gray 1903:206).

A.2 BDB, Ges., Ges.-18 and *HAL* (150) agree in attributing to the lexeme in Sir 16.16 the meaning "creatures", "Geschöpfe".

A.3 For the occurrences in the texts of Qumran, with the exception of the works of translation mentioned in *Lexical/Semantic Field(s)*, there does not exist any bibliography specifically concerned with our lexeme, and therefore no history of interpretation can be traced.

B.1 [nil]

7. Conclusion

A.1 The minimal bibliography concerning the lexeme, and especially the small and not always unanimous pieces of information that arise from the texts, do not allow us to provide a very varied picture of the semantic value of בריאה. At least it appears clear that the lexeme in Nu 16.30 may be categorized as an action of God. The presence of the feature of "extraordinariness" seems to exclude the possibility of commutability with the term מעשה, which was operative in the same functional language (EBH in historical prose), with the same categorizing features (action of God).

The relationship between the two terms may be considered as one of opposition between an unmarked term (מעשה) and a marked (exclusive) term (בריאה), these terms being opposed by the semantic trait "extraordinariness", which belonged only to בריאה.

The fact that the lexeme בריאה is a hapax legomenon within EBH of historical narrative, however, does not allow us to confirm full functionality for this opposition at the level of the system of this type of EBH.

In the occurrence in Sir 16.16 the lexeme seems to belong to the category <human being>. The possibility, displayed in the text, of substituting the syntagm כל בריותיו for the syntagm בני אדם, however, does not lead us to recognize the individual members of the syntagms as commutable. We should not exclude the possibility that the membership of the lexeme within the category <human being> is determined by the context, and that it would also be able to function as a term indicating all created beings, and not merely human creatures.

In the functional languages of Qumran the use of בריאה in the singular as a technical term for creation, belonging to the category <action of God>, seems to be fixed. Along with the development of such a specific meaning there probably went an ever more precise awareness of the very concept of creation. The occurrence of the expression יסוד הבריאה "the beginning of the creation" in legal texts, where the lexeme displays fewer signs of fixity, seems, for example, to display a feature of autonomy for the created, which is completely foreign to the biblical tradition. This leads us no longer to perceive in the creation merely the object of the action of God, but also a subject capable of imposing respect for the fixed principles of its creator. The meaning "extraordinary/miraculous event", which belongs to בריאה in Nu 16.30, turns out to be foreign to the different functional languages of Qumran. Such evidence speaks against the hypothesis that interprets בריאה in Nu as a later redactional insertion.

In Qumran exegetical and biblical texts and poetic texts the lexeme בריאות, in the plural, means "creatures", marked with the feature <work of God>. However, it is not possible to establish with certainty the distinguishing trait of such a term, since it seems in fact to be determined by contextual factors.

On the other hand, in legal texts בריאות appears as a term no longer specifically marked with the trait <work of God>, but rather as an unmarked term indicating "living beings", or perhaps (though caution is necessary due to the state of the texts) "human beings".

B.1 [nil]

BIBLIOGRAPHY

Böhl, F. 1913. *bārā* als terminus der Weltschöpfung. In A. Alt et al. (eds), *Alttestamentliche Studien* [Fschr R. Kittel]. Leipzig.

Foerster, W. 1933. Article κτίζω in *TWNT* 3:1015.

García Martínez, F. 1996. *Testi di Qumran*. Italian ed. (fuller than the English edn). Brescia.

Gray, G.B. 1903. Commentary on *Numbers* (ICC). Edinburgh.

Humbert, P. 1958. Emploi et portée du verb *bārā* (créer) dans l'Ancien Testament. In *Opuscule d'un hébraïsant*, 146-65. Neuchâtel.

Kutscher, E.Y. 1974. *The Language and Linguistic Background of the Isaiah Scroll (1QIsaᵃ)*. Studies on the Texts of the Desert of Judah, 6. Leiden.

Levine, B.A. 1993. Commentary on *Numbers 1-20* (AB). Garden City, New York.

Lohse, E. ⁴1986. *Die Texte aus Qumran*. München.

Ploeg, J.P.M. van der. 1946. Le sens du verbe hébreu *bārā* (étude sémasiologique). *Le Muséon* 59:143-57.

Qimron, E. 1986. *The Hebrew of the Dead Sea Scrolls*. Harvard Semitic Studies 29. Leiden.

Schmidt, W.H. 1971. Article ברא in *TH* 1:336-39.

The Historical Dictionary of the Hebrew Language. 1973. *The Book of Ben Sira: Text, Concordance and an Analysis of the Vocabulary*. Jerusalem.

Stefano Bindi
University of Florence
(Translated from Italian by Peter Williams, University of Cambridge)

דֶּרֶךְ

Introduction

Grammatical Type: n m/f.

Occurrences: Total 706x OT; 24x Sir; 258x Qum; 0x inscr.

Sir (numbering of Beentjes 1997): 3.31, 5.9 (MS A; not in MS C), 7.17 (MS A; doublet not in MS C), 8.16, 10.6, 26 (Bmg: ‎[ד]כרך‎), 11.14, 34a, 34c, 13.1, 14.21, 16.20, 32.20a (B, F), 20b (E, F; MS B reads ‎בנגף‎), 32.21a (MS B; doublet not in MSS E, F), 32.21c (B, E, F), 22 (B), 33.11, 37.7 (B, D), 9 (B, D), 42.3 (M; B reads ‎אדון‎, Bmg ‎ארח‎), 46.20, 48.22, 51.15.

Qum: CD 1.9, 11, 13, 15, 2.2, 6, 16, 3.15, 17, 7.19, 8.4, 5, 9, 11, 16, 11.1, 15.7, 19.17 (2x), 21, 23, 29, 20.18, 1QH 1.36, 2.10, 4.4, 18, 21, 24, 31 (2x), 32, 6.7, 20 (2x), 21, 24, 7.31, 8.9, 11.4, 12.34, 14.26, 15.13, 18, 17.21, 18.12, 22, 31.2, fr 1.5, 1QM 3.10, 14.7, 1QpHab 8.12, 11.13, 15.25, 1QS 1.13, 2.2, 3.3, 6, 10, 20, 21, 26, 4.1, 2 (2x), 10, 11, 15, 17, 19, 22, 5.4, 7, 11, 24, 8.10, 13, 14, 18, 21, 25, 9.2, 5, 9 (2x), 18, 19, 20, 21, 10.21 (2x), 11.2, 4, 10, 11, 13, 17, 14.7, 1QS^a i 2, 17, 28, 1QS^b v 22, 1Q17 1.4, 27.19, 1Q19 1.3, 1Q22 ii 18, 1Q30 2 i 2, 2QSir 2.7, 2Q22 1 ii 3, 3Q15 8.1, 4QPs^f 2 viii 4, 4Q158 1–2 10, 4Q161 1 ii 16, 2.7, 10, 27.10, 4Q162 i 5, 4Q163 1 i 3, 22 i 2, 4Q165 4.2, 4Q166 1.7, 4Q171 1+ i 17, 25, 1 ii 16, 17, 1 iii 14, 1 iv 10, 4Q174 1–2 i 14, 4Q175 1.12, 4Q176 1+ i 2, 7, 18.2, 4Q180 2–4 i 1, 5–6 i 3, 4Q183 1 ii 5, 4Q184 1.8, 9 (2x), 14, 16, 17, 4Q185 1–2 ii 1, 4Q200 2.5, 4.5, 4Q215 1 ii 6, 1 iv 6, 4Q219 21.22, 4Q222 1.3, 25.10, 4Q223-4 2 ii 6, 4Q227 2.5, 4Q256 5.4, 4Q258 1 i 3, 3 i 3, 6, 3 ii 2, 4, 5, 4Q259 1 iii 17, 4Q266 1 i 1, 2 i 4, 18 v 11, 4Q267 5.4, 4Q270 1 iii 17, 9 ii 20, 4Q271 1 i 9, 4Q286 2.1, 4Q299 5.2, 79.3, 4Q364 23.5–6, 4Q370 1 i 3, 4Q379 18.3, 4Q381 31 i 3, 4Q382 115.2, 4Q385 2 i, 3, 4Q390 1.3, 4Q391 9.3, 11.2, 32.2, 4Q392 1.4, 4Q397 14.12, 4Q400 1 i 14, 16, 4Q403 1 i 22, 2.3, 4Q404 2 i 3, 4Q405 13 i 6, 20 ii-21-22 12, 23 i 11, 4Q408 1.6, 4Q413 i 1, 4Q416 2 iii 10, 14, 4Q417 2 i 7, 2 ii 11, 4Q418 55 iii 4, 4Q419 1.12, 4Q420 1a ii-b 5, 4Q421 1a ii-b 12, 4Q422 C 1, 25.10, 4Q423 9.3, 4Q425 1–2 iii 6, 11, 4Q428 7.5, 10, 4Q432 9.2, 4Q434 2 i 4, 10, 11, 2 ii 4, 4Q436 1.6, 4Q464 5 ii 4, 4Q473 2.3, 2.4, 4Q486 1.4, 4Q491 8–10 i 5, 6, 4Q497 6.2, 4Q499 5.2, 4Q502 119.1, 4Q504 1–2 v 20 (2x), 8 recto 13, 4.13, 17 ii 4, 4Q505 121.1, 4Q509 296.1, 4Q510 1 i 9, 22, 4Q511 2 i 6, 10 i 8, 63 iii 3, 4Q517 17.2, 4Q524 5.4, 4Q525 3 ii 2 (2x), 4, 7, 3 v 8, 11, 5 viii 11, 12.3, 14 ii 6, 16, 11QJub 5.2, 11QMelch 1+ ii 24, 11QPs^a xxi 13, xxii 10, xxvii 3, 11QShirShab a 3, 11QT 31.6, 43.12, 52.14, 54.17, 56.18, 58.21, 65.2.

The figure of 706 in the OT is the correct number of occurrences in the MT and is that preferred by most scholars (e.g. Sauer 1971:456; Andersen - Forbes 1989:305; Dorsey 1991:212 & 249, n. 1), and corresponds to the number of citations in Lisowsky (1958:370–75). BDB give the number 715 (202) and *HAL* 710 (222). Mandelkern's list of 707 (1896:301–04) includes the one occurrence of the substantive ‎מִדְרָךְ‎ (Dt 2.5, st cst).

Text Doubtful:

A.1 Some commentators query the expression דֶּרֶךְ אֹרְחֹתֶיךָ at Is 3.12. Cheyne omits דֶּרֶךְ on rhythmical grounds (cited by Gray 1912:68), although Gray feels that the Heb is an "excellent balanced distich" (ibid.:68) and does not see any significant variant in the LXX (τὸν τρίβον τῶν ποδῶν). Wildberger (1972:129–130) renders the substantive דֶּרֶךְ as a vb, "the paths on which you walked".

A.2 At Is 35.8 the first דֶּרֶךְ in the expression וְדֶרֶךְ וְדֶרֶךְ, coming after the lexeme מַסְלוּל, should almost certainly be considered an interpolation, arising as a result of dittography. The repetition is absent from some Heb MSS and the Pesh. The suggestion that וְדֶרֶךְ should be emended to the vb הֹלֵךְ, "[the way of] the traveller" (e.g. Clines:II, 463) seems to be unnecessary. An emendation in accord with the LXX's rendering of מַסְלוּל by ὁδὸς καθαρά (e.g. בָּרוּר) is also not warranted. Chapters 30–35 in the LXX of Isaiah exhibit many variants from, and additions, to the MT, a number probably the result of exegetical concerns (see Horbury 1982:501).

A.3 It is often assumed that Jr 3.13, where דְּרָכַיִךְ "your ways" are said to be scattered "before strangers" (לַזָּרִים), should be emended. Rudolph (1968:59), therefore, proposes דּוֹדַיִךְ, "your love", and Duhm (1901:39) suggests that the expression refers to the spreading of the knees and accordingly emends דְּרָכַיִךְ to בִּרְכַּיִךְ, "your knees", comparing it with Ezk 16.25. Holladay (1986:59), however, says that the Ug *drkt*, meaning "your strength" (see Root and Comparative Material B.2), lies behind the meaning of דֶּרֶךְ here.

A.4 Some emend the reading at Ho 10.13 of דַּרְכְּךָ "your path" to רִכְבְּךָ "your chariot", as is suggested by the parallelism with גִבּוֹרֶיךָ "your warriors" later in the verse and by the LXX reading of ἐν τοῖς ἅρμασι (e.g. Davies 1992:248; BHS). Vaticanus reads ἁμαρτήμασιν, which is probably a later theological interpretation (cf. Mc 5.9), especially since Ambrose says that the original reading was ¤rmasi (cited by Wolff 1974:181). Wolff (1974:181), who accepts this emendation, interprets the MT (which is the same as Syr and Vg) as a misreading that generalizes the original, but he dismisses the hypothesized Ug background to דֶּרֶךְ without further qualification (see Root and Comparative Material B.2).

A.5 The דֶּרֶךְ of Beersheba in Am 8.14 could also be interpreted in the light of Ug *drkt* ("dominion"; see Root and Comparative Material B.2) as it is in the context of oaths being sworn to various deities, but suggestions for its emendation have included דֹּדְךָ "your beloved", דּוֹדְךָ denoting the patron deity of the holy place and דֹּרְךָ "your assembly" (see on all of these Wolff 1977:323–24). Harper (1905:184), however, thinks that דֶּרֶךְ may indicate that the oath is being taken on the manner of the practice of the cult for the god.

A.6 At Pr 31.3 דְּרָכֶיךָ is changed by Scott (1965:183) to יְרֵכֶיךָ, "your loins". On the same verse Toy (1899:541) suggests that one could possibly read דֹּדֶיךָ, "your love", or לְבָבְךָ, "your heart".

A.7 At Sir 42.3 MS B has the reading ואדון and MS M reads ודרך, whilst Bmg has written above it וארח. It is very probable that ארח was corrupted to אדון (Kister 1990:352) and that ארח was a variant for דרך in some manuscript traditions.

It seems likely in this instance that the reading of MS B/Bmg is superior to that of M, and that we should hence read here ארח and not דרך (see Exegesis B.6).

A.8 At Sir 49.9 most commentators reconstruct the text as דֶ[רְכֵי צ]דק, but Segal (1958:336, 339) prefers to read דבר ב- in place of דרך. LXX has ὁδός, the Vg *via* and the Syr *ʾurḥāʾ*, and they thus support the reading דרך. This verse should then probably be included in the number of occurrences in Sir.

Qere/Ketiv: There are 6 instances of Qere/Ketiv, all involving the correction of a pronominal suffix. In four cases (1Sm 8.3, Jr 17.10, Ps 10.5, Jb 26.14) the sing noun (דרכו) is changed to the pl (דרכיו), and in one the reverse happens (Pr 21.29). In one instance (2Sm 22.33) the 3p s suf becomes the 1p s suf (דרכי).

1. Root and Comparative Material

A.1 A cognate verb דָּרַךְ occurs 62 times in the OT, meaning in the qal (49x) "to step (on)". The hiph (13x) is causative. The cognate noun מִדְרָךְ, "footstep", also occurs once (Dt 2.5). The verb refers either to an individual case of stepping on something or to the stepping that combines into the process of walking (Dorsey 1991:214). It thus denotes the stepping upon (עַל) a threshold (1Sm 5.5) or a serpent (Ps 91.13), as well as the act of travelling along a דֶּרֶךְ (Ps 107.7) or through a land (Dt 1.36). It is also used of the act of stretching a bow by stepping upon it in order to string it (Jr 51.3, Ps 46.9), or for treading grapes in a wine press (Am 9.13) or corn on a threshing floor (Jr 51.33).

A.2 דֶּרֶךְ appears in RH, where it exhibits a similar range of meanings to BH and provides evidence for the continuance of some of these meanings, which are not attested at Qum. In the Mishna דֶּרֶךְ appears 285 times, often referring to a physical road, whether a private one through a field (e.g. mKet 13:7) or a public one (e.g. mOhal 16:2). It is also used of a journey (mPes 9:2, mShab 22:4) or a travelling enterprise (mBer 9:3). It may be used of a course of behaviour characteristic of a particular individual or group (e.g. mBer 1:2). It appears that the prepositional use exists (e.g. mTam 1:3), including the possibly additional (but see Davies 1979:98) prepositional meaning of "by way of, through" (mNid. 9:5, mZeb 6:3, mBesah 3:8), and that the sense "means" has been introduced (e.g. mZab 2:4, mNed 11:12, mYeb 15:6, 7). דֶּרֶךְ may also be used in a sexual context, where the natural gratification of the sexual appetite is "according to her way" (כדרכה, GenR 80), whereas the unnatural appetite is "not according to the way/manner" (שלא כדרכה, GenR 18).

A.3 In Ph the noun *drk* appears in the inscription of Azitawadda (*KAI* 26A ii 5), probably meaning "road", although others have suggested the meaning "dominion" (cf. Ug *drkt*; *DNWSI*:261). The vb occurs twice in Ph (*KAI* 27.7, 8) in reference to entering a courtyard. A possible verbal form *dᶜrkn* (*KAI* 145.10), interpreted as the qal pf 1p pl of *drk*, is classed as Pun in Jean & Hoftijzer 1965, and then in the *DNWSI* as Ph, but in both editions it is described as "highly uncertain" (*DNWSI*:261). Tomback (1978:75) presents another example from Ph in which the form *drk* appears to mean commander: "which ʾDNBʿL the commander (*drk*) vowed and er[ected]" (*KAI* 170. 1–2).

A.4 In early Arm the noun דרכא does not appear, although the Peʿal vb does (e.g. *Ahiqar* 108, 191; *Arsl.* 7s) with the meaning "to step (upon)", as the Heb vb דָּרַךְ. Among these cases there is one example of דרך with the object

קֶשֶׁת, a "bow" (*Ahiqar* 191). Later in Egyptian and JArm both the noun (e.g. bAZ 48b) and the verb (e.g TgO Dt 1.26, bShab 109a) are attested (Jastrow:323). The noun דרכא can mean either a physical road (e.g. bAZ 48b) or the manner of an action (e.g. bQid 2b). The verb, in addition to meaning "to step upon" (e.g. bKet 60b), can mean "to thresh" (e.g. Tg Is 28.27), "to lead" (e.g. Tg Pr 22.6) or "to trace, overtake" (e.g. AZ 15b).

A.5   In Syr the vb *drak* can be found with the meaning "to step upon" (Brockelmann:166), which in the Aphel conjugation can mean "to arrive at" or "to apprehend, understand". Derivatives from the vb are the m n *drākā*, "a step" and the f n *drāktā*, "a treading out (of corn)" (ibid.:166).

A.6   In Mandaic דירכא covers a similar range to the Heb: a) road, way, path, trodden way, step; b) moral, religious law, way of the law; c) tread; d) bank (Drower & Macuch 1963:109b).

A.7   In Geez the most likely cognates are *daraka* "to be hard" (Koch 1977:294), *deruk* "harsh, savage" (Lambdin 1978:396) and *madrak* "doorsill, threshold" (Dillmann:1095). A root idea of stepping or treading upon, as in the Heb vb, could have produced derivative forms meaning "to be hard" or "a (packed down) threshold" (Dorsey 1991:214).

B.1   The name of the Syrian goddess *derketō* of Ashkelon is perhaps derived from a second root דרך, meaning "to rule over", as in the Ug *drkt* (see B.2). This was first suggested by Albright (1934:130, n. 153), and has also been proposed as the interpretation of Am 8.14 (see Wolff 1977:323–24; cf. Introduction: Text Doubtful A.5).

B.2   The discovery and decipherment of the texts from Ras Shamra in 1929–30 led to the speedy identification of an Ug word *drkt* that appeared to have the meaning of "dominion" or "rule", a sense now assured for this Ug lexeme (see *DLU* I:137). In as early as 1931 Virolleaud (1931:220) observed the juxtaposition of *kht* (read by him as *khš*) and *drk*[*t*]*h* and concluded that the noun *drkt* expresses an idea analogous to that of royalty. He in turn connected this word with the Hebrew דֶּרֶךְ, explaining that this has the figurative sense of "way" (voie), meaning a mode of action. The deity's way is his rule over his kingdom. Other examples of a similar association were in time found in Ug, giving rise to the opinion that this lexeme had the specific meaning of "dominion, rule etc.", without necessarily imputing a figurative use comparable to that of דֶּרֶךְ. As the popularity grew for interpreting difficult Heb passages in the light of Ug syntax and lexicography (evidenced especially in the works of W.F. Albright and M. Dahood), many examples of where the Heb דֶּרֶךְ should be translated "dominion" were proposed. This has become pervasive in scholarship and Clines (II, 472–73), in his manner of listing all proposals made, lists this meaning of דֶּרֶךְ as a separate homonym (דֶּרֶךְ II).

It was in 1944 that the possible connection between the Heb root דרך and Ug *drkt* was first used to clarify the interpretation of an obscure Heb biblical passage. Albright (1944:219 and n. 82) derived a verbal form in Heb from the Ug noun *drkt* to explain the meaning of דָּרַךְ at Nu 24.17. דָּרַךְ in this instance is usually explained as "to go (up), rise" (of the star of Jacob), as implied by the Versions, or is emended to זרח (e.g. Wellhausen). Albright proposed that the word be vocalized דָּרְכוּ and rendered "shall sway, control", a sense derivable from the verb דָּרַךְ, "to step, tread", just as the Heb כָּבַשׁ, "to overcome, rule over", is derived from the verb "to tread". He had earlier (1934:130, n. 153) accounted for the Ug *drkt* as a derivation of a verbal form **drk* in the causative. This he compared with the Heb הִדְרִיךְ and Akk *šudruku* ("to tread, force, bend").

Albright (1955:7) later argued for the Canaanite features of Pr 8, comparing verse 22 (with the word דרכו) to the Canaanite 'L QNN R'ST DRKTH. He subsequently corrected his opinion that דרכו should be read as *drkt*, preferring to understand the form דרך as an infinitive construct or an abstract noun (Albright 1957:23, n. 6). Whatever the grammatical interpretation, the word was to be understood as referring to the Lord's dominion. Following from Albright's suggestion with regard to Balaam's oracle, other scholars observed possible cases of the noun דֶּרֶךְ with the meaning "dominion" in many books of the Old Testament. Dahood identified it in Ho 10.13, Jr 3.13, Pr 31.3, Ps 138.5 (1954:627–31), Jb 26.14, 40.19 (1952:593), Jb 36.23, Ps 67.3 (1957:320), Pr 19.16, Ps 119.37 (1963:40, n. 2), Jb 19.25 (Fisher 1972–81:I, 264). In his commentary on the Psalms he included some additional cases at Pss 77.14 (Dahood 1968:II, 230), 90.16 (1968:II, 326, reading הַ-דֶּרֶךְ for הֶהָדָר-ךָ), 101.2 (1970:III, 3), 102.24 (1970:III, 20) and 146.9 (1970:III, 342). Nober (1948:351–353) has suggested Ps 90.7 and 110.7, Bartina (1956:202–210) Am 8.14, Tidwell (1980:70, n. 33) Ps 1.6, and Muffs (1992:118, n. 11), with a sexual metaphorical meaning (cf. Syr and RH), Pr 30.19. In addition to the Old Testament, in recent years this meaning for the lexeme has also been observed in post-Biblical Hebrew. Lieberman (1967–68:90–92), on the basis of the context, notes an example in Sir 42.3 (see Exegesis B.6) and examples in RH have been suggested by Kutscher (1967–68:345–46), Lieberman (1967–68:90–92) and Muffs (1992:113–20). Although these cases require further analysis, it is not unknown for there to be a skipping of a linguistic generation between Ug and RH (see Greenfield 1969:92–101; Kutscher 1967:158–75).

To assess the evidence, we should begin with the Ug material. There are seven places in Ug texts where *drkt* is parallel to *mlk*: *KTU*² 1.1 IV 24–25, 1.3 IV 2–3, 1.6 V 5–6, 1.6 VI 33–35, 1.10 III 13–14, 1.16 VI 23–24, 1.22 II 17–18 (see Loretz 1979:493). These cases exhibit the parallel of *ksi mlk // kḫṯ drkt*, "throne of the kingdom // seat of dominion". In similar fashion "throne" (*ksu*) is parallel to "seat of dominion" (*kḫṯ drkt*) a number of times (*KTU*² 1.2 IV 12–13, 19–20), and the simple "kingdom" (*mlk*) in parallelism with *drkt* also occurs (*KTU*² 1.2 IV 10, 1.16 VI 37–38, 52–53, 1.108 I 6-7). The meaning of "dominion" (Aistleitner ³1967:792 renders "Herrschergewalt") may also be derived from some other texts where the context rather than the word pairs is the guide (*KTU*² 1.2 I 4–5, 1.4 VII 44, 1.14 I 42–43). The important factor in all these texts is that *drkt* is related only to *mlk*, "kingdom", or *ksu*, "seat, throne", indicating that the word expresses royal power or rulership. Therefore, to be true to the possible connection with certain uses of Heb דֶּרֶךְ, the Heb should also convey this precise meaning. The further away from the Ug meaning that one posits a Heb meaning, the less likely a connection there really is. In the case of the *drkt*/דרך connection, scholars often merely cite the connection without detailed argument.

Loretz (1979:493–94) has subjected the possible instances in the Psalms proposed by Dahood to an analysis and concluded that the connection is tenuous. The word pairs in the Psalms involving דֶּרֶךְ are not, in any of the cases concerned, the same as those exhibited by the Ug texts, calling the parallels into question. דֶּרֶךְ is in parallelism with יְשׁוּעָה in Ps 67.3 and with nothing in Pss 77.14, 101.2, 102.24 and 146.9. And at Ps 138.5 דִּרְכֵי יהוה, "the ways of the Lord", is in parallelism with the כָּבוֹד of the Lord. In the case of Ps 138.5, Dahood (1954:630) argues that verse 4 contains the expression מַלְכֵי־אָרֶץ, which he (contra MT's "kings") takes to mean "kingdoms of the earth", a rendering that, he argues, is favoured by the Ug parallelism of *mlk* and *drkt* (see also *HAL*:233). The argumentation in this example is weak since it is the Ug material that originally provides the evidence for the meaning of דֶּרֶךְ and should not then be used again for a reinterpretation of מַלְכֵי־אָרֶץ. More significant still is the fact that in Ug the expressions are in parallelism with each other, whereas in the Ps they are merely in the same context, and, as Loretz has indicated, are not in parallelism. A similar fault lies in Dahood's interpretation of Ps 102.23–24 (in Fisher 1972–81:Vol. 1, 264). One feature in favour of Dahood's arguments here is that the contexts at least are royal and in that respect similar to the contexts in the Ug texts.

The variety of translations offered for דֶּרֶךְ also raises questions regarding the validity of the identification of the Ug as a cognate. Gordon (*UT*:702), for example, notes for comparison with the Ug *drkt*, which he renders as "rule, dominion", that דֶּרֶךְ at Ho 10.13 can mean "power", adding Pr 31.3 as another possible example for this meaning. Dahood had also suggested this meaning for Ho 10.13, translating דֶּרֶךְ there as "might" or "resources" (1954:628). In the same article he translates דֶּרֶךְ at Jr 3.13 as "substance" (628), at Pr 31.3 as "strength, power, substance" (629), and at Ps 138.5 as "dominion" (629–30), the one case where the meaning is the same as that normally attributed to the Ug lexeme. Whilst these meanings are close to the Ug, which lies somewhere in the field of "dominion" or "rulership", they are not the same as the Ug and this appears to be a weakness. Dahood did in fact render the Ug *drkt* as "dominion, might" (1954:627), but the latter of these two translations cannot easily be inferred from the context of the Ug lexeme. Albright suggested for Nu 27.17 the translation "rule, dominion", which appears to be the closest to the Ug parallelism with *mlk*, but he understood this as a derivative of the verb.

The two most convincing examples according to Holladay (1986:59) for the link between *drkt* and דֶּרֶךְ can be found at Pr 31.3 and Ps 138.5. In Pr 31.3 some commentators propose an emendation of דרכיך ("your ways") to ירכיך ("your loins") or לבבך ("your heart"). Dahood (1954:629) points to the close parallelism in the verse in חֵילֶךָ וּדְרָכֶיךָ ("your strength") and the Vg's translation *divitias* ("riches"). From this he concludes that the word דֶּרֶךְ could carry some of the ideas found in חַיִל, namely "strength, power, substance". He reads the verse as "Give not your substance in the full measure [understanding Ph. *lmht*] of kings". In similar fashion McKane (1970:409) suggests the rendering "nor your dignity to those who destroy [reading לְמֹחוֹת] kings". This is once again stretching the meaning of דֶּרֶךְ beyond the Ug parallels, where it does not mean "substance" or "dignity". McKane (1970:409), however, prefers the reading

יְרֵכֶיךָ ("your loins") in place of דְּרָכֶיךָ ("your ways"), requiring alteration of only one consonant in the MT and implying the expenditure of strength in sexual intercourse. חַיִל ("strength, wealth") may refer to the enormous cost of keeping a harem.

Dorsey (1991:214) dismisses the association of *drkt* and דֶּרֶךְ, since the meanings of the two terms are too distinct to be etymologically related. Dahood (1954:627, n. 3) does relate this meaning of דֶּרֶךְ, however, to the Akk *durgu*, "fortress, stronghold", which he feels could convey a meaning similar to that of *drkt*. On the phonological connection between these lexemes see B.3 below. Muffs (1992:118–19, n. 11) suggests that there is an underlying metaphorical connection between the vb דָּרַךְ, "to exercise power", and דֶּרֶךְ, "road", based on a custom of stepping on something to establish ownership of it (e.g. pQid 1.3, 59d, bBB 100a). This is similar to the original suggestions of Albright and Virolleaud that if דֶּרֶךְ is to be understood as "power" then it is a metaphorical usage, perhaps derived from the vb דָּרַךְ.

B.3 The West Semitic form *drk* is often said to appear as the late Babylonian loan-word *daraggu*, "Weg [spur]" (*AHw*:163a), which occurs rarely in various forms in Akk (Sauer 1971:455; *HAL*:222; Koch 1977:II, 276). Koch also mentions the Babylonian adj *darku/derku* ("following, subsequent, next"), but adds that it is uncertain whether *durgu*, "innerster Teil (eines Gebirges) [innermost part (of a mountain range)]" (*AHw*:177), and *dariku*, "Dattelbehälter [receptacle or container for dates]" (*AHw*:63), belong to the same root (1977:II, 294). The meaning of *daraggu* may be inferred from a lexical list in which it is associated with other road words: *har.ra.an* = *ḫarrānu*, *urḫu*, *daragu* [sic], *mētequ* (Landsberger 1957:II, 270ff; Dorsey 1991:250, n. 4). The same applies to two other contexts (Landsberger 1957:II, 277; II, 279ff.). Sargon describes mountains so rugged that there was not path between them for even foot soldiers to pass through: *ina birīšunu ana mēteq zūk šepē lā išû daraggu* (TCL 3:325). In each of the two other occurrences of the word (AS 5, 16 V:6; Gadd 1954:192, l. 51) it is governed by the negated verb *šakānu*, expressing the establishment of a *daraggu* (von Soden renders "Weg herstellen" [*AHw*:163]).

Although the meaning "path" would fit all of these occurrences of *daraggu*, and therefore imply that it could be cognate with דֶּרֶךְ, it is difficult to account for the *g/k* interchange in the third radical (so Dorsey 1991:250, n. 4). The g may, however, be due to partial assimilation of an original *kaph* to the *resh*, or, as Haupt suggests (1904:132), assimilation to the initial *daleth*. Dorsey suggests that an equally probable cognate is the Semitic root *drg*, which is widely attested (1991:250, n. 4). The root appears in the Arabic words *daraja*, "step, stair, flight of steps" (Wehr 1971:277) and *daraja* "way, route, course" (ibid.:276–77). In BH it is found in the word מַדְרֵג, "mountain ascent" (Ct 2.14) and in later Heb, Arm and other languages it has meanings such as "stairs" or "ascents" (*DNWSI*:259; Jastrow:735). A meaning of *daraggu* as "[mountain] ascent" would be compatible with all the occurrences of the word (except possibly Gadd 1954:192, l. 51) and would account for its regular association with mountains and its collocation with the noun *mētequ*, another word for road associated with mountains (Dorsey 1991:250, n. 4). The same can be argued for *durgu*, sometimes connected with דֶּרֶךְ (*HAL*:222; Koch 1977:294), and interpreted as "remote [mountain] region" (CAD 4:191). Dorsey (1991:250, n. 4) admits that *durgu* could be defined as a "path" or "pass" (e.g. King 1902:64 iv 56), observing that it is often governed by the verb *petû*, "to open", which often governs words for "road" (e.g. CAD 6:107). Von Soden (*AHw*:177) does, however, relate the term to the Arb *durj*, "box", and not to דֶּרֶךְ. It most likely should be understood as a synonym of *daraggu*, meaning "[mountain] ascent", appearing as it does always in a context where mountains are involved (Dorsey 1991:250, n. 4).

B.4 In Arb there is no certain cognate. One possibility is the verb *drk*, which in the fourth conjugation means "to reach, overtake, catch up" and the nouns *darak*, which means "attainment, achievement", and *darakāt*, "descending steps" (Wehr 1971:322–23). Another is the verb *daraja*, "to go, walk" (Wehr 1971:319; Koch 1977:294) and its related nouns *daraj*, "way, route, course" and *madraj*, "way that one follows; course, route, road, path" (Wehr 1971:320). *HAL* also lists the noun *durj*, a "Schublade" (222). The difficulty with all these suggestions is that the shift in the third radical, although possible, need not be inferred when there is an alternative root extant (Dorsey 1991:214). As with the possible cognates in Akk, they should probably be related to the Semitic root *drg*.

2. Formal Characteristics

A.1 *qatl*

A.2 The morphology of the dual, with its pre-stress *qamets* of the plural of segholate nouns דְּרָכִים (Pr 28.6, 28), is probably on the analogy of the plural (BL:571 *v*; JM:§ 91 *b*). The same feature is found with קֶרֶן: קְרָנַיִם alongside קְרָנִים. In view of this rare vocalization Kahle wished to read at Pr 28.6, 28 the plural form דְּרָכִים (1902:82).

A.3 The omission of the *yodh* in the plural before a suffix, as in דְּרָכֶךָ (Ex 33.13), is a feature displayed by many lexemes (BL:252 *r*).

B.1 דֶּרֶךְ is double gendered in BH, although the plural is always found with masculine agreement (Albrecht 1896:54–55). Albrecht proposes that the lexeme was originally feminine, but used with masculine agreement from the time of Ezekiel onwards (1896:55). Michel repeats this theory (1977:77), making reference to Albrecht. The suggestion, however, does not seem to concur with the evidence where there are many examples of דֶּרֶךְ with masculine agreement in early books (e.g. Gn 28.20, Dt 14.24, 17.16, 1Kg 18.6; see Ratner 1983:81). Two recent explanations of the applications of each gender have appeared at the same time, but differ greatly. Both explanations list the identifiable cases of the masculine and feminine forms, with a high degree of agreement. There are, however, some anomalies between the two presentations. Ratner notes 61 cases of דֶּרֶךְ with masculine agreement and 55 with feminine (1987:471). Dorsey, on the other hand, notes 54 cases of masculine and 58 (although he only lists 56) of feminine (1991:220). In the citations of masculine forms, there are 13 instances of disagreement between those listed by Ratner and those by Dorsey. Ratner (1987:471, n. 1) includes the following that are not in Dorsey: Ex 13.17, Dt 17.16, 2Kg 6.19, 17.13, Jr 23.12 (which Dorsey classes as feminine), Ho 14.10

(3x rather than 1x), Ps 10.5, 18.33, 49.14, 101.6, 2Ch 28.26 (2x). Dorsey (1991:221) includes these ones absent from Ratner: 2Kg 12.13, Ezk 16.27, 18.29 (3x rather than 2x), Pr 16.2, 21.2, 8. In the citations of feminine forms, there are 6 instances of disagreement between those listed by Ratner and those by Dorsey. Ratner (1987:471, n. 1) includes the following that are not in Dorsey: Josh 3.4, Ezk 33.9. Dorsey (1991:220–221) includes the following that are not in Ratner: Jr 23.12 (which Ratner classes as masculine), Ezk 3.19, Ps 107.7, Pr 28.18. Dorsey's 1Ch 6.27, 20.32 can only be a misprint for 2Ch 6.27, 20.32, as is Ratner's Neh 9.18 for Dorsey's Neh 9.19. The differences do not affect Ratner's argument, but it is uncertain whether Dorsey's interpretation of the evidence would be affected. If the citations of the two writers are combined, the identifiable occurrences of דֶּרֶךְ with a gender are as follows. Masculine: Gn 28.20, Ex 13.17, Nu 22.32, Dt 14.24, 17.26, 19.6, 28.7 (2x), 25 (2x), Jdg 2.22, 2Sm 22.31, 1Kg 13.10, 18.6 (2x), 19.7, 22.43, 2Kg 6.19, 12.13, 17.13, Is 30.21, 65.2, Jr 6.16 (?), 23.12, 22, 31.9, 32.39, Ezk 13.22, 16.27, 18.25 (2x), 29 (3x), 20.44, 21.24, 26, 23.13, 33.11, 17 (2x), 20, 36.31, Ho 14.10 (3x), Zc 1.4, Ps 10.5, 18.31, 33, 36.5, 49.14, 101.2, 6, 119.5, Pr 2.12 (?), 4.26, 8.13, 12.15, 14.12, 16.2, 25, 29, 21.2, 8, 28.10, 2Ch 7.14, 17.3, 28.26 (2x); Feminine: Gn 24.42, 42.38, Ex 18.20, Nu 9.10, Dt 1.22, 33, 13.6, 28.68, Josh 3.4, 24.17, Jdg 2.19, 18.5, 6, 1Sm 9.6, 12.23, 24.20, 1Kg 8.36, 13.10, 17, 33, 2Kg 7.15, 19.28, 33, Is 37.29, 34, 40.27, Jr 6.16, 12.1, 18.11, 15, 25.5, 26.3, 31.9, 35.15, 36.3, 7, 42.3, Ezk 3.18, 19, 33.9, 36.17, Jn 3.8, 10, Ps 1.6, 107.7, 119.33, Pr 12.26, 14.12, 16.25, 22.6, 28.18, Jb 3.23, La 1.4, Ezr 8.21, Neh 9.12, 18, 19, 2Ch 6.27, 20.32. One disputed case is Jr 23.12. From this evidence we may note that Watson's view that דֶּרֶךְ is normally feminine (1980:335) cannot be substantiated.

Ratner concludes that the syntactic environment affects the gender of דֶּרֶךְ, and states that, in the book of Deuteronomy (which he takes as a sample), "[t]he employment of one gender or the other does not produce any discernible semantic differences" (1987:471). He also notes that דֶּרֶךְ is the only epicene lexeme in Dt. According to Ratner, in relative clauses דֶּרֶךְ governs only feminine agreements, while in independent clauses and in some dependent clauses it may govern either masculine or feminine agreements (1987:471–72). The noun governs masculine agreements seven times in Dt (14.24; 17.16; 19.6; 28.7 [2x] 25 [twice]) and feminine four times (1.22, 33, 13.6, 28.68). In ten of these eleven passages דֶּרֶךְ refers to a physical road or path, Dt 13.6 alone referring to a "spiritual" path. Hence, he is able to conclude that there is not any discernible semantic difference in Dt in the employment of any particular gender (Ratner 1987:471) and that this applies to other parts of the OT as well. The use of the feminine in relative clauses, therefore, accounts for the change in gender within the same verse at 1Kg 13.10 and Jr 31.9. In Jr 31.9 and Ex 18.20 the relative marker is absent, but it is to be understood (Ratner 1987:472). It does, however, seem unlikely that such a syntactic feature would affect the gender agreement of the noun, and perhaps other reasons should be sought, such as the feminine ending being used in these cases for euphonic or poetic effect.

Dorsey, by contrast, argues that the gender of דֶּרֶךְ is not determined by grammatical considerations but by meaning. He distinguishes between physical and figurative meanings of the lexeme. It is feminine when it denotes a physical road (e.g. 1Kg 13.10, 17), a course of physical travel (e.g. Dt 1.22, 33), a metaphorical road or course conceived in physical terms (e.g. Ex 18.20, Dt 13.6) and a journey or enterprise (e.g. Gn 24.42, 42.38). It is masculine when denoting a figurative course of travel not conceived in physical terms (mostly referring to moral conduct or behaviour; e.g. Pr 16.2), direction (e.g. Dt 28.7, 25) or journey where the דֶּרֶךְ is long or great (Dt. 14.24, 19.6, 1Kg 19.7) (Dorsey 1991:220–21). Dorsey notes certain exceptions, most of which he finds to be explicable. In 1Kg 13.10 דֶּרֶךְ is masculine despite referring to a physical road, although the text is questionable and BHS prefer a reading making it feminine. Is 30.21 may either not refer to a physical road, explaining the masculine gender, or perhaps express direction. The exceptions to be found in Ezekiel (13.22, 16.27, 21.24, 26, 36.17) are not surprising since that book generally exhibits peculiarities and inconsistencies in gender. This only leaves one unexplained case in Gn 28.20 where דֶּרֶךְ is masculine but referring to a journey. If Dorsey's interpretation is correct it explains why in Pr 14.12 and 16.25 דֶּרֶךְ is treated as masculine and feminine within the same sentence. The first דֶּרֶךְ denotes the course of behaviour of a man (and therefore is masculine), the second denotes the road to death, conceived as a more physical journey or road and therefore is feminine.

Dorsey (1991:223) also observes that, as in the case of דֶּרֶךְ, אֹרַח appears to be feminine when denoting a physical road or course of travel (Jdg 5.6, Pr 15.19), but masculine when denoting moral behaviour or other non-physical aspects (Ps 119.101, 104, 128, Pr 2.15). This may add greater weight to his theory, since he observes it in both lexemes. However, the identifiable cases of the gender of אֹרַח are so few that it is not possible to draw any firm conclusions. These instances of אֹרַח cannot be used to assist Ratner's theory, as none of them are be found in relative clauses. In his PhD thesis Ratner cites some instances of the masculine of אֹרַח in Gn 18.11, Joel 2.7, Ps 119.101 (cited by Dorsey as well), Pr 2.15, Jb 6.18, 30.12 (1983:78). In the case of אֹרַח Ratner (1983:91) suggests that, since it has a plural form in -ōt, the speaker or writer thought at times that words in agreement should be feminine by analogy (cf. לָשׁוֹן, מָקוֹם, עָווֹן, אָרוֹן, חַלּוֹן and possibly אוֹר). He also notes that the plural forms may be the result of vowel harmony (1983:99, n. 11).

When Ratner considers דֶּרֶךְ in his PhD thesis he comes to some different conclusions from those of his later article. He suggests, for example, that there may be a possible semantic variation between the genders (1983:111), although the opposite to that determined by Dorsey. He cites for this examples only from 1Kg, suggesting it is masculine in 1Kg 13.10 (= f?), 12, 17 (= f?) when denoting a literal "path" and feminine in 1Kg 13.33 when referring to Jeroboam's "evil ways". Another feature that he observes is a variation for reasons of style (1983:112). This may account for changes of agreement in close proximity to each other in Jdg 2.19 and 22, 2Ch 6.27 and 7.14, Ezk 33.9, 11, 17 and 20, and Ezk 36.17 and 31. A third feature is a change of gender used to indicate a change of speaker. In 2Ch 6.27, for example, when Solomon is speaking דֶּרֶךְ is used in the feminine, but when God speaks in 7.14 דֶּרֶךְ is used in the masculine (1983:117). This approach in his dissertation, although not without some doubtful interpretations, is probably a better approach than that of his 1987 article.

The context in each instance is more likely to determine which gender is chosen. There may be poetic or euphonic reasons, or the author may be wishing to highlight or emphasize a feature of the narrative by changing gender (cf. Watson 1980:321–41). The attempt to discover one system that accounts for all the occurrences is probably futile. An example containing דֶּרֶךְ of the poetic use of gender has been observed by Watson at Is 43.16, where the unusual event is emphasized by the interchange between masculine and feminine forms (1980:428). In this example, however, the gender of דֶּרֶךְ is not specified, but Watson takes it to be feminine since it his belief that דֶּרֶךְ is normally feminine. A simple example is Pr 12.26, where the action of the righteous person (צַדִּיק) is contrasted with the way of the wicked (דֶּרֶךְ רְשָׁעִים). This contrast is brought out by the use of a masculine verb with צַדִּיק and a feminine verb with דֶּרֶךְ. Boling has noted the "high preponderance of feminine forms employed in second position *metri causa*" (1969:122), and this may be another clue to the gender of דֶּרֶךְ. The appearance of the feminine in relative clauses may be due to the position of the pronominal suffix at the end of the clause in pause (e.g. Gn 24.42, Dt 13.6) or at least with the accent *zāqeph qāṭōn* (e.g. Gn 42.38, Josh 3.4). In Jr 31.9 we find a masculine ending on the adjective, but a feminine suffix at the end of the clause, perhaps from a wish to end with the feminine suffix: בְּדֶרֶךְ יָשָׁר לֹא יִכָּשְׁלוּ בָּהּ.

3. Syntagmatics

A.1 Verbs of motion tend to govern דֶּרֶךְ directly (e.g. Nu 20.17; see Dorsey 1991:215), and this is especially pronounced where the road is named (e.g. Dt 3.1). The verbs בוֹא (e.g. 2Kg 11.16, 19), הָלַךְ (e.g. Gn 28.20, 2Sm 4.7), hif הלך (e.g. Dt 8.2), יָצָא, נָחָה (Ex 13.17), נָסַע (e.g. Nu 10.33, Dt 1.40), נוס (e.g. Dt 28.7, 25), סָבַב (e.g. Ex 13.18), עָבַר (Dt 2.8b, Is 35.8), עָלָה (e.g. Nu 21.33), פָּנָה (1Sm 13.18), רָדַף (e.g. Gn 31.23), רוץ (2Sm 18.23) and שׁוּב (Ezk 44.1, 46.9) all govern דֶּרֶךְ directly when it is named (Dorsey 1991:215). Likewise, the ptc of עָבַר is used with דֶּרֶךְ to denote a "traveller" (e.g. Ps 80.13[12]). To go on one's journey may also be expressed by the verb עָשָׂה followed by the direct object (Jdg 17.8).

A.2 After some of the verbs of motion דֶּרֶךְ may also be governed by a preposition: בוֹא + מִן (e.g. Jdg 9.37), בּוֹא + ב (e.g. 2Kg 19.33), הָלַךְ + ל (e.g. Gn 19.2), הָלַךְ + ב (e.g. Gn 35.3), הָלַךְ + עַל (e.g. Jdg 5.10), נָחָה + ב (e.g. Gn 24.27), עָלָה + ב (2Sm 15.23), עָבַר + עַל פְּנֵי (e.g. Dt 2.8a), עָבַר + מִן (e.g. Ex 32.8), שוב + מִן (e.g. Dt 1.22), שׁוּב + ב (e.g. Dt 17.16), שׁוּב + ל (e.g. Gn 33.16), שׁוּב + מִן (e.g. 1Kg 13.26). The verb יָשַׁר governs דֶּרֶךְ with the prepositions ב and עַל (1Sm 6.12). To "turn onto" a דֶּרֶךְ is expressed by the vb פָּנָה followed by the direct object דֶּרֶךְ (1Sm 13.18), or by the preposition אֶל and דֶּרֶךְ (Jdg 20.42, 1Sm 13.17). The two constructions appear to be synonymous. For further examples, see Clines II:472a–b.

A.3 דֶּרֶךְ is the subject of the verbs אָבַד "to perish" (Ps 1.6), גָּבַהּ "to be high" (Is 55.9), היה "to be" (e.g. Jr 23.12), חִיל "to be firm" (Ps 10.5), יָרַט "to be precipitate" (Nu 22.32), nif כון "to be established" (e.g. Ps 119.5), pual כפר "to be atoned" (1QS 3.6), passive כתב "to be written" (e.g. 2Ch 13.22), מָלֵא "to be full" (2Kg 7.15), passive סלל "to be raised" (Jr 18.15), nif סתר "to be hidden" (e.g. Is 40.27), עָשָׂה "to do" (Jr 4.18), nif פלא "to be wonderful" (Pr 30.19), פָּנָה "to turn" (Ezk 47.2), צָלַח "to be prosperous" (Jr 12.1), רָבָה "to be great" (Dt 14.24, 19.6), hif שחת "to be corrupt" (CD 15.7), nif שמם "to be made desolate" (Lv 26.22), תָּמַם "to be perfect" (e.g. 1QS 8.25), hof תמם "to be made perfect" (4Qse 1 iii 17) and hif תעה "to lead astray" (Pr 12.26).

A.4 דֶּרֶךְ is the direct object of such verbs as piel בלע "to swallow up" (Is 3.12), זָכַר "to remember" (Dt 8.2), יָדַע "to know" (Josh 3.4), hif ידע "to make known" (e.g. Ex 18.20), hif ירה "to teach" (1Kg 8.36, Is 2.3), piel ישר "to make straight" (Is 45.12), hif כבד "to make glorious" (Is 8.23), hif כון "to establish" (Dt 19.3), hif נבט "to look" (1Kg 18.43), hif נגד "to tell" (1Sm 9.6), hif נתר "to loosen" (2Sm 22.33), נָתַן "to give" (1Kg 8.32), עָזַב "to forsake" (Is 55.7), piel פנה "to prepare" (Is 40.3), צִוָּה "to command" (e.g. Ex 32.8, Dt 5.33), hif צלח "to prosper" (e.g. Gn 24.21), רָאָה "to see" (Dt 28.68), שִׂים "to set [a distance]" (Gn 30.36), שָׁמַר "to keep" (e.g. Gn 3.24, 18.19). For further examples, see Clines II:467b–68a.

A.5 דֶּרֶךְ is the indirect object or adverbial adjunct of בָּקַשׁ + ב "to seek" (Josh 2.22), יָצָא + ב "to depart" (e.g. Ex 18.8), hitp יצב + ב "to oppose" (Nu 22.22), מוּל + ב "to circumcise" (Josh 5.7) מָצָא + ב "to find" (Gn 16.7), hif נדח + מִן "to drive away" (Dt 13.6), נָפַל + ב "to fall" (Dt 22.4), hif נפל + מִן "to let fall" (Jdg 2.19), נִצַּב + ב "to take one's stand" (e.g. Nu 22.23, 31), עָמַד + עַל "to stand" (1Kg 20.38), קָבַר + ב "to bury" (Gn 35.19), קרה + ב "to encounter" (Dt 25.18), שָׁלַח + ב "to send" (1Sm 15.18), hif שגה + ב "to err" (Dt 27.18), שָׁמַר + ב "to keep"(e.g. Gn 28.20). For further examples, see Clines II:471b–72a

A.6 דֶּרֶךְ is governed by the prepositions אַחֲרֵי (Dt 11.30), אֶל (e.g. 2Ch 6.27), עַל (e.g. Gn 38.21), לְ (e.g. Gn 42.25), בְּ (e.g. Gn 45.24), כְּ (e.g. Nu 11.31) and מִן (e.g. Pr 21.16). For the range of verbs used with these prepositions, see Clines II:471a–72b. The lexeme also appears once each with the prepositional expressions עַל־יַד, "beside" (+ עָמַד, 2Sm 15.2), עַל־פִּי, "according to" (+ חָנַךְ, Pr 22.6), עַל־פְּנֵי, "towards" (2Sm 15.23) and בֵּין ...וְ "between" (4Q423 1.8). With verbs of motion, the preposition governing דֶּרֶךְ is most often ב (e.g Ex 4.24). The prepositions אֶל (Gn 38.16), עַל (e.g. Gn 38.21), עֲלֵי (Gn 49.17) and יַד (1Sm 4.13 Qere) also express position by the side of a דֶּרֶךְ.

A.7 דֶּרֶךְ is described by various adjectives. A physical דֶּרֶךְ may be רָחֹק, "distant" (Nu 9.10), רַב "great" (1Kg 19.7), יָשָׁר, "straight" (e.g. Ezr 8.21), מָלֵא "full" (2Kg 7.15), or חֹל "profane [in purpose]" (1Sm 21.6) or it may be qualified by the adjectives אֶחָד, "one" (e.g. Dt 28.7, 25), אַחֵר, "another" (1Kg 13.10, 18.6), רִאשׁוֹן, "former" (2Ch 17.3, 18.26), אַחֲרוֹן, "latter" (2Ch 28.26) or זֶה, "this" (e.g. Gn 28.20). For further examples, see Clines II:467 a–b, 470b–71a.

A.8 A figurative דֶּרֶךְ may be טוֹב, "good" (e.g. 1Sm 12.23), יָשָׁר, "upright" (1Sm 12.23, Sir 11.15), קָשֶׁה, "stubborn" (Jdg 2.19). It may be תָּמִים, "blameless" (Ps 101.2, 6), תָּם (e.g. Pr 10.29), or רַע, "evil" (e.g. 2Kg 17.13) or רָשָׁע, "wicked" (Ezk 3.18, 19).

A.9 דֶּרֶךְ may appear as the nomen regens of a place name: אֱדוֹם "Edom" (2Kg 3.20), אֶרֶץ פְּלִשְׁתִּים "the land of the Philistines" (Ex 13.17), אֶפְרָתָה "Ephratah" (Gn 35.19. 48.7), הָעֲרָבָה "Arabah" (Dt 2.8), אַשּׁוּר "Assyria" (Jr 2.18), הָאֲתָרִים "Atharim" (Nu 21.1), בְּאֵר שָׁבַע "Beer-Sheba" (Am 8.14), הַבָּשָׁן "Bashan" (Nu 21.33, Dt 3.1), בֵּית הַגָּן "Beth-Hagan" (2Kg 9.27), בֵּית חוֹרֹן "Beth-Horon" (1Sm

13.18), בֵּית הַיְשִׁמוֹת "Beth-Jeshimoth" (Jo 12.3), בֵּית שֶׁמֶשׁ "Beth-Shemesh" (1Sm 6.12), חוֹרֹנַיִם "Horonaim" (Is 15.5), הַיַּרְדֵּן "the Jordan" (Josh 2.7), יַם־סוּף "the Red Sea" (e.g. Nu 21.4), צִיּוֹן "Zion" (La 1.4), מִצְרַיִם "Egypt" (Is 10.24, 26), עָפְרָה "Ophrah" (1Sm 13.17), שַׁעֲרַיִם "Shaaraim" (1Sm 17.52), שׁוּר "Shur" (Gn 16.7) or תִּמְנָתָה "Timnah" (Gn 38.14).

It may likewise be the nomen regens of a location, as, for example, הַגְּבוּל the "border" (1Sm 6.9, 13.18), הַמִּדְבָּר "the wilderness" (e.g. Ex 13.18), הָר "a mountain" (e.g. Dt 1.19), מְבוֹא הַשֶּׁמֶשׁ "the setting sun" (Dt 11.30). For further examples, see Clines II:469a–b.

A.10 דֶּרֶךְ may appear as nomen regens of יוֹם both in the singular (Nu 11.31, 1Kg 19.4) and with a number expressed (e.g. Gn 30.36, 11QT 43.13, 52.14), in order to denote length of journey. For further examples, see Clines II:470a.

A.11 דֶּרֶךְ may be the nomen regens of an abstract noun, such as אֶמֶת "truth" (e.g. Gn 24.48, 4QSᵉ 1 iii 4), אוֶלֶת "folly" (4Q525 3 ii 2, 7), חָכְמָה "wisdom"(Pr 4.11) or תְּבוּנָה "understanding" (Is 40.14). For further examples, see Clines II:469b–70a.

It may also be found as the nomen regens of concrete nouns: אֹרַח "way" (Is 3.12), כָּל־הָאָרֶץ "all the earth" (e.g. Gn 19.31), מַעֲלֵה "ascent" (Josh 10.10), רֶגֶל "foot"(Sir 51.15), עֵץ הַחַיִּים "tree of life" (Gn 3.24). For further examples, see Clines II:469a–b.

A.12 דֶּרֶךְ is the nomen regens of a PN: אָסָא "Asa" (e.g. 1Kg 22.43), דָּוִד "David" (e.g. 2Kg 22.2, Sir 48.22), יהוה "the Lord" (e.g. Gn 18.19, Jdg 2.22), יְהוֹשָׁפָט "Jehospaphat" (2Ch 21.12), יָרְבְעָם "Jeroboam" (e.g. 1Kg 16.2, 19) and שְׁלֹמֹה "Solomon" (2Ch 11.17). These names indicate that the דֶּרֶךְ may either be a good example to be followed or a bad example.

דֶּרֶךְ is also the nomen regens of nouns denoting people: אָב "father" (1Kg 15.26), אֵם "mother" (1Kg 22.53), מֶלֶךְ "king" (Nu 21.22), נָשִׁים "women" (Gn 31.35), עַם "people" (Is 8.11). For further examples, see Clines II:468b–69a.

A.13 The construction or preparation of a דֶּרֶךְ is expressed by the verbs סָלַל and piel פנה (Is 40.3, 57.14, 62.10, Ml 3.1). The maintenance ("instand setzen/halten") or measuring up ("abmessen") of a דֶּרֶךְ is termed in Dt 19.3 by הכין (*HAL*:222).

A.14 The "side" of a דֶּרֶךְ is the יָד (e.g. Ezk 48.1), whilst another section is called the רֹאשׁ, "head" (e.g. Ezk 16.25, 31, 21.26), and a third its אֵם, "mother" (Ezk 21.26). These latter two expressions probably denote junctions.

A.15 The repetition of דֶּרֶךְ appears at Dt 2.27 in the form בַּדֶּרֶךְ בַּדֶּרֶךְ the interpretation of which is disputed (see Exegesis A.10, and Clines II:472b).

B.1 Koch (1973:295) thinks that the use of the preposition בּ with verbs of motion indicates that a דֶּרֶךְ was tridimensional and not flat. This is an inaccurate interpretation of the preposition, which has a far wider range of meanings than "in".

4. Versions [A full listing of translation equivalents and references may be found in APPENDIX] *a*. LXX:

A.1 The LXX for the most part renders דֶּרֶךְ by the word ὁδός, the most general word in Greek for "road". The LXX of Pr, as with other words in the semantic field of "road", and, in one instance in Is, is idiosyncratic, choosing τρίβος rather than ὁδός.

A.2 The LXX is aware of a possible prepositional use of דֶּרֶךְ in construct phrases, as indicated by translations with ἐπί (Ezk 21.2, 42.4), κατέναντι (Ezk 40.10, 42.1αβ), πρός (e.g. Ezk 8.5), βλέπω ἀπέναντι (Ezk 42.7), βλέπω εἰς (Pr 16.25b), βλέπω κατά (Ezk 40.32, 47.2b), and βλέπω πρός (Ezk 40.24αβ, 42.15b). Sometimes this sense is conveyed by a preposition with the noun ὁδός: καθ' ὁδόν (Ezk 42.15a) or κατὰ τὴν ὁδόν (e.g. Ezk 43.2).

A.3 In 1Kg 13.33 the expression דַּרְכּוֹ הָרָעָה is translated by κακία, capturing the sense if not the lexical equivalents. Likewise, דֶּרֶךְ alone at Jr 15.7 is translated by κακία and the דֶּרֶךְ of Jeroboam is rendered by ἁμαρτία at 1Kg 22.53.

A.4 In the LXX to Is 35.8 the first דֶּרֶךְ of the MT does not seem to have a translation equivalent (except perhaps for καθαρά; see Introduction: Text Doubtful A.2), and probably is the result of dittography. For the third occurrence of דֶּרֶךְ in the verse the translation seems to be the pronoun αὐτή. The expression ὁδὸς ἀκάθαρτος in the preceding colon appears to be part of an inserted colon, which emphasizes the concentration on purity of the LXX in this verse and creates a balanced structure in the verse. The verse opens in the LXX with the statement that there shall be a pure road, and so continues later that there shall not be there an impure road.

A.5 At Is 62.10, the LXX omits an earlier clause containing מְסִלָּה, and translates the phrase פַּנּוּ דֶּרֶךְ by the one verb ὁδοποιεῖν. In similar fashion the LXX translates עֹבְרֵי־דָרֶךְ at Pr 9.15 by πάρειμι [ἰέναι]. This Greek verb only occurs elsewhere in the LXX at Pr 15.10 where it also renders the Heb עָבַר. In some MSS of LXX Pr the noun ὁδός has been added, but the Greek verb probably includes דֶּרֶךְ within its semantic range (Cook 1997:276–77).

A.6 Is 40.14 is not reproduced in the LXX, whilst Pr 9.15 is paraphrased.

A.7 In Jr 18.11 and 23.22 דֶּרֶךְ is collocated with מַעֲלָל, and the phrase as a whole is translated in both cases by ἐπιτήδευμα, providing no obvious translation equivalent. By contrast at Jr 32.19, where the same collocation may be found, the LXX appears to render דֶּרֶךְ by ὁδός and then to omit מַעֲלָל.

A.8 πολυοδία at Is 57.10 is a neologism, rendering the Hebrew phrase דֶּרֶךְ רֹב. There are many compound words in Greek with πολυ-, which may indicate that it already existed in Greek and is only not attested in our extant sources. It does, nonetheless, render the Heb closely. It is surprising that the LXX has few such compounds when the OT has many pairs with רבה (as noted by Tov 1977:194). Tov suggests that the literary taste of the translator led him to coin the word πολυοδία (ibid.:194).

A.9 The translation καρδία "heart" (Ps 37.14 [=36.14]) is appropriate to the context where it refers to those who are upright in their lifestyle, but in the next verse the word καρδία does appear and there may have been some contamination from that verse into the previous.

A.10 In Pr 10.29 the translation φόβος "fear" suggests that the LXX read דֶּרֶךְ as the construct of the tetragrammaton that follows, "the way of the Lord".

McKane, however, proposes that the tetragrammaton is the predicate and that דֶּרֶךְ should go with חָם (1970:427).

A.11 The LXX of Jb 13.15 (λαλέω, "to speak") appears to have misread Heb דרך as דבר. The LXX of La 3.11 (καταδιώκω, "to pursue"), on the other hand, has read the consonants correctly, but understood it to be from the Arm דרך (Lust 1996:233), presumably afel.

A.12 For the LXX readings at Ho 10.13, see Introduction, Text Doubtful A.4.

A.13 The MT of Am 8.14 is difficult to interpret and the LXX translator rendered דֶּרֶךְ there as θεός "god" in accommodation to the previous colon.

B.1 Hatch & Redpath (1897:1240) indicate that the translation of דֶּרֶךְ at Pr 14.12b and 16.25b is πυθμήν, "depth, bottom". It seems more likely that the expression πυθμένα ᾅδου translates מָוֶת "death" and that דֶּרֶךְ is understood in its prepositional sense and hence is translated by ἔρχομαι εἰς in Pr 14.12b and by βλέπω εἰς in 16.25b.

B.2 The LXX to Sir 11.34a reads διαστρέψει σε ἐν ταραχαῖς "he will lead you astray in disorder" in place of the Heb זָהִיר דרכיך (MS A). Skehan suggests that the Greek has rendered the sound rather than the sense of דרכיך (Skehan and di Lella 1987:244).

b. Peshitta:

A.1 The most common rendering for דֶּרֶךְ in the Pesh is ʾurḥāʾ, the most frequent and general word for "road" in Syr. דֶּרֶךְ is translated by šḇīlāʾ only very rarely. The second most frequent rendering, merdāʾ "journey", is found in only a few instances. One should also note the one instance of hlaḵtāʾ at Ezk 42.4.

A.2 It is difficult in some cases of דֶּרֶךְ to determine whether the Pesh has provided a translation equivalent or not, especially when it seems to have a prepositional sense. This prepositional sense is conveyed in the translations *b*, *b* + ʾurḥāʾ, *d*, *l*, *l* + ʾurḥāʾ and *mn*. The two cases of maʿlānāʾ "entrance" (Ezk 42.10, 46.2?) seem to be places where the Pesh had difficulty with the prepositional meaning. At Ezk 46.2 maʿlānāʾ may in fact be the translation of the Heb אוּלָם.

A.3 In Gn 38.14 and 38.21, where we find pālšaṭ ʾurḥāʾ, "the head of the roads", the Pesh seems to have read רֹאשׁ דֶּרֶךְ; cf. Vg, TgO, TgPsJ and BHS.

A.4 The Heb of Ezk 46.2 דֶּרֶךְ הַפּוֹנֶה is the reverse of the more common הַפּוֹנֶה דֶּרֶךְ. The Pesh seems to have omitted it, perhaps through difficulty in understanding it.

A.5 In Jr 32.39 the Pesh translation of ruḥāʾ "spirit" seems to be a contextual rendering, since in the MT דֶּרֶךְ is in parallelism with "heart" (לֵב; Pesh: lebbāʾ). The Syr may also be a corruption internal to the Pesh of ʾurḥāʾ to ruḥāʾ, aided by the parallelism.

A.6 The Pesh translation reʿyānāʾ "opinion, counsel" at Ps 1.1 is probably the translation of Heb עֵצָה earlier in the verse, which itself is translated by urḥāʾ. The Pesh has reversed the first noun of each of the construct pairs.

A.7 The translation brīṭāʾ "creation" at Pr 8.22 is understandable in the context (cf. TgHag). The same translation at Jb 40.19 can be accounted for by the presence there also of רֵאשִׁית preceding דֶּרֶךְ in that verse (see also B.1).

B.1 Cook (1997:221) suggests that the rendering *briṭaʾ* "creation" in the Pesh of Pr 8.22 is evidence of the translator making use of the LXX, which itself speaks of creation (using the verb κτίζω to render קָנָה), since it is an interpretation, he says, that occurs in none of the other versions. In fact the rendering can also be found in the Tg to this verse (בְּרִיתָא) so that it is not unique to the Pesh, and the Pesh chooses the same noun for the similar phrase at Jb 40.19 (where the LXX has πλάσμα), indicating that it may be an interpretation by the Pesh translator(s).

c. Targum:

A.1 The primary translation for דֶּרֶךְ in its meaning "road" or "way" in the Tg is the lexeme א(וֹ)רְחָא. The only exceptions to this are the translations שְׁבִילָא (Ho 13.7, Jb 24.18), כְּבִישׁ (Ps 138.5) and the loan-word א(יׁ)סְרַטָא, "street", used by TgPsJ (Nu 22.22, 23aα, 23b, 31, Dt 22.6). One should also note the odd expressions א(וֹ)רְחָא כְּבִישׁ (Dt 2.27aβ [PsJ]) and שְׁבִילֵי א(וֹ)רְחָא (Gn 3.24 [PsJ]). When דֶּרֶךְ is found in parallelism with the Heb אֹרַח in Pr, both lexemes are translated in the Tg by א(וֹ)רְחָא (e.g. 9.15, 12.28). If דֶּרֶךְ is found in parallelism with another lexeme from the semantic field of "road", דֶּרֶךְ is still translated by א(וֹ)רְחָא, but the other lexeme is translated by שְׁבִילָא (e.g. מְסִלָּה at TgPr 16.17).

A.2 The Tg is sensitive to the meaning of דֶּרֶךְ as "journey" and accordingly translates it by מַהְלַךְ a number of times.

A.3 In the Pentateuchal Tg there are no renderings of דֶּרֶךְ with a prepositional sense. In TgHag there is one instance of לְאַפֵּי אָרְחָא "in the direction of the road" (2Ch 6.38), which translates the prepositional meaning of דֶּרֶךְ, but still retains an equivalent for דֶּרֶךְ as a noun. Often in Ezk and once in 2Sm (18.23) the Tg overcomes the difficulty of rendering דֶּרֶךְ with a prepositional meaning by adding the preposition ל or ב before א(וֹ)רְחָא, often alternating between the two.

A.4 The Tg at Is 15.5 translates דֶּרֶךְ by מְחוֹתִית, "descent", perhaps under the influence of מַעֲלֶה "ascent" earlier in the verse.

A.5 The two occurrences of דֶּרֶךְ in Jr 2.18 have no obvious translation equivalents. The verse in the Tg describes the treatment of Israel by Egypt and the threat posed by the Assyrians. The word דֶּרֶךְ may have conjured up something of this action in expressing the way Israel is treated by Egypt, and that Israel *went* to Assyria and will be punished in an Assyrian *manner* by going into exile (see Hayward 1987:51, n. 22).

A.6 In a large exegetical paraphrase in the Tg, the expression דֶּרֶךְ הַיָּם in Is 8.23 is translated as גְּבוּרַת יַמָּא "prodigy of the sea". This is part of the translation of the verse relating it to the events of the Exodus. In another exegetical portion those who return to the דֶּרֶךְ of their heart are said to wander "after the fantasy" (בָּתַר הִרְהוּר) of their heart (Is 57.17).

A.7 The translation at Ezk 16.25, 31, and 21.26 and in PsJ to Gn 38.14, 49.17, Nu 24.25 (a doublet) of פָּרָשׁוּת א(וֹ)רְחָא, "crossroads", is comparable to the Pesh's *palšaṭ ʾurḥaʾ* (Gn 38.14, 21).

A.8 The Tg to Am 2.7 refers to the perversion of the "cause" (דִּין) of the needy, a repeat of a phrase from the Tg at Am 5.12, where it accurately translates the MT.

A.9 The meaning of דֶּרֶךְ in the MT at Am 8.14 is obscure and the Tg renders it there by נִימוֹסֵי "laws" (a Greek loan-word: νόμος).

A.10 The Tg at Nah 1.3 appears to understand דרך as a verb, translating it by דבר, "to go forth". This is the usual verb in the Tg for denoting the going forth of God (cf. Zc 9.14; Cathcart & Gordon 1989:132, n. 13).

A.11 The translation שָׁעֲתָא "moment" at 2Ch 18.23 is a contextual interpretation by the Tg. The same may be said of the translations בְּרִיתָא "creation" (Pr 8.22), אַתְרָא "place" (Nu 24.25 [Neo]) and אַרְעָא "earth" (Gn 49.17 [Neo], Ex 23.20 [Neo]).

B.1 [nil]

d. Vulgate:

A.1 The most frequent rendering for דֶּרֶךְ in the Vg is *via*. There is, as in all the other Versions, no consistency whether it is rendered by the s or pl. The meaning of as a "journey" is conveyed by the translation *iter*. It is only rarely that *semita* is used to translate דֶּרֶךְ (Nu 22.23c, Is 57.14? [see A.3], La 3.11). There is one case of דֶּרֶךְ being translated by a word for a street in a city, namely *vicus* (Jdg 4.9).

A.2 The prepositional use of דֶּרֶךְ is rendered by various means in the Vg: *ad* (Ezk 40.22, 43.4b), *ad viam* (Ezk 40.46, 44.1, 47.2aβ), *directus* (Jr 31.21), *duceo ad* (Pr 14.12b, 16.25b), *quae ducit ad* (Dt 2.1), *per viam* (Ezk 42.12, 15a, 43.4a, 44.4, 46.2, 8a, 9 [4x]), *per viam quae ducit ad* (Nu 21.4, Josh 2.7, 2Kg 25.4b), *per viam quae ducit* (Josh 12.3, 1Sm 6.12aβ, Jr 52.7), *per* (Nu 10.33b, 2Kg 3.8b, 46.9, 47.2aα), *quae respiciebat ad* (Ezk 40.24aβ), *via respiciens ad* (Ezk 42.1, 12). In many of these cases the Vg translator included a nominal equivalent of דֶּרֶךְ (*via*) as well as rendering a prepositional sense by means of prepositions and sometimes verbs (*duceo*, *respicio*).

A.3 In Is 57.14 the second דֶּרֶךְ is clearly rendered by *via*. However, the first דֶּרֶךְ appears to have been translated three times: first, by the usual *via*, then by *iter*, suggesting the different nuance of "journey", and finally by the word *semita*, which is rarely used to render דֶּרֶךְ.

B.1 [nil]

5. Lexical/Semantic Field(s)

A.1 The lexeme דֶּרֶךְ appears frequently in both prose and poetry of the OT, and can be found in every book of the OT except for Obadiah, Habakkuk, Zephaniah, Song of Songs, Esther, Daniel and 1Chronicles (Dorsey 1991:212). It is also found frequently in Sir and in a range of literature from Qum.

A.2 Other lexemes in the field are אֹרַח, חוּץ, מוֹרָד, מְסִלָּה, מַסְלוּל, מַסַּע, מַעְבָּר/מַעֲבָרָה, מַעְגָּל, מַעֲלֶה, מִשְׁעוֹל, נָתִיב/נְתִיבָה, עֲבָרָה, רְחוֹב, שְׁבִיל, and שׁוּק.

A.3 Of those lexemes that denote a road or course שְׁבִיל, נְתִיבָה, נָתִיב/נְתִיבָה, מַעְגָּל, and שׁוּק never appear in prose, whilst אֹרַח can be found only once in a prose text (Gn 18.11), but frequently in poetry. Tidwell (1980:68, n. 14), therefore, raises the question whether Gn 18.11 should not be understood as a poetic expression in a prose context. מְסִלָּה likewise occurs primarily in poetry, although it can be found in prose (Nu 20.19). מַסְלוּל and מִשְׁעוֹל, found in prose, are both *hapax legomena*. מְסִלָּה may perhaps be used in prose exclusively of an important road or "highway", whilst דֶּרֶךְ denotes a road of any kind outside a city. Although some lexica (e.g. *HAL*:691; BDB:677) render נְתִיבָה/נָתִיב as "Pfad" or "path", there is no evidence to suggest that it is any different from "Weg" or "road, way", their renderings for דֶּרֶךְ and אֹרַח. When נְתִיבָה/נָתִיב is in parallelism with the other lexemes, it is in no way portrayed as being of a lesser size or importance (Dorsey 1991:226). Little can be said of שְׁבִיל from its total of five appearances (2x OT, 1x Sir, 2x Qum), but in MH it appears ten times as an independent substantive (in addition to the prepositional expression בשביל, "for the sake of"), and seems to designate a "path" and should, in that respect, be distinguished from דֶּרֶךְ, which is used of roads in general (Dorsey 1991:237–38).

A.4 דֶּרֶךְ has a figurative as well as a literal sense. In BH נְתִיבָה/נָתִיב is rarely used of a course of travel, whilst in Qum it is mostly used in this sense (Dorsey 1991:228). An exception at Qum is 4Q400 I 2.10. In prose the meaning "journey" may also be conveyed by the lexeme מַסַּע. All the lexemes in A.3 may denote in poetry the figurative sense of "course of life".

A.5 The lexemes מַעֲלֶה, מַעְבָּרָה/מַעֲבָר, מוֹרָד, and עֲבָרָה all denote a specific type of road. חוּץ, רְחֹב, and שׁוּק denote parts within a city, town or village. Although many of the other lexemes are not used of streets within urban areas, it does not mean that they could not have been, as indicated by the use of אֹרַח for "street" in Qum (4QapLam[a] 2.7) and Sir (49.6). The expression דֶּרֶךְ עִיר at Ezk 21.24 and Ps107.4 seems to denote in both cases a road leading to a city rather than in the city itself (see also A.8).

A.6 Of all the words in the semantic field of "road", דֶּרֶךְ alone is bound in a cstr relationship with another lexeme from the field (דֶּרֶךְ אֹרְחֹתֶיךָ at Is 3.12 and perhaps דֶּרֶךְ נְתִיבָה at Pr 12.28).

A.7 Tidwell (1980:57) indicates that דֶּרֶךְ is the only lexeme from the field used in parallelism with itself (e.g. Ps 1.6, Pr 41.1). With other lexemes from the field דֶּרֶךְ takes the position of the A-word 32 times, and of the B-word 10 times (Tidwell 1980:57).

A.8 דֶּרֶךְ is never in parallelism with the most common word for "street", חוּץ (occurring 164x OT), which itself is often in parallel with רְחֹב and once with שׁוּק (Ct 3.2) (Dorsey 1991:240).

B.1 Dorsey notes that מַעְגָּל is "regularly in parallelism with אֹרַח and דֶּרֶךְ, both of which can mean 'course', but never with מְסִלָּה or נָתִיב" (1991:235), which, he says are more restricted to the meaning "road". Although he is correct that מַעְגָּל is never in parallelism with these latter lexemes, it does occur in passages with them in neighbouring verses (Is 59.7–8) or in the same sentence (4Q184), suggesting that there is not so sharp a distinction between the lexemes.

6. Exegesis

A.1 *HAL* (222), on the basis of the derivation of the noun from the verb, summarize its meaning as a "Strecke Land, die durch Beghen fest u. so z. Weg (אֹרַח) geworden ist". Dorsey suggests that the various meanings of דֶּרֶךְ may be subsumed under three categories: road, journey and course of travel (both physical and in life) (Dorsey 1991:213). These categories may in turn be subdivided.

A.2 A דֶּרֶךְ denotes any stretch of terrain that may be used as a thoroughfare, whether a public highway carrying many people (Nu 20.17) or a private road to a house (Pr 7.8). It may be a path that leads to an object, such as a tree (דֶּרֶךְ עֵץ הַחַיִּים, Gn 3.24) or a road to a named place (דֶּרֶךְ שׁוּר, Gn 16.7). In similar fashion it may be used metaphorically for the way to wisdom (Jb 28.13).

A.3 In a second meaning of דֶּרֶךְ as "journey" (Reise), the focus rests on the travelling itself, and not the surface upon which the travelling is done. It may involve journeying along several roads (Ezr 8.22) or none (Nu 11.31). Included within this category is דֶּרֶךְ expressing the direction of travel (Dt 28.7). Dorsey (1991:213), however, classifies this with behaviour under his third category of "course of travel (in life)". This seems to blur the distinctions.

The length of the journey is expressed by a cstr state with temporal modifier; e.g. דֶּרֶךְ שְׁלֹשֶׁת יָמִים, "three days journey" at Gn 30.36.

A.4 דֶּרֶךְ denoting a course in life can be expressed in terms of the conduct by man, by God or required by God:

a) Characteristic behaviour, as that of the ant (Pr 6.6) or of a woman (דֶּרֶךְ נָשִׁים, Gn 31.35; cf. אֹרַח at Gn 18.11). The way of all the earth (דֶּרֶךְ כָּל־הָאָרֶץ) is death (e.g. Josh 23.14) (Zorell:179).

b) One's daily pattern (course) of life; e.g. a man should commit his דֶּרֶךְ to God (Ps 37.5).

c) Moral course followed by someone, as that of Jeroboam I (1Kg 13.33).

d) A prescribed moral course, as the דֶּרֶךְ of righteousness (Pr 16.31).

e) A course prescribed by God expressed as the דֶּרֶךְ יהוה (e.g. Dt 9.16). This is particularly associated with the course laid down in the divine decrees and laws (e.g. Ex 18.20).

A.5 A דֶּרֶךְ may be an enterprise or business ("Unternehmung, Geschäft"; *HAL*:222) (e.g. 2Ch 13.22), and in this manner is a course undertaken in business. It may also refer to a military campaign (1Sm 15.18) and perhaps to a pilgrimage (in Am 8.14 according to Budde 1925:98–99).

A.6 Construct expressions using דֶּרֶךְ as the *nomen regens* are common, but present problems of interpretation. The construct in many cases could be understood either as a preposition or as the designation of the name of a road. For example, the expression at Dt 1.40, "and journey ... *derekh* the Suph Sea" (וּסְעוּ ... דֶּרֶךְ יַם־סוּף) could mean either "towards the Suph Sea" (as RSV) or "on the Suph Sea Road" (e.g. Aharoni 1979:57–58). This use of דֶּרֶךְ to form road names is clear in Ex 13.17 where the expression כִּי קָרוֹב הוּא confirms that דֶּרֶךְ is here used in a nominal sense, as הוּא must refer to the noun (Davies 1979:98). That דֶּרֶךְ could be used with prepositional force is indicated by Ezk 8.5, where the prophet is told to lift up his eyes "towards the north" (דֶּרֶךְ צָפוֹנָה), and similar expressions may be found elsewhere in Ezekiel, especially chapters 40–48. There are in total approximately eighty occurrences where דֶּרֶךְ could be taken as a preposition, with דֶּרֶךְ in each case preceding a geographical name, a cardinal point, or a noun designating a geographical or architectural feature (Dorsey 1991:216). These instances should be subdivided before analysis.

Examples involving verbs of looking but not physical movement are found mostly in Ezk 40–48, where the nomen rectum is either a point of the compass (e.g. Ezk 41.11) or a noun representing a geographical or architectural feature (e.g. Ezk 43.1). In these instances, דֶּרֶךְ appears to be functioning as a preposition and Dorsey, therefore, renders it as "toward" or "in the direction of" (1991:217). All other cases where דֶּרֶךְ may serve as a preposition involve a verb expressing travel followed by דֶּרֶךְ. The phrase is then followed either by a geographical name or by a noun designating a geographical or architectural feature. In the cases where דֶּרֶךְ is followed by a geographical name Dorsey (1991:218) argues that, if דֶּרֶךְ is taken as a noun, the passage makes geographical sense, whilst, in certain instances (2Sm 2.7, 18.23, 2Kg 3.8b), if it is taken as a preposition it would be geographically absurd. He adds that in all other cases where a verb of travel governs דֶּרֶךְ, it functions as a noun (e.g. Nu 20.17: דֶּרֶךְ הַמֶּלֶךְ נֵלֵךְ).

The majority of the examples where דֶּרֶךְ is followed by a noun denoting a geographical or architectural feature and is governed by a verb of travel display similar characteristics. In a number of cases (e.g. 2Kg 11.16, Ezk 42.15a) the nomen rectum is a gate or entrance-way and the verb is one denoting travel. It is likely that דֶּרֶךְ can be translated as "via, through" in these instances. Such a meaning would make the best sense in the passages and the usage does occur in later Heb. Dorsey, however, argues that the common substantival function of דֶּרֶךְ in these passages is preferable (1991:219).

Davies (1979:98), however, shows that "towards" may not be the only rendering of the prepositional force of דֶּרֶךְ. He argues that the expression דֶּרֶךְ הַר שֵׂעִיר at Dt 1.2 is not intended to locate Horeb or Kadesh on a map, but to express the time taken to travel between the two places. The phrase should, therefore, be translated as either "via Mount Seir" or "along the Mount Seir road". For the interpretation of the passage, either alternative is possible, both denoting that the time stated in Dt 1.2 is calculated according to a journey via Mount Seir or on the road that leads to Mount Seir. It is possible that דֶּרֶךְ can mean "via", but this is not conclusive.

A.7 In five occurrences דֶּרֶךְ is governed by the preposition מִן (Jdg 9.37, 2Kg 3.20, Ezk 9.2, 43.2, 44.3) and the verb בּוֹא. In these cases מִדֶּרֶךְ could mean "from the way", but in view of the use of the prefix מִן in Heb before prepositions it could also mean "from the direction of". In 2Kg 3.20, where water comes מִדֶּרֶךְ אֱדוֹם, the expression must be prepositional since water would hardly be coming "from the road" of Edom, but rather "from the direction of". The same applies to Ezk 43.2 where the glory of God comes from the east. On the other hand, the other two uses in Ezk appear to be substantival (Dorsey 1991:219–20). Jdg 9.37 is the most ambiguous. Gaal spies Abimelech's men coming down from the mountains, one company of which approaches "from the direction of" or "along the road of" Elon-meonenim. Dorsey (1991:220) argues that since Abimelech's men were not interested in the element of surprise, to approach along the road would be expected. This argument, however, is very weak. It proves that there is no reason why they should not be coming along a road, but does not discount the possibility that the expression means "from the direction of". Commentators and translations are understandably divided on this passage.

A.8 An additional meaning set out by *HAL* (222) is "condition, situation"

(Is 40.27, Hg 1.5). According to Jr 10.23, man determines his own condition.

A.9 At Qum the meaning "journey" does not occur, nor does the prepositional use, but this probably reflects the limited range of the corpus rather than a late development (as can be seen from the appearance of these usages in RH). The term occasionally refers to a physical road (e.g. 1QH 16 [= formerly 8] 9), but more often to a course of travel (e.g. 1QH 19 [=11] 4), man's behaviour (e.g. 1QH 9 [=1] 36) or a course to be followed (e.g. 1QH 12 [=4] 18).

A.10 At Dt 2.27 Moses promises to King Sihon that he will pass through his land בַּדֶּרֶךְ בַּדֶּרֶךְ. The repetition of a substantive expresses emphasis, and therefore at Dt 2.27 Moses intends to travel "only by the road" (GK:§ 123 *c*, 133 *k*). BDB render it as "straight (or steadily) along the way" (202), which appears to convey a different sense from the more generally accepted emphatic one.

A.11 The starting point of a דֶּרֶךְ is called the רֹאשׁ, "head" (Ezk 16. 25, 31, 21. 24, 26), which Dorsey suggests indicates the junction of roads rather than the isolated starting place of one road (1991:242). This may be shown by the presence of passers-by in Ezk 16.25 and is comparable to the meaning of רֹאשׁ חוּצוֹת(Is 51.20, Nah 3.10, La 2.19, 4.1). As the place where two roads separate it was the logical place for a sign pointing the way to a city (Ezk 21.24). The one reference to a road's אֵם, "mother" (Ezk 21.26), also seems to indicate the junction (Dorsey 1991:243; cf. Versions).

A.12 Held (1973:179–80) has shown that the pairing of בַּיִת with דֶּרֶךְ (Pr 5.8, 7.19, cf. 7.27) corresponds to that of בַּיִת with מַעְגָּל (Pr 2.18, 7.27). One may find the comparable pairing in the Akk words *bītu* and *ḫarrānu* (CT 15, 45:3–6) and there is a tradition in Akk of the netherworld being associated with the road leading to it (e.g. *ḫarrān lā tāri* "road of no return" appears alongside *erṣet lā tāri* "land of no return" in STT 73:35–38). Many commentators have wished to emend בֵּיתָהּ at Pr 2.18 and 7.27 to נְתִיבָתָהּ, especially in view of its being paired with מַעְגְּלֹתֶיהָ אֶל־רְפָאִים, "the road to death", later in the verse (e.g. Steuernagel 1923:281 [cited by Held]). The comparable pairing of בַּיִת with דֶּרֶךְ would render this unnecessary. Further evidence may be noted in 4Q184, which speaks of the דרכי שוחה, "the roads of the pit" (1.17). In Sir דרך denotes the "fate" of Saul (46.20), suggesting an association with death, whilst the LXX and Vg at Sir 3.31 understand דרך there also to denote one's death.

A.13 The trade route between Damascus and Aqaba is called the דֶּרֶךְ הַמֶּלֶךְ (e.g. Nu 20.17). This may be compared with Akk *girru šarri*, Arm ארח מלכא (Porten & Yardeni 1989:B2.10:6–7), Gr ἡ ὁδὸς ἡ βασιληίη (Hrdt V 53; the whole route is described in V 52–54) (*HAL*:222) and Arb *darb/ṭarīq as-sulṭānī* (Ges.-18:259).

B.1 Sauer (1971:457–58) presents a hypothesis on the development of the different meanings of דֶּרֶךְ. He argues that the primary meaning ("Grundbedeutung") of דֶּרֶךְ was a "(betretener und dadurch festgetretener) Weg". In time this meaning developed to become "Bewegung auf dem Wege [movement on the road]" and "Reise, Unternehmung ... Kriegszug ... Wegstrecke [journey, venture, military campaign, stretch of road]". From this, he suggests, the figurative meaning of דֶּרֶךְ arose: "Wandel, Verhalten [conduct, behaviour]" and "gewisse

Grundtatsachen im Leben der Menschen oder der Natur [fundamental facts in the life of man and nature]" (e.g. Pr 30.19–20, Gn 19.31, 31.35, cf. Gn 18.11). Koch (1977:289) avoids any use of the terms "konkrete" ('literal') and "übertragene Bedeutung" ('figurative use'), which, he says, in the case of דֶּרֶךְ is the product of a judgement based on modern Western languages. He prefers to distinguish between the terms *vordergründiger* ("foreground") and *hinter-gründiger* ("background"), the former referring to a spatial stretch of road, the latter to behaviour or condition. Dorsey (1991:213) likewise says that the meaning of דֶּרֶךְ as "journey" or "trip" is not necessarily derived from the meaning "road". Both meanings may be derived from the verb דָּרַךְ "to travel".

B.2 Merrill (1997:989) states that a covenant overtone is "fundamental" to the figurative meaning of דֶּרֶךְ. This seems to be a theological interpretation in what is for the most part a theological presentation of the lexeme. דֶּרֶךְ is used of the course in life to be followed according to the laws of God. From this it comes to be used in covenantal contexts, but its meaning still remains the course to be followed.

B.3 Nober (1959:178–80) proposes that the meaning of דֶּרֶךְ at Is 49.9 should be pasture land, suggested by its parallelism with 1QIs[a] here. In 1QIs[a] דרכים is replaced by הרים and this serves as a fitting parallel to שפיים (written שפאים in 1QIs[a]), probably meaning "fields", later in the verse. He is followed in this by Clines (1995:466), who suggests the rendering "hill, mountain, pasture". The scribe, however, of 1QIs[a] is prone to harmonize parallelisms (e.g. 41.8), and in Is 49.9 we need not expect a synonymous parallelism. In the LXX, which also tends to harmonize, דרכים is rendered by τρίβοις and שפיים by ὁδοῖς. The combined evidence of the LXX and 1QIs[a] witness to the validity of the MT (see Kutscher 1974:130–31) and to the fact that the scribe and translator did not understand דֶּרֶךְ to mean "pasture", and therefore it should probably not be interpreted with this meaning.

B.4 In 1Kg 18.27 the דֶּרֶךְ is said to belong to Baal, and this is understood in the LXX as meaning that he has business to transact (cf. A.4). Hayman (1951:57–58) notes that Baal is Lord of the produce of the soil (cf. Ho 2.10), and that דֶּרֶךְ, therefore, should here be understood as the "treading of grapes", a meaning derivable from the vb דָּרַךְ as it is used in Am 9.13, Mic 6.15, and Is 16.10 (and specifically used of producing wine without an object at Jdg 9.27 and Jr 25.30). The use of the segholate form in Heb as a noun of action is attested with other nouns (e.g. אֹסֶף, Is 33.4; אֵבֶל, Jr 6.26; בְּכִי, Ps 6.9, Jr 31.15, Is 22.12). Hayman suggests that this uncommon meaning of the lexeme דֶּרֶךְ in the verse explains the paraphrastic rendering of the LXX (Hayman 1951:58). The meaning of דֶּרֶךְ at 1Kg 18.27 as "treading of grapes" is listed, probably incorrectly, as a separate lexeme by Clines (II, 473).

B.5 De Savignac (1954:429–32) suggests, on the basis of Philo (*de conf. ling*. 63), that דֶּרֶךְ at Pr 8.22 should be understood as "modèle, image idéale". Such an understanding of the verse is, however, more informative for Philonic scholarship and New Testament tradition than for the interpretation of the Heb (see Bauer 1958:91).

B.6 Sir 42.3 presents particular problems (see Introduction: Text Doubtful A.7). It is unclear whether the variants ארח (in Bmg) and דרך (in M) should be read as verbs (as Yadin 1965:22) or as nouns (as Clines:I, 375; Skehan & di Lella 1987:477). And, if דרך is the correct reading, it is also unclear what it denotes. Falk takes it as a caution not to embezzle one's partner, linking it with the rabbinic concept of *ḥavura* (1978:230). Indeed, MS B contains the reading חובר which seems to clarify the Akk loan-word שותף to be found in MS M. Lieberman (1967–68:90–92) interprets דרך in the light of the MS B reading, אדון, and suggests that it is an old Heb term for "guardian". He compares this with the form נדרך found in Sifre to Deuteronomy with the meaning "delegated". It is more probable, however, that אדון is a corruption of ארח (Kister 1990:352). Kister suggests that the reading in MS B of חובר is original and that the lexeme collocated with it is the verbal form of ארח (from Bmg). He makes comparison with the similar collocation וְאָרַח לְחֶבְרָה עִם־פֹּעֲלֵי אָוֶן ("and goes in company with evildoers") in Jb 34.8. The text in Sir seems to be speaking of the taking of expenses from a "friend" or "traveller". אֹרֵחַ appears a number of times with the meaning "traveller", and this seems to be the more likely form here than the vb דרך. Hence, the reading here should be ארח and not דרך, and it should be interpreted as a verbal form and not as a noun.

7. Conclusion

A דֶּרֶךְ can be either a literal road or a metaphorical course of behaviour. As a physical road, it is the most general and common word for road, being used to refer to many different types. It also is the one word consistently paired with the other words in the semantic field of "road". It may mean a "journey" or "course of travel", and it is in this respect that it appears to have a prepositional sense, expressing the direction of travel. As a course of behaviour דֶּרֶךְ can refer to habitual behaviour, good or bad ways of life and to the moral course prescribed by God or followed by those who are faithful to him. In a related sense to that of a course of behaviour, it may refer to a business enterprise.

The range of meanings exhibited by דֶּרֶךְ is also reflected by the primary words for "road" in other Semitic languages. One may, for example, compare Akk (as Dorsey 1991:249, n. 2), in which the word *ḫarrānu* has an even wider range of meanings. It may mean a highway, road, path; or a course of travel (not distinguished in CAD 6:107–109); a journey; a business trip or venture (involving travel); a military campaign, expedition; a caravan, or expeditionary force. The Arm and Syr *ʾwrḥ* exhibit similar meanings (Jastrow:33; Brockelmann:47), as does Arb *ṭarīq* (Wehr 1971:559).

Since דֶּרֶךְ is never in parallel to חוּץ, the most common word for "street", it is uncertain whether דֶּרֶךְ could ever denote a street within a city. Therefore, although דֶּרֶךְ has a generally similar range of meanings to Heb אֹרַח, it is possible that there is a difference in that אֹרַח could be used of a city street in at least the Heb of Qum (4QapLam[a] 2.7) and Sir (49.6).

BIBLIOGRAPHY

Aharoni, Y. 1979. *The Land of the Bible: A Historical Geography*, rev. edn. translated and edited by A.F. Rainey. Philadelphia.

Aistleitner, J. ³1967. *Wörterbuch der ugaritischen Sprache*. Berlin.

Albrecht, K. 1896. Das Geschlecht der hebräischen Hauptwörter. *ZAW* 16:41–121.

Albright, W.F. 1934. The North-Canaanite poems of Al'Êyân Ba'al and the "Gracious Gods". *JPOS* 14:101–40.

_____ 1944. The Oracles of Balaam. *JBL* 63:207–33.

_____ 1955. Some Canaanite-Phoenician Sources of Hebrew Wisdom. In *Wisdom in Israel and in the Ancient Near East: Presented to Harold Henry Rowley by the Society for Old Testament Study in association with the editorial board of Vetus Testamentum in celebration of his sixty-fifth birthday, 24 March 1955*. Edited by M. Noth and D. Winton Thomas (VTS 3). Leiden:1–15.

_____ 1957. The Refrain «and God saw ki ṭôb» in Genesis. In *Mélanges Bibliques Rédigés en l'honneur de André Robert* (Travaux de l'Institut Catholique de Paris, 4). Paris:22–26.

Andersen, F.I. and A. Dean Forbes. 1989. *The Vocabulary of the Old Testament*. Rome.

Bartina, S. 1956. «Vivat Potentia Beer-Sheba» (Amos 8,14). *VD* 34:202–10.

Bauer, J.B. 1958. Encore une fois Proverbes viii 22. *VT* 8:91–92.

Beentjes, P.C. 1997. *The Book of Ben Sira in Hebrew: A Text Edition of all Extant Hebrew Manuscripts and a Synopsis of all Parallel Hebrew Ben Sira Texts*. Leiden.

Boling, R.G. 1969. Review of R.C. Culley, *Oral Formulaic Languages in the Biblical Psalms*. *JSS* 14:119–22.

Budde, K. 1925. Zu Text und Auslegung des Buches Amos. *JBL* 44:63–122.

Cathcart, K.J. & R.P. Gordon. 1989. *The Targum of the Minor Prophets, Translated with a Critical Introduction, Appendix and Notes*. The Aramaic Bible, 14. Edinburgh.

Cook, J. 1997. *The Septuagint of Proverbs. Jewish and/or Hellenistic Proverbs? Concerning the Hellenistic Colouring of LXX Proverbs* (VTS, 69). Leiden-New York-Köln.

Dahood, M. 1952. Review of Gustav Hölscher, *Das Buch Hiob*. *TS* 13:593–94.

_____ 1954. Ugaritic drkt and Biblical derek. *TS* 15:627–31.

_____ 1957. Some Northwest-Semitic words in Job. *Bib* 38:306–20.

_____ 1963. *Proverbs and Northwest Semitic Philology*. Rome.

_____ 1965–70. Commentary on *Psalms*. 3 vols. (AB, 16, 17, 17a). Garden City, NY.

Davies, G.I. 1979. The significance of Deuteronomy 1.2 for the location of Mount Horeb. *PEQ* 111:87–101.

_____ 1992. Commentary on *Hosea* (New Century Bible Commentary). Grand Rapids, Michigan.

Díez Merino, L. 1984. *Targum de Proverbios: Edicíon príncipe del Ms Villa-Amil no. 5 de Alfonso de Zamora* (Bibliotheca Hispana Bíblica). Madrid.

Dorsey, D.A. 1991. *The Roads and Highways of Ancient Israel*. Baltimore and London.

Drower, E.S. & R. Macuch. 1963. *A Mandaic Dictionary*. Oxford.

Duhm, B. 1901. *Das Buch Jeremia* (Kurzer Handcommentar zum Alten Testament, Abt. 11). Tübingen.

Falk, Z.W. 1978. *Introduction to Jewish Law of the Second Commonwealth*, part 2. Leiden.

Fisher, L.R. (ed.). 1972–81. *Ras Shamra Parallels: The Texts from Ugarit and the Hebrew Bible* (Analecta Orientalia, 49-51). Rome.

Gadd, C.J. 1954. Inscribed prisms of Sargon II from Nimrud. *Iraq* 16:173–201.

Gray, G.B. 1912. Commentary on *Isaiah, I–XXXIX* (ICC). Edinburgh.

Greenfield, J.C. 1969. Amurrite, Ugaritic and Canaanite. In *Proceedings of the International Conference on Semitic Studies held in Jerusalem, 19–23 July 1965*. Jerusalem.

Harper, W.R. 1905. Commentary on *Amos* and *Hosea* (ICC). Edinburgh.

Hatch, E. & H.A. Redpath. 1897–1906. *A Concordance to the Septuagint and the Other Greek Versions of the Old Testament*, 2 Vols. Oxford.

Haupt, P. 1904. *The Sacred Books of the Old Testament, Part 9: The Books of Kings, with notes by B. Stade, assisted by F. Schwally*. Leipzig-Baltimore-London.

Hayman, L. 1951. A note on I Kings 18.27. *JNES* 10:57–58.

Hayward, C.T.R. 1987. *The Targum of Jeremiah, Translated, with a Critical Introduction, Apparatus, and Notes*. The Aramaic Bible, 12. Edinburgh.

Held, M. 1974. Hebrew *ma'gal*: A study in lexical parallelism. *JANES* 6:107–16.

Holladay, W.L. 1986. Commentary on *Jeremiah* 1 (Herm). Philadelphia.

Horbury, W. 1982. 1 Thessalonians ii 3 as rebutting the charge of false prophecy. *JTS* ns 33:492–508.

Jean, C.F. & Hoftijzer, J. 1965. *Dictionnaire des Inscriptions Sémitiques de l'Ouest*. Leiden.

Kahle, P.E. 1902. *Der Masoretische Text des Alten Testaments*. Leipzig.

King, L.W. 1902. *The Annals of the Kings of Assyria*, I. London.

Kister, M. 1990. A contribution to the interpretation of Ben Sira [in Hebrew]. *Tarbiẕ* 59:303–78.

Koch, K. 1977. Article דרך in *TW* 2:288–312.

Kutscher, E.Y. 1967. Mittelhebräisch und Jüdisch-aramäisch im neuen Koehler-Baumgartner. In B. Hartmann, E. Jenni & E.Y. Kutscher (eds.). *Hebräische Wortforschung: Festschrift zum 80. Geburstag von Walter Baumgartner* (VTS, 16). Leiden:158–75.

_____ 1967–68. Marginal notes to the Biblical lexicon [in Hebrew]. *Leš* 32:343–46.

_____ 1974. *The Language and Linguistic Background of the Isaiah Scroll (1QIsa^a)*. Leiden.

Lagarde, P. de. 1872. *Prophetae Chaldaice*. Leipzig.

Lambdin, T.O. 1978. *Introduction to Classical Ethiopic (Ge'ez)* (Harvard Semitic Series, 24). Missoula, MT.

Landsberger, B. 1957. *Materialien zum sumerischen Lexicon* V: The Series ḪAR-ra » ḫubullu, Tablets I–IV. Roma.

Lieberman, S. 1967–68. Forgotten meanings [in Hebrew]. *Leš* 32:89–102.

Lisowsky, G. ²1958. *Konkordanz zum hebräischen Alten Testament*. Stuttgart.

Loretz, O. 1979. *Die Psalmen II: Beitrag der Ugarit-Texte zum Verständnis von Kolometrie und Textologie der Psalmen. Psalm 90–150* (AOAT, 207/2). Kevelaer.

Lust, J. et al. 1996. *A Greek–English Lexicon of the Septuagint. Part II K–W.* Stuttgart.

McKane, W. 1970. Commentary on *Proverbs* (OTL). London.

Mandelkern, S. 1896. *Veteris Testamenti concordantiae hebraicae atque chaldaicae.* Leipzig.

Merrill, E.H. 1997. Article on דרך in W.A. VanGemeren (ed.). *The New International Dictionary of Old Testament Theology and Exegesis.* Vol. 1, 989–93. Carlisle.

Michel, D. 1977. *Grundlegung einer hebräischen Syntax: Sprachwissenschaftliche Methodik Genus und Numerus des Nomens.* Neukirchen-Vluyn.

Muffs, Y. 1992. *Love and Joy: Law, Language and Religion in Ancient Israel.* New York.

Nober, P. 1948. «De torrentia in via bibet» (Ps 110.7a) (Nota ugaritica in V.T.). *VD* 26:351–53.

Nober, P. 1959. Review of F. Nötscher, *Gotteswege. VD* 37:176–80.

Porten, B. & A. Yardeni. 1989. *Textbook of Aramaic Documents from Ancient Egypt, Newly Copied, Edited and Translated into Hebrew and English*, Vol. II: Contracts. Winona Lake, IN.

Ratner, R. 1983. Gender problems in Biblical Hebrew. Unpublished PhD dissertation. Cincinnati.

_____ 1987. DEREK: Morpho-syntactical considerations. *JAOS* 7:471–73.

Rudolph, W. 31968. Commentary on *Jeremia* 1 (HzAT, 1, 12). Tübingen.

Sauer, G. 1971. Article on דרך in *THAT* 1:456–60.

de Savignac, J. 1954. Note sur le sens de verset VIII 22 des Proverbes. *VT* 4:429–32.

Scott, R.B.Y. 1965. Commentary on *Proverbs* and *Ecclesiastes* (AB, 18). Garden City, NY.

Segal, M.H. ²1958. *The Book of Ben Sira* [ספר בן סירא השלם]. Jerusalem.

Skehan, P.W. & A.A. di Lella. 1987. Commentary on the *Wisdom of Ben Sira* (AB, 39). Garden City, NY.

Tidwell, N. 1980. A road and a way: A contribution to the study of word-pairs. *Semitics* 7:50–80.

Tomback, R.S. 1978. *A Comparative Semitic Lexicon of the Phoenician and Punic Languages.* Missoula.

Tov, E. 1977. Compound words in the LXX representing two or more Hebrew words. *Bib* 58:189–212.

Toy, C.H. 1899. Commentary on *Proverbs* (ICC). Edinburgh.

Virolleaud, Ch. 1931. Un poème phénicien de Ras-Shamra: La lutte de Môt, fils de dieux, et d'Aleïn, fils de Baal. *Syria* 12:193–224.

Watson, W.G.E. 1980. Gender-matched synonymous parallelism in the OT. *JBL* 99:321–41.

Wehr, H. 31971. *A Dictionary of Modern Written Arabic*, ed. J.M. Cowan. Wiesbaden.

Wildberger, H. 1972. Commentary on *Isaiah 1–12* (BK, X/1). Neukirchen-Vluyn.

Wolff, H.W. 1974. Commentary on *Hosea* (Herm). Philadelphia.

_____ 1977. Commentary on *Joel* and *Amos* (Herm). Philadelphia.
Yadin, Y. 1965. *The Ben Sira Scroll from Masada*. Jerusalem.

James K. Aitken
University of Cambridge

הֲדֹם

Introduction
Grammatical type: n m.
Occurrences: Total 6 occurrences BH: Is 66.1, Ps 99.5; 110.1; 132.7, Lm 2.1,
1Ch 28.2. No occurrences. Ep, Sir. 2 occurrences Q: 4Q ShSh (4Q403) 1 ii 2,
11Q ShSh 2-1-9 5-6.

Text doubtful: none.

Qere/Kethiv: none.

1. Root and Comparative Material

A.1 The root הדם does not appear in AH except in this noun form.

A.2 The noun has no known Sem etymology (Cohen:376). Ug *hdm*,
'footstool', provides a close parallel, and also Eg *hdm rdwy*, 'footstool of the
feet'. The Ug and Eg are first found at approximately the same time, the period
of the Eg 18th Dynasty (1580–1350). Earlier scholars tended to see the Eg as
the original behind Ug and Heb (KB^2 1958:225; Ellenbogen 1962:66; de Savignac
1951:114–15; de Vaux 1960–61:118; Gössmann 1967:36 n12), but the majority
of scholars now think that the Eg is a loanword from Can (Görg 1977; Hintze
1954, coming from Ug via Heb to Eg; Nötscher 1940:32; Albright 1943:42 [Eg
*hadmu]; Gardiner 1947:68; Caquot 1956:35; Gordon 1965:751; *HAL* 229;
WbÄS II:505; *BRL*^{2} 521a; Dahood 1968:369).

A.3 In addition to the uncertainty over the origin of הֲדֹם, there are questions
concerning the root of the word. Some relate it to Arb *hadama* 'overthrow,
overturn, cast down' (e.g. BDB 213), on the analogy of כֶּבֶשׁ 'footstool' of LBH
and Arm (sometimes Tg uses *kiḇšā* and Pesh uses *kuḇšā* to render הֲדֹם) and כבש
'subdue', a meaning implied by Ps 110. (In Arm the homonymous root הדם
means 'dismember' as a verb and 'limb' as a noun, so bears no relation to Heb
הֲדֹם.) Others suggest that the root is related to דום I, 'be still, quiet', cf. Ug *dm* II
'remain', with a prefixed ה for the hiph, giving a basic meaning for the word as
'place to rest' (of the feet): the parallels to *hdm* in Ug are נחת 'rest' and in Heb
מְנוּחָה (Fabry 1977:348).

A.4 Gordon (1934:751) says of the Ug word that it is an East Mediterranean
one, appropriate for a term of craftmanship.

2. Formal Characteristics

A.1 *qitāl*(?)

A.2 Always in cons., perhaps even in Ps 110.1 (see Syntagmatics).

3. Syntagmatics

A.1 6 times (depending on reconstruction of 11Q ShSh) in construct with

רַגְלַיִם, once לְ + רַגְלַיִם (possibly construct also: GK § 130 [1]). רַגְלַיִם has a possessive suffix each time except 1Ch 28.2 where it is in construct with אֱלֹהֵינוּ.

A.2 Pred of הָאָרֶץ Is 66.1.
Result of שׁוּת Ps 110.1
Location of שׁחו hith Ps 99.5; 132.7.
Obj of זכר qal Lm 2.1
Dative of בנה qal 1Ch 28.2.

A.3 The possessor of the footstool is the Lord in 7 occurrences, and the king ('my lord') in Ps 110.1, though even in this last case it is the Lord who promises to provide the footstool. Similarly, in Ug texts, *hdm* occurs as the footstool of El, Baal and King Danel (KTU^2 1.5 VI 13; 1.6 I 60; 1.17 II 11: Caquot 1956:35).

4. Versions

All the versions agree on the translation 'footstool', though some renderings display an anti-anthropomorphic reluctance to speak of God's feet, e.g. LXX Ps 132(131).7, 1Ch 28.2; Tg and Pesh 1Ch 28.2, Tg Is 66.1, but oddly enough, not Tg Lm 2.1. LXX Ps 132(131).7 implies the commemoration of a past theophany, rather than a continued physical presence in the sanctuary.

LXX
A.1 ὑποπόδιον (τῶν ποδῶν) 'footstool (of the feet)', with possessive pronouns: Is 66.1; Ps 99(98).5; 110(109).1; Lm 2.1.

B.1 εἰς τὸν τόπον οὗ ἔστησαν οἱ πόδες αὐτοῦ 'to the place where his feet stood' Ps 132(131).7 (theological rendering): Aq and Sym (recon-structed from Syh) ὑπόποδιον (τῶν ποδῶν αὐτοῦ).

B.2 στάσις ποδῶν (κυρίου ἡμῶν) 'position of feet' 1Ch 28.2 (theological rendering?): some MSS καὶ στάσιν τῷ ὑποποδίῳ τῶν ποδῶν (τοῦ θεοῦ ἡμῶν).

Tg
A.1
לכבשא (דרגלוי) כֵּיבַשׁ קֳדָמַי 'footstool before me' Is 66.1, cf. כביש (לרגלך) Ps 110.1, Ps 132.7.
כבש כורסי ליקרא 'footstool of the throne of glory' 1Ch 28.2.
בית מוקדשא דהוה גלונדקא דריגלוהי 'his sanctuary that was the footstool (?) for his feet' Lm 2.1 (Sokoloff 128b: גלנטק 'sedan chair'), cf. לבית מוקדשיה 'to the place of his sanctuary' Ps 99.5.

Pesh
A.1
kubšā (*dreḡlē*) 'footstool (of the feet)' with possessive suffixes: Is 66.1 (cf. Matt 5.35), Ps 99.5; 132.7, Lm 2.1.
kubšā (*lreḡlē*) 'footstool (for the feet)' Ps 110.1.

B.1 *ʾaṯrā dašḵintā* 'place of the Presence' 1Ch 28.2(3) (theological rendering).

Vg

A.1 *scabillum pedum* + possessive/owner.

5. Lexical/Semantic Fields

A.1 In parallellism with כִּסֵּא Is 66.1 (cf. Ug *kht* (throne) // *hdm* (footstool) in *KTU²* 1.4. I 33–34 (van Selms 1975:472): with מִשְׁכָּנוֹת 1Ch 28.2: with אֶרֶץ בַּת־צִיּוֹן and תִּפְאֶרֶת יִשְׂרָאֵל Lm 2.1; with אֲרוֹן בְּרִית־יהוה 1Ch 28.2.

A.2 As a pair with כִּסֵּא Is 66.1, parallel to בַּיִת and מְקוֹם מְנוּחָה (cf. 1Ch 28.2 בֵּית מְנוּחָה)

6. Exegesis

A.1 הֲדֹם is never used literally (BDB 213). Apart from Ps 110.1, the 'footstool of the feet' is a metaphorical reference to God's sanctuary, or to Zion, as can be seen from the parallels. However, in Is 66.1 the Lord is depicted as saying that no human-built temple is adequate for him, since the cosmos itself enthrones him.

A.2 It is commonly supposed that the Ark of the covenant served as the Lord's footstool in the Temple (Haran 1959:255, de Vaux 1960-61:96–97, Mettinger 1982:21–23). To do obeisance at the sanctuary would thus be to bow down before the feet of Yahweh. Görg (1977) derived the term כַּפֹּרֶת from another Eg term for a footstool, *kp (n) rd(wy)*, pointing out that many of the priestly terms have an Eg derivation.

A.3 However, de Vaux believes that in the case of the tabernacle in the desert, the Ark served as a pedestal for a standing deity, not as a footstool, with the tablets of stone inside it as a sign of the עֵדוּת/בְּרִית between God and Israel, in line with Ancient Near Eastern custom (1960-61:118–24), followed by Mettinger 1982:21–23. In contrast, Fohrer (1969:100f; ET 109f) and Noth (1969:179) say that the position of the ark in the Jerusalem temple makes it impossible that it was perceived as God's footstool. In any case, as notions of the divine developed, it was the temple and later the earth itself that were considered to be the place of God's feet (Davies 1962:309). (For further discussion and bibliography on this subject, see under *Exegesis* for כִּסֵּא.)

A.4 Ps 110.1 is metaphorical, of Davidic dominion (Davies 1962:309). The enemies come to do obeisance at the ruler's feet. A good illustration of this is the footstool of Tutankhamun, described in *Art* below, which represents the Pharaoh's traditional foes. Similarly, in the Amarna letters Rib Addi of Byblos calls himself the footstool of Pharaoh's feet (Broshi 1962:219).

A.5 Although the word in AH is never used of an actual footstool, such an object undoubtedly existed, both in palaces and in ordinary homes, cf. Ug. poetry, and the many depictions in Ancient Near Eastern art (Brettler 1989:82 for refs. in *ANEP*). It was the place at which obeisance was performed (hence Ps 110.1): as the suppliant or subject bowed down, the king's or deity's feet were higher than he. There was a practical need for a footstool, too, when the throne was large or raised (see *Exegesis*, כִּסֵּא), because the king would need it in order to mount the throne and then to prevent his feet from dangling in an undignified fashion from the high seat (note that Athtar's feet do not even reach the footstool of Baal's throne in the Ug text *KTU²* 1.6. I 57–65, and consequently he is not worthy to replace him).

A.6 Van Selms (1975:472) translates the Ug passage in *KTU²* 1.4 I 34 *kḥt.* *ʾil.nḥt bẕr.hdm.ʾid dpršʾa.bbr* as 'the throne of Ilu, a golden seat, a solid footstool which he overlaid with electrum', on the basis of biblical parallels, e.g. Jb 26.9 and 1K 10.18 // 2Ch 9.18.

A.7 There are other places where there may be an allusion to a footstool without the word הֲדֹם being used, e.g. מְקוֹם כִּסְאִי // מְקוֹם כַּפּוֹת רַגְלַי) (Ezk 43.7) and מְקוֹם מִקְדָּשִׁי // מְקוֹם רַגְלַי) (Is 60.13) (Zimmerli [1969:1072, 1079; ET II:415]; Davies 1962:309). כֶּבֶשׁ בַּזָּהָב לַכִּסֵּא (2Ch 9.18). (See כִּסֵּא, *Exegesis*–Davies, Japhet, Williamson).

Art and archaeology

A.1 Tutankhamun's throne (c.1350 BCE) has a footrest decorated with nine bound human figures representing the nine traditional enemies of Egypt, and symbolising conquest. The footstool is of solid wood veneered with ebony, ivory, faience, glass, and natural stone. The shape is that of the top, front and back of a low rectangular box, not closed at the sides or at the bottom. The footstool of Tutankhamun's golden throne has six figures, and another footstool has two. There are also examples of Egyptian footstools apparently resting on the necks or backs of representations of enemies (Baker 1966:81, Pl. 91; Metzger 1985:II, figures 272, 274).

A.2 In contrast, Assyrian footstools of the 9th–7th centuries have four legs, and are truly stools. Often the legs terminate in pine- or cedar cones, as chair and table legs from the region often do. There are stretchers, sometimes with scroll work. Sometimes there are projections to hold a cushion in place. (Baker 1966:182 figure 291; 185 figure 297; 187 figures 299–300; 189 figure 302; 190–91 figures 304–5). Layard decribes the remains of a throne and footstool at Nimrud: the footstool was of wood overlaid with embossed metal, decorated with the heads of rams or bulls. The feet had lion's paws and pine cones (Baker 1966:188).

A.3 Syrian footstools of the 8th century were plainer, either solid with a little decoration, or with an arch beneath, e.g. the triple-staged footstool depicted on Ahiram's sarcophagus (*ANEP* 456, 458: Ahiram of Byblos). However, that of Bar Rekub at Zinjirli is Assyrian in style, with four feet, scroll work on the stretcher and pine-cone feet. (Baker 1966:207–208, figures 336–339). See also *ANEP* 515 (Hammurabi and Shamash), 518 (Meli-Shipak and goddess), 630–631 (women, from Zinjirli and Marash), 635 (Agbar the priest from Nerab), and Laser (1968:55 figures 11, 12).

A.4 Footstools were not luxury items in themselves. Lists from Alalakh demonstrate that they could be ordinary items of household furniture (Baker 1966:208), though Wyatt (1983:275) believes that even here they may have cultic connotations.

7. Conclusion
Although footrests undoubtedly existed all over the Ancient Near East, the use of הֲדֹם in AH is solely metaphorical, conveying the idea of obeisance and submission. It is symbolic of the conquest of one's enemies on the one hand (Ps

110), and of the place where Yahweh is worshipped as sovereign on the other.

BIBLIOGRAPHY

Albright, W.F. 1943. The furniture of El in Canaanite mythology. *BASOR* 91:39–44.

_____. 1934/1966. *The Vocalization of the Egyptian Syllabic Orthography.* American Oriental Series 5. New Haven, CT.

Baker, H.S. 1966. *Furniture in the Ancient World. Origins and Evolution 3100–475 BC.* London.

Bernhardt, K.-H. 1966. Article 'Schemel' in *BHH* III:1690.

Brettler, M.Z. 1989. *God is King. Understanding an Israelite Metaphor.* JSOTSS 76. Sheffield.

Broshi, M. 1962. Article כִּסֵּא in *EM* IV:216–20.

Caquot, A. 1956. Remarques sur le Psaume CX. *Semitica* 6:33–52.

Curtis, E.L. 1910. Commentary on *Chronicles* (ICC).

Dahood, M. 1968. Commentary on *Psalms* II (AB).

_____. 1970. Commentary on *Psalms* III (AB).

Davies, G.H. 1962. Article 'Footstool' in *IDB* II:309.

Ellenbogen, M. 1962. *Foreign Words. Their Origin and Etymology.* London.

Fabry, H.-J. 1977. Article הדם in *TWAT* II:347–57.

Fohrer, G. 1969. *Geschichte der israelitischen Religion.* Berlin. ET 1972, *History of Israelite Religion.*

Gardiner, A.H. 1947. *Ancient Egyptian Onomastica.* I. Oxford.

Gordon, C.H. 1965. *Ugaritic Textbook.* Rome.

Görg, M. 1977. Eine neue Deutung für Kapporaet. *ZAW* 89:115–19.

Haran, M. 1959. The ark and the cherubim: their symbolic significance in the biblical ritual. *IEJ* 9:30–38, 89–97.

_____. 1978. *Temples and Temple Service in Ancient Israel. An Inquiry into the Character of Cult Phenomena and the Historical Setting of the Priestly School.* Oxford.

Hintze, F. 1954. *Hdm rdwj* ,Fußsehemel'. *Zeitschrift für ägyptische Sprache und Altertumskunde* 79:77.

Japhet, S. 1989.*The Ideology of the Book of Chronicles and its Place in Biblical Thought.* Beiträge zur Erforschung des Alten Testaments und des antiken Judentums 9. Frankfurt am Main.

_____. 1993. Commentary on *Chronicles* (OTL).

Kyrieleis, H. 1969.*Thronen und Klinen. Studien zur Formgeschichte altorientalischer und griechischer Sitz- und Liegemöbel vorhellenistischer Zeit.* Berlin.

Laser, S. 1968. Hausrat. *Archaeologia Homerica.* Vol. P. Eds. F. Matz and H.G. Buchholz. II:44–56. Göttingen.

Mettinger, T.N.D. 1982. *The Dethronement of Sabaoth. Studies in the Shem and Kabod Theologies.* CBOT 18. Lund.

Metzger, M. 1966. Article 'Thron' in *BHH* III:1976.

_____. 1970. Himmlische und irdische Wohnstatt Jahwes. *UF* 2:139–58.

_____. 1985. *Königsthron und Gottesthron. Thronformen und Thron-darstellungen in Ägypten und im vorderen Orient im dritten und zweiten Jahrtausend vor Christus und deren Bedeutung für das Verständnis von Aussagen über den Thron im Alten Testament.* AOAT 15; Neukirchen-Vluyn.

Nötscher, F. 1940. *Biblische Altertumskunde.* Bonn.

Salonen, A. 1963. *Die Möbel des Alten Mesopotamien nach sumerisch-akkadischen Quellen. Eine lexicalische und kulturgeschichtliche Untersuchung.* AnAcScFen ser. B 127. Helsinki.

Savignac, J. de. 1951. Essai d'interpretation du Psaume cx à l'aide de la littérature égyptienne. *OTS* 9: 107–35.

Selms, A. van. 1975. A guest-room for Ilu and its furniture. *UF* 7:469–76.

Vaux, R. de. 1960–61. Les chérubins et l'arche d'alliance, les sphinx gardiens et les trones divins dans l'ancient Orient. *Mélanges de l'Université S. Joseph* 37:93–124, esp. 118.

Williamson, H.G.M. 1982. Commentary on *Chronicles* (NCBC).

Wyatt, N. 1983. The stele of the seated god from Ugarit. *UF* 15:271–77.

Zimmerli, W. 1969. Commentary on *Ezekiel* (BK). ET 1979 *Ezekiel* II (Herm).

Alison Salvesen
University of Oxford

Introduction

Grammatical type: n m.

Occurrences:

BH—135 occurrences: Gn 41.40, Ex 11.5; 12.29, Dt 17.18, Jdg 3.20, 1Sm 1.9; 2.8; 4.13,18, 2Sm 3.10; 7.13,16; 14.9, 1Kg 1.13,17,20,24,27,30,35, 37(2x), 46, 47(2x),48; 2.4,12,19 (2x),24,33,45; 3.6; 5.19; 7.7; 8.20,25; 9.5(2x); 10.9,18, 19(2x); 16.11; 22.10,19, 2Kg 4.10; 10.3,30; 11.19; 13.13; 15.12; 25.28(2x), Is 6.1; 9.6; 14.9,13; 16.5; 22.23; 47.1; 66.1; Jr 1.15; 3.17; 13.13; 14.21; 17.12,25; 22.2,4,30; 29.16; 33.17,21; 36.30; 43.10; 49.38; 52.32(2x), Ezk 1.26(2x); 10.1; 26.16; 43.7, Jn 3.6, Hg 2.22, Zc 6.13(2x), Ps 9.5,8; 11.4; 45.7; 47.9; 89.5,15, 30,37,45; 93.2; 94.20; 97.2; 103.19; 122.5(2x); 132.11,12, Pr 9.14; 16.12; 20.8,28; 25.5; 29.14, Lm 5.19, Jb 26.9; 36.7, Neh 3.7, Est 1.2; 3.1; 5.1, 1Ch 17.12,14; 22.10(9); 28.5; 29.23; 2Ch 6.10,16; 7.18; 9.8,17,18(2x); 18.9,18; 2Ch 23.20);

Sir—4 occurrences: 10.14A; 11.5A (B); 40.3B; 47.11B.

Q—17 occurrences: 4QCommGen (4Q252) V.2, 4QDibHaMeor 4.7, 4QFlor (4Q174) 1.10f, 4QpIs^a 8–10.19, 11QPs^aCreat (11Q5) 26.11, 4QShSh (4Q405) 20 ii 21-22 2; 20 ii 21-22 8; 23 i 3, 11QShSh 2-1-9 5–6; 3-4 1; f 5; k 5; 4QSongs of the Sage (4QShir^b/4Q511) 2 i 10, 4QWarScroll 11 i 12, Temple Scr 56.20; 59.14; 59.17.

Ep—no occurrences.

Text doubtful:

A.1 Ex 17.16: כִּי־יָד עַל־כֵּס יָהּ: usually emended to *נֵס, 'banner' (*HAL* 465; Childs 1974:311–12; S.R. Driver 1918:161). Though LXX reads ὅτι ἐν χειρὶ κρυφαίᾳ as < *כסה 'hide', MS F^b has ὅτι ἡ δύναμις ἐπὶ θρόνον ἄχραντον 'on an immaculate throne'. Pesh has hā ʾidā ʿal kursyā, 'see, the hand upon the throne', suggesting that the translator read *כֵּסֵה, and Ephrem the Syrian (c.360 CE) has the reading hā ʾidā dyāh ʿal kursyā, 'see, the hand of Yah upon the throne'. The influence of Jewish exegetes on the early Syr is the most likely explanation: note TgO ʿal kursē yqārā, 'on the Throne of Glory', cf. also TgNeo and TgPsJ (Geiger 1857: 277, Komlosh 1973:195, Mekhilta on Ex 17.16 [Amalek 2; Lauterbach II,160], PRE 44).

A.2 Ps 45.7: כִּסְאֲךָ אֱלֹהִים עוֹלָם וָעֶד שֵׁבֶט מִישֹׁר שֵׁבֶט מַלְכוּתֶךָ. Because of the change in address, from king (as God?) to God, Gunkel (1926:194) suggested reading either *כִּסְאֲךָ כִּסֵּא אֱלֹהִים 'your throne is God's throne (forever)' or *כִּסְאֲךָ יְהְיֶה 'your throne shall be (forever)', which was misread as the Divine Name, then changed to אֱלֹהִים. However, North (1932) suggested that the original text was *כִּסְאֲךָ כֵּאלֹהִים, and the second Kaph was omitted: 'your throne is (as) God('s throne)'. Noth (1957:225–26) followed him, observing that the Hebrew Bible never addresses the king as God. See also Kraus (1966:I,331;ET 451f).

A.3 Ps 122.5: Gunkel (1926:544), following Grimme (1902:114), deletes the second כִּסְאוֹת.

A.4 Jb 26.9: Driver and Gray (1921:179) read as suffixed form *כִּסְאֹה, or *כִּסְאוֹ, as Theod and the versions except Pesh. Ibn Ezra and 19th century commentators suggested *כֶּסֶא 'full moon' for כֵּסֶה, on the basis of Ps 81.4, Pr 7.20, and are followed by Dhorme (1926:340; ET 372f.), NJB and NEB. The emendation is possible if, as Dhorme suggests, pi אחז is taken in the same sense as Ass *uḫḫuzu*, 'cover' (an object with gold or silver), cf. the BH usage in the hoph in 2Ch 9.18. It is possible that the latter passage has influenced the form of Jb 26.9, changing כֶּסֶא to כֵּסֶה, or that we should retain the sense 'his throne' and use the verb in the same way as 2Ch 26.9: 'he has covered the face of his throne', to which Dhorme objected on the ground that it would be the base or back of God's heavenly throne that was covered in cloud. But the idea may be that the aspect of God's throne is concealed from those on earth.

A.5 Jb 36.7: Dhorme (1926:493;ET 540) emends וְאֶת־מְלָכִים to *וְשָׁת־מְלָכִים, due to the orthographic confusion of Shin and Aleph, following Perles (1922:41), cf. Ps 132.11 אָשִׁית לְכִסֵּא־לָךְ.

B.1 Ps 45.7: Dahood (1965:I,272) points as a denom pi: 'the eternal and everlasting God has enthroned you', commenting 'the only evidence for this proposal is its manifest good sense'. The problem is that it is without parallel anywhere else in AH, or even in Ug, it seems. There are also alternative locutions for the concept that are more familiar in AH, Ug and Akk such as the hiph (and cognate forms) of כִּסֵּא + עַל + ישׁב, e.g. 2Ch 23.20, Sir 11.5A, 11QT 59.14, 4QDibMeor 4.7.

1. Root and Comparative Material

A.1 The word כִּסֵּא and its cognates are found very widely in all Semitic languages. It derives ultimately from Sum *gu-za* 'seat', via OAkk *kussium* (= Standard Bab *kussû*) 'throne, saddle, stool' (e.g. Ellenbogen 1962:89, Murtonen I Bb 235). There may also be some relation to the Sum verb *guz* 'cower, squat, be lowered' etc., and though J. Black (personal comm.) doubts this, he supports the Sum etymology against the objections of Kaufman and Lipiński (1988:67) (see B category).

A.2 The variant Akk spelling with *-rs-* for *-ss-* is the normal form in Arm, and represents the dissimilation of sibilants to a liquid plus sibilant (Salonen 1963:58, Lipiński 1988:67).

A.3 Lipiński (1988:67) explains the Heb vocalization as due to assimilation of the vowel of the first syllable (*u*) to the vowel of the second syllable (*i*), and Murtonen suggests that the original AH form was KUS'. The suffixed form (ου)χεσσω appears in the transliteration column of the Hexapla of Ps 89.30,37 (Murtonen, I Ba 189).

A.4 Ug *ks'*, 'throne, seat, saddle'; Ph *ks'*, NeoPun *ks'h*; AH and RH כִּסֵּא 'seat, stool, throne'.

A.5 In Arm the geminated sibilants were dissimilated, *-ss-* to *-rs-*, hence Zinjirli כרסא, BibArm כָּרְסֵא, and cf. 'Damascus', דַּמֶּשֶׂק > דַּרְמֶשֶׂק in late BH and Arm. However, Fraenkel (1960:78f) argues that the Resh is a lengthening sound (Dehnlaut), and compares other roots in Arm that appear to have had a Resh introduced in the middle when compared with cognates in Arb. The word is also found in OldArm, ImpArm, EgArm, JArm (כּוּרְסְיָא) 'seat, privy', Syr and CPA (kursyā) 'throne, head of region, bishop's seat', Mand (kursia) 'throne'

A.6 Arb *kursī* 'throne, seat, chair', of ruler, God, bride.

A.7 South Semitic languages: Tigre *kursī* , 'little bed, seat', Tigri *kōras*, Mehri *karsī*,'chair, rifle butt', Shauri *kersī* , Socr *korsiy*, 'throne', Harari *kursi* 'chair, lectern', though Leslau (1958:27) says that the Harari is a loanword from Arb; Bedouin *kursi* 'chair, bench', Somali *kursi* 'chair', Saf *kōrō* 'saddle', Hausa *kujēra* 'chair'.

B.1 Kaufman (1974:28) objects to a Sum origin, stating that the doubled sibilant (*ss*) and 'final Aleph' are inexplicable on the hypothesis of a loan from Sum: rather, the Sum word could conceivably be a borrowing from Akk. He goes on to argue that if the NWSem languages borrowed it in turn from Akk, it would have to be an early loan, since the Akk word has a final uncontracted diphthong only in OAkk and OAss. But if the Akk is not < Sum, all the NWSem languages may have obtained the word from another non-Sem source, independently (Kaufman, ibid., and see Salonen 1963:58). A Semitic etymology is just possible (e.g. **ksî* > Akk *ksû* 'tie, bind': see Salonen (ibid.), who points to the earliest Mesopotamian seats, which are tied bundles of reeds or rushes), but the form is an unusual one for Sem. Perhaps **kussi'* is a foreign or substrate word, hence the odd Ug spelling *kśu*, using a sibilant normally reserved for foreign words (Kaufman (1974:29).

Lipiński (1963), too, is dubious about a Sumerian etymology on account of the dual spelling of the word in syllabic script: Akk *kussû(m)* or *kussi'um*. However, according to J. Black (personal communication) OAkk, OBab, OAss *kussium* contracts naturally to Standard Bab. *kussu*, which resolves Lipiński's problem. Regarding Kaufman's objections, Black's response is that the doubled sibilant and uncontracted diphthong are not inexplicable, just rather unusual, and that the Akk is indeed a loanword from Sum.

2. Formal characteristics

A.1 Form: m, sg. כִּסֵּא, var. כִּסֵּה 1Kg 10.19(2x), Jb 26.9; cons כִּסֵּא; pl כִּסְאוֹת, Q possible 'm' form pl. cons כסאי 11QShSh 2-1-9 5-6; f 5; k 5, 4QShirShab^f (4Q405) 23 i 3.

A.2 *qittil*

3. Syntagmatics

A.1 כִּסֵּא is the *nomen regens*

a) of (כִּסֵּא מַמְלַכְתּוֹ) Dt 17.18 cf. 11QT 56.20; 2Sm 7.13, 4QFlor 1.10f; abs 2Ch 23.20; (pl) Hg 2.22:

of הַמְּלוּכָה 1Kg 1.46:

of מַלְכוּת Est 1.2; 5.1; 1Ch 22.10(9); 28.5; 2Ch 7.18, 4Q405 20 ii 21–22, 11QT 59.17 + יִשְׂרָאֵל:

of הַמְּלָכִים 2Kg 11.19; 25.28, Jr 52.32:

b) of דָּוִד 2Sm 3.10, Is 9.6, Jr 17.25; 22.2; 29.16; 36.30: of יִשְׂרָאֵל 1Kg 2.4; 8.20,25; 9.5; 10.9; 2Kg 10.30; 2Ch 6.10,16; 4QDibMeor 4.7: of בֵּית יִשְׂרָאֵל Jr 33.17: of אָב (אבותיו) 11QT 59.14:

c) of יֽ Jr 3.17; 1Ch 29.23

d) of כָּבוֹד 1Sm 2.8, Is 22.23, Jr 14.21; 17.12, 4QpIsᵃ 8–10.19, 4Q405 23 I 3 (pl); 11QShSh 2-1-9 5–6 (pl):

of קֹדֶשׁ Ps 47.9: of פלא 11QShSh f 5 (pl): of עז 4QWarScroll 11 i 2; of עולמים 11QShSh k 5 (pl).

e) of שֵׁן 1Kg 10.18//2Ch 9.17:

f) of הַוּוֹת Ps 94.20:

g) of דִּין Pr 20.8:

h) of מֶרְכָּבָה 4Q405 20 ii 21–22 8

A.2 כִּסֵּא is the *nomen rectum*

a) of אוּלָם 1Kg 7.7:

b) of דְּמוּת Ezk 1.26²; 10.1: of תַּבְנִית 4Q405 20 ii 21–22 8

c) of מָקוֹם Ezk 43.7: of מָכוֹן Ps 89.15; 97.2; 11QPsᵃCreat 26.11

d) of פְּנֵים Jb 26.9

e) of גאים Sir 10.14

f) of יוֹשֵׁב Sir 40.3, 4QComm Gen (4Q252) V.2.

A.3 כִּסֵּא appears very frequently with *pronominal suffixes*. Whereas the article alone occurs in 5 of the 8 occurrences of כִּסֵּא in Gen, Ex, Jdg, 1Sm, in 2Sm—1Kg—2Kg the 1ps (6x) and 3pms (9x) occur regularly, and 2pms (3x 1Kg), espcially in the 'Succession Narrative'. A suffix is very common in Psalms too (2pms 3x, 3pms 7x). The 3pms occurs in Pr (3x of 6), 1x Est, 2x 1Ch, 3x 2Ch, 1x Sir, 1x Q). The pl form with mpl suf occurs at Is 14.9, Ezk 26.16.

A.4 Verbs:

a) כִּסֵּא is the direct *object* of

ישב qal Ps 122.5, Lm 5.19.

קום hiph 2Ch 7.18; + על 2Sm 3.10, 1Kg 9.5

חון po 2Sm 7.13, Ps 9.8, 1Ch 17.12:

hiph Ps 103.19, 1Ch 22.10(9), 4QFlor 1.10f, Sir 47.11

סעד qal Pr 20.28

בנה qal Ps 89.5

עשה qal 1Kg 10.18//2Ch 9.17

נתן qal + מעל 2Kg 25.28; + על Jr 1.15; + ממעל Jr 52.32

שׂים qal 1Kg 2.19, 2Kg 4.10, Jr 49.38, Ps 89.30; + מעל Est 3.1; + ממעל Jr 43.10:

רום hiph Is 14.13

גדל pi + ccomparative מן 1Kg 1.37,47

נחל hiph 1Sm 2.8

צפה pi 1Kg 10.18//2Ch 9.17

נבל pi Jr 14.21

הפך qal Hg 2.22, Sir 10.4

מגר pi Ps 89.45.

b) כִּסֵּא is governed by עַל:

ישב qal Ex 11.5; 12.29, Dt 17.18, 1Kg 1.13,17,20,24,27,30,35; 8.25; 16.11; 22.10//2Ch 18.9; 1Kg 22.19//2Ch 22.19, 2Kg 10.30; 11.19; 13.13; 15.12, Is 6.1; 16.5, Jr 13.13; 17.25; 22.2,4,30; 29.16; 33.17, Zc 6.13?, Ps 47.9, Pr 9.14; 20.8; Est 1.2; 5.1; 1Ch 28.5; 29.23; 2Ch 6.10,16; 18.18: hiph 2Ch 23.20, Sir 11.5A,

11QT 59.14, 4QDibMeor 4.7.

   נתן qal 1Kg 5.19; 10.9, 2Ch 9.8:

   שׂים qal 2Kg 10.3:

   מלך Jr 33.21; 36.30;

   משׁל qal Zc 6.13:

   היה Zc 6.13

c) כִּסֵּא is governed by מֵעַל:

   קום qal Jdg 3.20:

   נפל qal 1Sm 4.18:

   כרת niph 1Kg 2.4; 9.5:

   ירד qal Ezk 26.16

d) כִּסֵּא is governed by מֶן:

   קום hiph Is 14.9: qal Jn 3.6

e) כִּסֵּא is governed by ל:

   ישׁב qal Ps 9.5; 132.12

   חזק hiph Neh 3.7

   שׁית qal Ps 132.11

A.5 כִּסֵּא is *subject* of

   חבר pi Ps 94.20:

   היה 2Sm 7.16, 1Kg 2.45; Ps 89.37, 1Ch 17.14; ל + 2Ch 9.18[2]

   כון hoph Is 16.5; niph Pr 16.12; 25.5; 29.14:

   (with אין Is 47.1)

A.6 predicate of הַשָּׁמַיִם Is 66.1: לְבֵית דָּוִיד Ps 122.5

A.7 with adjectives:

   נָכוֹן 2Sm 7.16, 1Kg 2.45, 1Ch 17.14, Ps 93.2:

   רָם וְנִשָּׂא Is 6.1:

   גָּדוֹל 2Ch 9.17

A.8 The commonest verb associated with כִּסֵּא is ישׁב (cf. Akk *wašābu*, Ug *yṯb*: Fabry 1984:250–51) but sometimes the idea of sitting is present even if not expressed by a verb (e.g. 1Kg 2.4; 9.5b, with the construction לֹא יִכָּרֵת ... מֵעַל כִּסֵּא). Similarly, there are phrases where the notion of a throne or seat is implicit but the word כִּסֵּא does not appear (e.g. Ps 9.8, where כִּסֵּא appears in the second half of the verse; Is 10.13 וְאוֹרִיד כָּאבִּיר יוֹשְׁבִים). However, it is often difficult to determine whether ישׁב refers to dwelling or sitting/enthronement in the absence of כִּסֵּא: e.g. does God dwell or does he sit enthroned in the heavens or sanctuary? (Brettler 1989:81). (For more on ישׁב used of God, see Preuss 1991:I,175; ET I,153).

A.9 The usual preposition used with כִּסֵּא and ישׁב is עַל, but in Ps 9.5 the phrase occurs with ל Kraus (1966:80; ET I,194) interprets this as 'an old theophanic formula, referring to the appearance and effective intervention of God, with ל normally meaning 'direction towards a target''. However, the parallels with similar expressions in Ug may be more illuminating, e.g. *yṯb l-kḥt aliyn bʿl* 'he was enthroned on the throne of ʿAliyan Baʿl', *KTU*[2] 1.6 I 58 (Dahood 1965:I,55).

A.10 The phrase יוֹשֵׁב כִּסֵּא later comes to mean 'king', e.g. Sir 40.3B.

A.11 The commonest context for כִּסֵּא is within a discussion of a king's succession or as a description of his royal position. The phrase 'he will sit on [someone's] throne' frequently occurs in parallelism with 'he will be king in someone's place/after someone' in the 'Succession Narrative': 1Kg 1.17,24,30, 35 (cp. vv. 20,27, Ps 132.12, 11QT 59.14), and operates as a formula to express legitimate succession. The two ideas are conflated in Jr 33.21 'reigning upon his throne'. A very common expression, especially in Jr, is 'the throne of David': Jr 17.25; 22.2,30; 29.16; 36.30, cf. 13.13; 22.4, also 33.17,21: in all these the Deuteronomic aspect of the perpetuation or failure of the Davidic dynasty is emphasised (Weinfeld 1972:7 n.4,355; Holladay 1989:II,142). Because of this abstract use in a dynastic sense, there is no such AH expression 'throne of Solomon', but if it did occur, it would refer to his personal royal seat (Fabry 1984:257). In the 'Succession Narrative', the possessive suffix of כִּסֵּא or its nomen rectum generally refers to David: his kingdom and royal power are transmitted to his successors, primarily Solomon. But in the work of the Chronicler, the possessive suffix of כִּסֵּא (or of its nomen rectum 'kingdom', cf. Akk *kussî šarrūti* (Fabry 1984:250) generally refers to Solomon (1Ch 17.12,14; 22.10(9), 2Ch 7.18; 9.8), and the contexts in which כִּסֵּא is found refer to Solomon's kingship (1Ch 28.5; 29.23, 2Ch 6.10). וְיָשַׁב וּמָשַׁל עַל־כִּסְאוֹ (Zc 6.13), though differing from the usual formulation in Dt and Jr, deliberately alludes to the succession to the Davidic throne (Meyers and Meyers 1987:359).

A.12 The expression 'throne of Israel' is also found in 1–2Kgs (1Kg 2.4; 8.20, 25; 9.5b; 10.9, 2Kg 10.30; 15.12: Deuteronomic [Fabry 1984:257]) but in the Chronicler only in 2Ch 6.10, 16. Instead, we find substituted the expressions 'throne of the Lord's kingdom over Israel' (1Ch 28.5) and 'throne of the Lord' (1Ch 29.23, //1Kg 1.46 where the text has 'throne of the kingdom'). Japhet (1989:396,402) believes this indicates the Chronicler's identification of Israel's monarchy with the kingdom of Yahweh, the king functioning as God's representative, as expressed in 2Ch 9.8, 'to put you on his throne as king *for* the Lord your God'. To her, this identification resolves the dilemma expressed in Sm and Jdg that Israel cannot be ruled by both Yahweh and a king at the same time, and harmonizes it with the opposing view of a glorious monarchic past. In contrast, Williamson (1982:136) defines the sense of 1Ch 28.5 and 29.23 as forward-looking, referring to a throne legitimized by God and therefore permanent. Kuntzmann (1993:19–27) generally follows Japhet, but lays even greater stress on role of the king as Yahweh's representative and the subordination of the monarchy to Yahweh. Such beliefs on the part of the Chronicler means that in the exilic period the monarchy remains intact because Yahweh himself is king (Kuntzmann 1993: 22).

It should be noted that although Preuss (1991:I,175; ET I,153) states that there are 22 occurrences of Yahweh's throne in the Hebrew Bible, the actual expression 'throne of Yahweh' כִּסֵּא י׳ occurs only in two places, 1Ch 29.23 and Jr 3.17: the first has the meaning just discussed, i.e. the identification of Israel's monarchy with the Lord's rule, and the second refers to Jerusalem. Caquot (1956:34) argued on the basis of 1Ch 29.23, 2Ch 9.8, Ps 45.7 that Ps 110.1 implied a rite in which the king sat down in the empty throne of Yahweh and placed his feet on the necks of representatives of national enemies, but he overlooked the prevailing metaphorical use of both כִּסֵּא and הֲדֹם (Kuntzmann 1993:22–23). Neither 1Ch 29.23 nor Jr 3.17 refers to a throne on which the

Deity was thought to sit, either in the sanctuary or in heaven, though the disputed reading Ex 17.16 does appear to have this sense in several witnesses (see *Disputed Readings*).

A.13 Of human occupants of thrones, it is the king who sits on a (secular) throne, and not just Israelite and Judahite kings, since similar expressions are used of Pharaoh and other non-Israelite monarchs (e.g Gn 41.40, Ex 11.5, 12.29; Is 14.9; Jr 1.15; Est 1.2).

A.14 As for non-royal occupants of thrones, וְשָׂרִים in Jr 17.25 (מְלָכִים וְשָׂרִים יֹשְׁבִים עַל־כִּסֵּא דָוִד) is often regarded as an addition (Holladay 1986:I,508). The meaning of Zc 6.13 (וְיָשַׁב וּמָלַךְ עַל כִּסְאוֹ וְהָיָה כֹהֵן עַל כִּסְאוֹ) is also disputed: was the priest to sit on his own throne, occupy a double throne with Zerubbabel, or to stand by Zerubbabel's throne? Mitchell (1912:186–88) believes that the original reading was *עַל יְמִינוֹ, as suggested by LXX, and was changed to עַל־כִּסְאוֹ at a later date, when, as is often supposed, the high priest became the leader of the community in place of the king and sat and ruled on a throne. In contrast, Rignell (1950:231) thinks that the LXX translator felt that 'throne' was inappropriate for a priest and hence altered the translation to something fitting to a priest's station under Zerubbabel. Mastin (1976), developing suggestions by Sellin (1922:472) and Petitjean (1969:291ff), points out that since LXX may be interpreting the text under the influence of 1Kg 2.19, where Solomon offers the king's mother a כִּסֵּא at his right hand, and differentiating a royal seat (כִּסֵּא = θρόνος usually in LXX) from a priestly one (כִּסֵּא = δίφρος usually), it is unwise to reconstruct MT on the basis of LXX. Meyers and Meyers (1987:359–61) note the similarity of the phrase in Zc 6.13 to the Dtr succession formula, though the verb משל intrudes in the accustomed order, perhaps to suggest the extension of his reign beyond Judah. They explain the oddity of a priest with his own throne by reference to Eli's chair, the symbol of his priestly and judicial functions. Therefore the throne does not indicate royal status but an increase in responsibilities for the high priest in the postmonarchic period, with a precedent in the premonarchic era. Against this, Rose (1997:46–48) observes that the verb יָשַׁב does not occur, so there may be no suggestion that Joshua was sitting on a throne, i.e. ruling. Rose also points out that the phrase הָיָה עַל כִּסֵּא is unique. He compares the situation in 1Kg 2.19, where a king and another important person are each described as being seated on a כִּסֵּא, yet no one suggests that this implies a dyarchic rule consisting of Solomon and his mother, still less that the queen mother is given supremacy. Rose believes that the priest Joshua portrayed as being 'by' Zerubbabel's throne as a counsellor, in view of the rest of the verse.

A.15 Just once an angel is described as having a throne: Michael, in 4QWarScroll 11 I 2. Another non-royal, non-divine possessor of a throne is the governor of Transeuphrates in Neh 3.8, a reference to his judicial and administrative functions (Williamson 1985:197).

A.16 Usually the expression 'sit on the throne' is more or less metaphorical, referring to the exercise of royal power (e.g. Dt 17.18 = 11QT 56.20), but occasionally it is literal, as in Est 5.1 (as against Est 1.2), and 1Kg 2.19.

A.17 God is generally the agent in the enthroning of a king, in establishing his throne or in making it great (2Sm 3.10; 7.13, 1Kg 1.37,47; 2.24; 9.5; Jr

43.10, of Nebuchadnezzar; Ps 89.5, 30; 132.11, Sir 47.11B, 4QFlor 1.10f): contrast the arrogance of the king of Babylon in Is 14.13, who seeks to rival the Lord by raising his own throne higher than God's stars. When the subject of a similar phrase is human, it seems that the meaning is 'seat of honour' rather than the supreme royal throne: Evil-Merodach places Jehoiachin's seat higher than the seats of other kings in Babylon (Jr 52.32 = 2Kg 25.28), and Ahasuerus sets Haman's seat higher than that of other officials (Est 3.1): both of these subjects are kings who have it in their power to promote those beneath them. At Jr 1.15 all the northern kingdoms are to set up their thrones at the gates of Jerusalem, an assertion of royal authority, but this is at the Lord's instigation, as also in Jr 43.10, of Nebuchadnezzar (Holladay 1986:I,41).

A.18 God's power to bring human rule to an end is expressed in Hg 2.22 (וְהָפַכְתִּי כִּסֵּא מַמְלָכוֹת), Sir 10.14, Ps 89.45 (cf. Ug *hpk ks' mlk*, cited by Fabry 1984:252). He promises to establish his own throne, i.e. his rule, over a far-off nation in Jr 49.38 (וְשַׂמְתִּי כִסְאִי בְעֵילָם). God's power to reverse fortunes is expressed in Sir 10.14, 1Sm 2.8 (though these may refer to a seat of honour rather than a royal throne).

A.19 The expression לֹא יִכָּרֵת לְךָ אִישׁ מֵעַל כִּסֵּא יִשְׂרָאֵל, is translated by NJB 'you will never lack for a man on the throne of Israel', by NEB 'you shall never lack a successor on the throne of Israel'. It represents the assurance that a dynasty will be perpetuated (1Kg 2.4; 9.5 = 2Ch 7.18; 11QT 59.17: for variants see 1Kg 8.25 = 2Ch 6.16; Jr 33.17, 4QCommGen [4Q252] V.2 and 11QT 59.14). It is regarded as a Deuteronomic trait (Weinfeld 1972:5,355: Holladay 1989:II,228).

A.20 Rising, descending or falling from a throne or seat can be seen as signifying humiliation or deposition: Eglon rises from his throne and is assassinated by Ehud (Jdg 3.20), Eli falls backwards from his seat (1Sm 4.18), signifying both his own death and the end of power for his dynasty (for further discussion of these two passages see below in *Exegesis*), the king of Nineveh descends from his throne along with other gestures of self-abasement in response to God's message through Jonah (Jn 3.6), the 'daughter of Babylon' is told to get down and sit on the ground without a seat (Is 47.1), and similarly the princes of the sea will get down from their thrones, strip off their finery and sit on the ground (Ezk 26.16). Zimmerli (1969:II,38) believes that the verb ירד denotes descent from a throne raised on steps, cf. 1Kg 10.18–20. Fabry (1984:252) cites the use of *yrd* in similar contexts in Ug.

A.21 There is an association between כִּסֵּא and judging in BH. 1Kg 7.7 describes Solomon building a hall for the throne from which he dispensed justice. But a כִּסֵּא in the sense of a ruler's seat is not necessarily in a palace, and it is sometimes described as being at the city gates (1Kg 22.10, Jr 1.15). The only time when a negative word is attached to כִּסֵּא is at Ps 94.20, where it seems to mean 'seat of iniquity', a place where justice is perverted (see Kraus 1966:657; ET II, 242). Whether Deborah in Jdg 4 was thought of as sitting on a כִּסֵּא beneath the palm of Deborah is unclear (וְהִיא יוֹשֶׁבֶת תַּחַת־תֹּמֶר דְּבוֹרָה ... וַיַּעֲלוּ אֵלֶיהָ בְּנֵי יִשְׂרָאֵל לַמִּשְׁפָּט), but it is possible that the fact that Absalom *stands* by the road to the city gate (וְעָמַד עַל־יַד דֶּרֶךְ הַשָּׁעַר) to offer his services as a judge underlines his lack of official status (וַיֹּאמֶר אַבְשָׁלוֹם מִי יְשִׂמֵנִי שֹׁפֵט בָּאָרֶץ 2Sm 15.4).

However, McCarter (1980:114) believes that both Eli and Absalom are on the top of the city wall beside the gate.

A.22 The expression כִּסֵּא כָבוֹד in BH may not refer to a royal throne, but instead to a seat of honour: 1Sm 2.8 refers to God seating the poor with nobles, and making them inherit a כִּסֵּא כָבוֹד, though Carlson (1964:96) regards this as a Deuteronomic reference to David's throne. In Is 22.23 Eliakim son of Hilkiah is promised the stewardship of the royal palace, and he is to be לְכִסֵּא כָבוֹד for his father's house, which is presumably not a royal throne. But in Jr (14.21; 17.12) the expression seems to refer to the temple in Jerusalem, and would more easily be translated 'glorious throne' (Holladay 1986:I,438,502). The meaning of כָבוֹד כִּסֵּא varies in Qumran texts. In Pesher Isaiah it is one of the accoutrements of the Branch of David along with the holy נֵזֶר and embroidered garments. In the Songs of the Sabbath Sacrifice it is apparently in the plural, 'glorious thrones', and refers to the chariot throne of God (Newsom 1985:308,325).

4. Versions [A full listing of translation equivalents and references may be found in APPENDIX]

LXX
A.1 The LXX translators distinguish between 'throne' and 'chair', and sometimes emphasise the aspect of kingship and rule.
There are very few alternative renderings of כִּסֵּא recorded for 'The Three', probably because the normal rendering θρόνος was uncontroversial and needed no revision. However, at Is 47.1, where LXX renders כִּסֵּא as σκότος, Aq and Thd have θρόνος.

B.1
σκότος 'darkness' Is 47.1 (as from *כסה)
ἐκ δεξιῶν 'at the right hand' Zc 6.13 (see Petitjean 1969:291ff: LXX usually renders as θρόνος for a king, and δίφρος for a priest, but the contrast between the seats is too great here to be fitting: so the priest becomes Zerubbabel's 'right-hand man' instead).
ἔδαφος 'ground' Sir 11.5 (contextual rendering)

Tg
A.1 The addition of *malkuṭa* to qualify *kursyā* is connected with the meaning of כִּסֵּא in RH and JArm: 'chair', or even 'privy'. It therefore needed to be defined as a royal throne.

B.1
אֲתַר בֵּית שְׁכִינְתָּא ('place of the house of the divine Presence': theological rendering) Jr 3.17.
2Ch 18.9: this phrase is missing in Tg.

Vg
A.1 Jerome likes to vary his translation between the Greek loan *thronus* and the native Latin *solium*. To him, Eli sits on a chair, as do Elisha and

Wisdom. But God has the heavens as a seat, *sedes*, not as a throne (Is 66.1), cf. the princes of the sea in Ezk 26, and there are seats of judgment in Ps 94.20; 122.5, and a seat for David Ps 132.11. (Latin Sirach is not the work of Jerome.)

B.1 Neh (2 Esd) 3.7 is not represented.

Pesh
A.1
kursyā ('seat, throne') throughout: for the exception, see B.1 below.

B.1
taksiṭā ('covering' < *כסה*) Jb 26.9

5. Lexical/Semantic Field(s)

A.1 In parallelism with הֲדֹם: Is 66.1 הַשָּׁמַיִם כִּסְאִי וְהָאָרֶץ הֲדֹם רַגְלָי, 11QShSh 2–1–9 5–6: cf. Ug *yrd l ksi yṯb l hdm w l hdm yṯb KTU*² 1.5 VI 12–13; *yṯb krt l ᶜdh yṯb l ksi mlk KTU*² 1.16 VI 22–23 (Loretz 1994a:230ff.). Similarly, Ezk 43.7 אֶת־מְקוֹם כִּסְאִי וְאֶת־מְקוֹם כַּפּוֹת רַגְלַי.

A.2 In parallelism with כֶּבֶשׁ, 2Ch 9.18
A.3 In parallelism with מוֹשָׁב 4Q405 20 ii 21–22 2.
A.4 In parallelism with קָדְשׁוֹ Ps 11.4
A.5 In parallelism with מַמְלָכָה, בַּיִת 2Sm 7.16
A.6 Schmid (1968:85,86,146) notes the association of כִּסֵּא and מֶלֶךְ with מִשְׁפָּט וּצְדָקָה (1Kg 10.9), יָשַׁב עַל־כִּסֵּא with צְדָקָה, חֶסֶד and יְשָׁרֵת לְבַב (1Kg 3.6), and שֹׁפֵט, מִשְׁפָּט, צֶדֶק, with יָשַׁב, + כִּסֵּא in Jr 22.2–4; מֶלֶךְ with מִשְׁפָּט וּצְדָקָה and יָשַׁב עַל־כִּסֵּא, יָשַׁב + כִּסֵּא (Ps 9.5), מִשְׁפָּט, דִּין, שׁוֹפֵט, צֶדֶק with יָשַׁבְתָּ + כִּסֵּא (Is 16.5), חֶסֶד, אֱמֶת, צֶדֶק וּמִשְׁפָּט, חֶסֶד וֶאֱמֶת with כִּסֵּא (Ps 45.7), כִּסֵּא with מִישֹׁר (Ps 9.8), מַלְכוּת with כִּסֵּא, שֵׁבֶט, מִשְׁפָּט (Ps 89.15), כִּסֵּא with צֶדֶק וּמִשְׁפָּט (Ps 97.2). However, one might argue that these passages describe an idealized situation with even messianic or divine features, and are not necessarily descriptive of the nature of monarchy in Israel (see Kissane 1943:193, Gray 1912:289, Proksch 1930:218, Feldmann 1925:203, Fischer 1937:129f, on the context of Is 16.5). Similar connections between the king's throne and justice are made in Ug (Schmid 1968:29, 85, 86).

B.1 Dahood (1968:II, 317) suggests that עַד in Ps 89.30 should be understood as 'seat' in parallelism with כִּסֵּא, since a similar word appears in Ug (ᶜdh) in parallellism with *ksi*: *yṯb krt lᶜdh yṯb lksi mlk* (UT 127.22–23). He believes that עַד is 'seat' in Ps 89.38; 93.5; 94.15; 110.1, Is 47.4; 57.15, Jr 22.30, Zp 3.8. However, there is no support for this idea outside Ug.

6. Exegesis

A.1 כִּסֵּא is rather unusual in that, although its primary application is a concrete one, 'throne' or 'chair', most occurrences are in a metaphorical sense (in the meaning 'throne' especially), and denote regal power. The expression יָשַׁב עַל־כִּסֵּא also occurs very frequently, and means 'to have royal power'; with suffixes and some *nomina recta* it means 'to succeed someone'. The metaphorical use is particularly common in the work of the Deuteronomic historian, and McCarter (1980:II, 347-48) sees 2Sm 14.9 (especially the phrase וְהַמֶּלֶךְ וְכִסְאוֹ נָקִי) as a Deuteronomic expansion added in order to protect the house of David from guilt arising from the interview with the wise woman and from David's oath in v.11.

A.2 כִּסֵּא can have connotations of judgement, since, presumably, the judge and later the king sat on a chair of state to judge cases (Pr 20.8, 1Kg 7.7) while petitioners and others sat or squatted on the ground or remained standing. (Perhaps Deborah was envisaged as sitting on a כִּסֵּא in Jdg 4.5 when she sat beneath the palm tree to judge the Israelites?)

A.3 The only time when we can be completely sure that כִּסֵּא refers to an ordinary household chair is in 2Kg 4.10, where it is listed with a lamp, bed and table as furnishings for the room that Elisha is to occupy on his visits. However, Spina (1994:70) believes that the inclusion of כִּסֵּא calls attention to the prophet's status and office.

Other non-royal occurrences are ambiguous: 1Sm 1.9, where Eli may be sitting on a) a special chair to denote his priestly status, b) on an ordinary chair because of his age (Willis 1979:207), c) on an ordinary chair to preserve order in the sanctuary ('Ordnungshüter', Fabry 1984:259), hence his attempt to dismiss the apparently inebriated Hannah, d) on an ordinary chair 'idly and unobtrusively', like 'a rather simple country clergyman attached to a sanctuary which is really rather modest', since Hannah does not notice him at first (Cody 1969:69). At 1Sm 4.13,18 Eli seems to be sitting on an ordinary כִּסֵּא because of his age during the long wait for news of the Ark, and it is presumably backless in view of the fact that he falls off backwards and breaks his neck: a campstool is possible. However, McCarter (1980:I,114) takes יַד (Qere, 1 Sm 4.13) not in a prepositional sense but with the concrete meaning 'hand, side', indicating the wall to which the gate is attached. Hence, Eli's chair is 'atop the gate' in 1Sm 4.18, with the result that he falls 'over the hand of the gate', i.e. over the wall to the street below, which perhaps explains better the breaking of his neck in the fall. Against this, the text in 1Sm 4.13,18 is doubtful where it describes the position of Eli's chair and the circumstance of his fall (1Sm 4.13 Qere וְהִנֵּה עֵלִי יֹשֵׁב עַל־הַכִּסֵּא יַד דֶּרֶךְ; 1Sm 4.18 וַיִּפֹּל מֵעַל־הַכִּסֵּא אֲחֹרַנִּית בְּעַד יַד הַשַּׁעַר וַתִּשָּׁבֵר מַפְרַקְתּוֹ וַיָּמֹת), and the interpretation of בְּעַד (usually 'through, among' in such contexts) is difficult. It is also to be doubted whether the writer really envisaged the elderly, half-blind and infirm Eli as able to reach the top of the wall. Klein (1983:44) rejects McCarter's interpretation because he is unconvinced by the parallels cited.

A.4 1Sm 4.18 mentions that Eli judged Israel, and the chair may have been a part of his judicial insignia. This is the view of Spina (1994:68–70), who disagrees with the many scholars who consider כִּסֵּא in 1Sm 1.9; 4.13,18 to be an ordinary seat. He believes that since the verb יָשַׁב so often occurs without the addition of עַל כִּסֵּא, when כִּסֵּא is added it is a significant detail. Spina sees Eli as a priest who judged Israel (1Sm 4.18). The כִּסֵּא is a symbol of his office as priestly ruler, a dynastic appointment in contrast to the individual charismatic judges of the Book of Judges. His fall from the כִּסֵּא represents the deposition of this type of rulership, to be replaced by that of the prophet Samuel, and

subsequently of King Saul, neither of whom is described as having a כִּסֵּא, until
the ideal rule of David and his dynasty, of which כִּסֵּא is used very frequently
indeed (ibid. 70–75). Spina's argument is interesting, but he may carry it too far
in its symbolism in the developing pattern of Israelite rulership. Polzin takes a
similar line (1989:23,31,44): Eli is portrayed as a royal figure, who because he
sits on the כִּסֵּא in the הֵיכָל, acts as a metaphor for Israel's kingship, doomed to
fail from the perspective of the Deuteronomist, hence Eli's collapse and demise
in ch. 4. In contrast, McCarter (1980:I,115) rejects the notion that Eli was a
judge, putting it down to a Deuteronomic expansion. In addition, much depends
on the significance of the definite article: is a specific chair intended, or does
הַכִּסֵּא have a more general sense? GK § 126 suggests that the article does have a
defining sense, and is more often indefinite in poetic texts (Is 16.5; 47.1, Ps 9.5;
122.5; 132.11,12, Pr 16.12, Jb 26.9 [si vera lectio], Sir 11.5; 40.3), compared
with prose: 2Kg 4.10, Is 6.1, Ezk 1.26; 10.1 (the last three being theophanic).

A.5   There is a similar problem for the interpretation of 1Kg 2.19: Solomon
is sitting on a throne, it seems, but it is unclear whether the כִּסֵּא he obtains for
his mother Bathsheba and places at his right hand is a chair offered to a visitor
who is important and also elderly, or a throne specifically for the Queen Mother.
A chair is placed at his right hand after the king has done obeisance to her, both
gestures being signs of great honour, but there is no definite article for כִּסֵּא,
which may suggest that no special seat was reserved for the king's mother.

A.6   Caquot (1966:34) suggests that royal thrones were a borrowing in
Israelite culture from the Canaanites (cf Ug and Ph *ksʾi*), since no throne is
mentioned for Saul, and one first appears in connection with David in 2Sm
3.10. However, this occurrence has a metaphorical sense in a speech of David's,
and it could be argued that it is due to a later editor.

Much the same could be said of the occurrence in 2Sm 14.9, where David's
throne is again mentioned and has a figurative sense. However, for the argument
that Israelite royal thrones were influenced by Canaanite practice, Eglon king
of Moab (Jdg 3.20) is seated on a כִּסֵּא.

A.7   The significance of Eglon's rising from his כִּסֵּא (Jdg 3.20) has been
discussed. Polzin sees it as symbolic, 'as if to foreshadow that this word of God
signified the end of his role' (1980:157), but Lindars takes it as a 'predictable
response to Ehud's words and therefore part of the plan' (1995:145). For Halpern
(1988:59), Eglon stands up in bewildered horror: Halpern denies that it was
normal to stand when receiving an oracle (1988:75 n.66). Brettler (1995:82)
perceives a scatological side to the Ehud story, with sexual overtones to Ehud's
visit to Eglon. Although Brettler does not remark on the significance of כִּסֵּא in
the passage, it could be seen as having humorous overtones as well, since
Eglon's servants assume that he is relieving himself. But this would depend on
כִּסֵּא in AH sometimes having the same meaning, 'privy', as in RH.

A.8   *The form of Solomon's throne*
The form of Solomon's throne is described in 1Kg 10.18–20//2Ch 9.17–18, but
there are doubts concerning the reliability of MT at that point. Because the
reading of LXX 3Kgdms (προτομαὶ μόσχων τῷ θρόνῳ ἐν τῶν ὀπίσω αὐτοῦ
καὶ χεῖρες ἔνθεν καὶ ἔνθεν ἐπὶ τοῦ τόπου τῆς καθέδρας 'bulls' heads for the
throne behind it, and arms here and there on the place of the seat', 10.19)

suggests that the translator read *רָאשֵׁי עֲגָלִים, it is generally thought that the rabbis later changed the vocalisation of the word עגל to avoid the notion that Solomon had a bull's head on the top of his throne: the bull was a symbol of Baal, hence the biblical writers' disapproval expressed in Ex 32 and concerning the career of Jeroboam (see Geiger 1857:343; Curtis 1910:359; North 1932:28; Gray 1964:266, 269 note g; Montgomery 1951:221–22; Japhet 1993:640ff). This hypothesis is further strengthened by the equivalent passage in Josephus *Ant.* VIII § 140, ἀνακέκλιτο δ' εἰς μόσχου πρωτοτομὴν τὰ κατόπιν αὐτοῦ βλέποντος, 'it rested on the head of a calf which faced toward the back of the throne'.

In an earlier theological alteration, also to avoid suggestions of bull-worship, the Chronicler at 2Ch 9.18 changed 'calf' to 'lamb', כֶּבֶשׂ. This in turn was read as the graphically similar and appropriate כֶּבֶשׁ , 'footstool'. מֵאַחֲרָיו of 1Kg was then altered to מָאֳחָזִים, since a footstool would not be behind a throne (Canciani and Pettinato 1965:90ff; Noth 1968:204; Williamson 1982:235; Japhet 1993:640ff). There is no support in the versions for an original reading כֶּבֶשׂ, however: LXX A and B suggest a reading *חבשׁ (ἐνδεδεμένοι, 'bound'), and the Lucianic recension adds the words καὶ ὑποπόδιον ὑπέθηκεν ἐν χρυσῷ τῷ θρόνῳ, 'he placed a footstool in gold beneath the throne', which is even closer to MT. However, LXX 1–2Ch is a relatively late translation of the Hebrew, and the Lucianic recension later still, so alteration of the Heb may have preceded the Old Greek translation.

Discussing the problem from the perspective of Ancient Near Eastern parallels, Metzger (1985:298ff) believes that one cannot compare the description of Solomon's throne with Assyrian and late Hittite bull heads on thrones, as these appear only on the thrones of gods, which lack lion armrests. The proposed Egyptian parallels predate Solomon's throne by two millennia. Metzger infers that the LXX translator simply made a mistake, since the word עָגֹל 'round' appears so rarely in the Hebrew Bible, and often with plene spelling, that they supposed the word 'calf' was intended. Metzger (1985:300) takes MT to refer to the sort of backrests found in the Egyptian New Kingdom, which curl over at the top, and likewise Canciani and Pettinato (1965:102 figure 5). As for the passage in 2Ch, Metzger points out that there are no archaeological parallels to this design apart from rams on the sides of the armrests, but Solomon's throne has lions in this position.

It is difficult to come to a definite conclusion on the matter of possible censorship of Solomon's throne. The argument that the text has been altered from 'calf' to 'round', or from 'calf' to 'sheep' in Ch, makes very good sense, though there is no versional support in the case of Ch. However, the evidence from Ancient Near Eastern art tends to support the round-backed throne of MT.

'Ivory throne' (1Kg 10.18) does not mean that Solomon's throne was made entirely of ivory (Kittel 1900:92). Metzger (1985:300-301) compares the expressions in Am 6.4 and 1Kg 22.39, and the archaeological finds from Syria and Palestine, to show that beds and chairs could be decorated with ivory intarsias or ivory plates carved in relief on the backrest, feet or side panels. He explains v.18b as meaning not that Solomon had the whole chair gold-plated, but that either the ivory plates were partially inlaid with gold, as with one of

Tutankhamun's thrones and as found at Samaria, or that the woodwork was plated with gold in a similar way to another of Tutankhamun's thrones. Canciani and Pettinato (1965:108) conclude that Solomon's throne reflects Syro-Phoenician art (cf. the role of Hiram king of Tyre in helping with the building of the Temple), which itself was influenced by Egypt.

As for the 'two lions standing by the armrests' (v.19c), symbols of royal might like the bull (Kittel 1900:92), the armrests could be enclosed, with lion reliefs on the outside of the infilled side pieces, like sphinx reliefs on some Egyptian thrones. However, the preposition suggests lion figures standing alongside (אֵצֶל) each side of the throne, either at the height of the armrests (as in the Egyptian New Kingdom examples) or at a lower level (as at Ur) (Metzger 1985:302). The presence of lion pairs and the six steps plus golden podium (כֶּבֶשׁ) on which the throne sat would demonstrate a mixture of Egyptian and Mesopotamian influences, since the seven levels would resemble the ziggurat typology found in Mesopotamia (Metzger 1985:303). Fabry (1984:261; ET VII:247) takes issue with this interpretation of the dais, and, following Canciani and Pettinato (1965:107), points to the Egyptian throne estrade, symbolising the cosmic order.

A.9 *Other royal thrones*

In Jr 43.9–10 Jeremiah places stones in the pavement in front of Pharaoh's palace at Tahpanes in readiness for Nebuchadnezzar's throne, over which Nebuchadnezzar would spread his canopy (Holladay 1989:II,302). The expression בַּמַּלְבֵּן (בְּמֶלֶט) is unclear, but if it is understood as 'clay', it may be that the stones were to serve as a firm base for the throne. The passage appears to depict the setting up of a throne out of doors, following a siege or victory, and indicating the assertion of authority over a city (cf. Jr 1.15).

A.10 *God's throne*

The idea is widespread throughout the Ancient Near East that deities reign from a throne, and Israel is no exception. Since the king sat on a ceremonial chair on solemn occasions, gods were depicted in the same way (Krebs 1974:3–4,7). Brettler (1989:82) observes that in BH the notion appears in all periods of biblical writing from the early prophetic literature to the postexilic psalms.

In the Psalms, many of the occurrences of כִּסֵּא refer to God's throne (Ps 9.5, 8; 11.4; 45.7; 47.9; 89.15; 93.2; 97.2; 103.19) rather than that of a king (89.5,30, 37,45; 122.5[2]; 132.11,12). God's throne is associated with justice and judgment (Ps 9.5,8) as is the royal throne at times, and is described as being founded on righteousness and justice (Ps 89.15; 97.2, cf. Pr 16.12, 20.8,28; 25.5; 29.14 of the royal throne): Gunkel (1926:389) suggested that these attributes were seen as supporting the throne, since on Ancient Near Eastern thrones subjects or figures of demons are often depicted as supporting the seat. However, Brunner believes that this is the influence of Egyptian thought, where royal and divine thrones rest on a plinth or steep ramp, the hieroglyph for which means both 'ancient hill/throne base' and 'righteousness, truth', Ma'at (see also Preuss 1991:I,198–99; ET I,173, Schmid 1968:76,79–80, Kraus 1966:621,672–73; ET II,207, Ringgren 1947:87). In contrast, Dahood (1968:II,315) sees the abstract virtues as the four personified sacred mountains of Canaanite tradition. (See also Paas [1993] on Egyptian comparative material for dais and throne, in relation to Am 9.6a.) Handy (1992:1065–66), cf. Rosenberg (1965), points to the position of the minor deities Sedheq and Misor (according to the classical sources on Phoenician history), the dual divinity *ṣdq mšr* at Ugarit, and Kittu and Mesharu sons of Shamash in Babylonian. They appear either to function as attendant deities to a more important god, or to be the deified characteristics of divine qualities such as justice and equity. In any case, this provides a useful context for the qualities of Yahweh and of the king in various passages, especially in Ps 97.2 (Ringgren 1947:83–88, 151; Schmid 1968:146,148f,155).

A.11 God's throne is described as firmly established and enduring (Ps 45.7, 93.2, Lm 5.19), and holy (a word not used of a royal throne: see Ps 47.9), but where is it considered to be? One view is that at an earlier stage of Israelite religion Yahweh was considered to be enthroned in his sanctuary, first in the tabernacle, and then in the Temple, but after the Exile he was thought to be seated in heaven. Thus Loretz (1994b) suggests that though in Ps 11.4 and 103.19 God's throne is in heaven, the text of 11.4 once had *יֹשֵׁב עַל instead of בַּשָּׁמַיִם: the later corrector wanted God in heaven, rather than on the throne of the Jerusalem temple. Dahood's understanding of the same psalm includes both concepts: 'Yahweh – in the temple is his holy seat: Yahweh — in the heavens is his throne' (1965:I, 69–70). But Preuss believes that earlier texts also speak of the heavens as the place where God sits enthroned and dwells, e.g. 1Kg 22.19, Ps 2.4, though sometimes it is Zion (Ps 9.12, cf. Jr 8.19, Ps 132.5,13–14), with the influence of Deuteronomic thinking on the inaccessibility of God affecting other texts (e.g. 1Kg 8.30,39,43,49: 2Ch 6.21,30,33,39; cf. 2Sm 7.5–7, with the late Pss 33.14; 103.19; 123.1 presupposing the Deuteronomic notion of God). But the earthly and heavenly dwellings are often thought of as closely connected, with something like the vision of Isaiah linking them together, the throne in the sanctuary rising into heaven at the same time (Preuss 1991:I,175, 286–89; ET I,153, 251–53).

A.12 Mowinckel (1922:II) was the first to suggest that certain psalms, termed 'enthronement psalms') were part of an ancient New Year ceremony in which Yahweh was enthroned as king of the world for the coming year. Many scholars have accepted his basic thesis, and include a number of psalms containing the word כִּסֵּא among these 'enthronement psalms': 45, 47, 93, 94, 103, 122, 132, though the list varies. A number of other scholars reject the idea of an enthronement ceremony for Yahweh, e.g. Michel (1956: 40–68), McCullough (1956), Schreiner (1963:191–216), Schmidt (1966:76–77), Johnson (1967:65 n.1), Kraus (1966: 647–48, 682–83; ET II,232–34, 268–70), one of the reasons being that the Ancient Near Eastern parallels were principally Babylonian and therefore were unlikely to have influenced early Israelite religion. Tengström (1993:37–58) observes that no myth of Yahweh's enthronement comparable to that of Marduk or Baal has come down to us. Another point of contention is the understanding of the phrase יְהוָה מָלַךְ (to be discussed in the SAHD entry on מָלַךְ). The various positions on a possible enthronement festival for Yahweh are set out in Ollenburger (1987:24–33).

A.13 Although the word כִּסֵּא does not appear in relation to the Ark of the Covenant, a great deal has been written concerning the notion that the Ark was considered to be the throne of the invisible Yahweh, largely on the basis of the phrase יֹשֵׁב הַכְּרֻבִים, and for that reason a brief discussion of the issues is in order. One view is that the Ark was considered God's throne, another that he was seated on the cherubim in the Temple while the Ark was his footstool, a third that he was enthroned in heaven with the Ark as his earthly footstool (see de Vaux 1960–61, and Ringgren 1963:43–44; ET 48; Haran 1959; Fritz 1977:135). Clements (1965:3–31) suggests that the Lord was considered by P to be enthroned on the cherubim of the Kapporet, and that the Ark was merely a box, as the term אָרוֹן implies. Similarly, others maintain that God was thought of as enthroned in heaven only: the Ark was a container for something of importance, such as the covenant. In particular, Noth (1968:179) rejects the idea that the Ark was either a throne or a footstool, since it was at the wrong angle in the Debir, with the short ends of the Ark facing forward. (For more detail on the various theories, see Haran 1978:248–50 and 1959:30–38, de Vaux 1960–61, Mettinger 1982:21–23, Tengström 1993:39–43, and biblio-graphies in Fohrer 1969:100; ET 109, and Fritz 1977:135 n.83). All this has some pertinence to the meaning of כִּסֵּא, especially if Is 6.1 is regarded as making explicit the concept of the Lord occupying the cherubim seat in the sanctuary. However, Knierim (1968:53–54) rejects any connection of the throne of the Lord with the ark or its cover, or with the cherubim, since כִּסֵּא never occurs in that context except in the late passage Ezk 10.1ff, and he argues that Is 6.1 is intended to express the notion of Yahweh as king, a transfer of the heavenly court to the Jerusalem temple in a theophany of judgement. Tengström (1993:41) takes a similar line, and regards the expression 'seated on the cherubim' as an allusion to Yahweh's chariot, not to a static throne.

Micaiah's vision of the heavenly court in 1Kg 22.19 clearly alludes to the terrestrial kings seated before the gates of Samaria, as described earlier on in 1Kg 22.10, but it also imitates the scene of Is 6.1 (Rouillard 1993:103). However, the exact location of Micaiah's heavenly court is not specified: it could be considered to be in the heavens generally or in the sanctuary. Metzger (1970:156) contends that Mount Zion is conceived of as God's throne, on the basis of Ancient Near Eastern art where the god sits on a mountain-throne, and Ps 9.12; 68.17; Jr 14.19,21. But the word כִּסֵּא appears only in Jr 14.21, and then would not necessarily refer to Zion (mentioned in v.19). The verb יָשַׁב does appear in Ps 9.12, but could equally mean 'dwell', and again in Ps 68.17 it occurs in parallelism with שָׁכַן, so the idea that Zion is God's throne cannot be proven.

It is generally held that the Ark eventually disappeared from the Temple—Ezekiel never mentions it (Haran 1959:30–38)—hence the statement in Jr 3.17, no doubt intended to reassure the people that the whole of Jerusalem would be the Lord's throne. But Ezk 43.7 expresses the different view that the Temple would again be the place of God's throne, the place of his feet (cf. 1Ch 28.2 'the place of rest for the ark' is also 'a footstool for the feet of our God' (Haran 1959:89–94). Bertholet sees this as a characteristic concept in Ezk, that the Temple and God's dwelling place are ultimately inseparable (1936:151). The postexilic writer of Is 66.1 takes a third view, that any human-built structure would be inadequate for the Lord who is enthroned on the heavens and uses earth as his footstool.

Ezk 1 and 10 depict a *moving* chariot-throne, not bound to stay in any place. Mettinger (1982:35) explains this by taking the Temple cherubim as originally representing the throne and then becoming a cloud-chariot of the coming God of theophanic tradition (Ps 18.10–11; 104.3, cf. Is 19.1), influenced by notions of the storm-god Baal and of El. The outstretched wings of the sculpted cherubim created the impression of 'frozen motion'.

So there is a tension in the late pre- and early post-exilic periods regarding the whereabouts of the Lord's throne. Some commentators therefore stress that the Temple is only a model of God's dwelling place on high (Brettler 1989:84, Haran 1978:257, Levenson 1985:38ff). Metzger 1970:158 draws attention to the views of Noth (1968:173–93) and de Vaux (1967:219–28) that there is a difference in terminology between Dt (where the Lord makes his name dwell) and the Deuteronomist (where a house is built for the Lord's name and his name is present): Metzger (1970:158) thinks that this does not spiritualise the idea of God or reject outright the idea of the Lord living in the Temple, but rather stresses the lasting presence of the Lord.

A.14 This leads on to the description of God's throne in theophanies. Regarding Ezk 1.26, 10.1, commentators agree that the throne is not made of sapphire, which was unknown in the Ancient Near East before the Romans, but of lapis lazuli, which resembled the night sky sprinkled with golden stars (Cooke 1936:21,111; Zimmerli 1969:122ff, Keel 1977:255ff): God is enthroned on the splendour of the floor of heaven (רקיע) which acts as a platform for his seat, as perhaps also in Ex 24.10 (to which LXX Ezk assimilates this passage) or alternatively (and less convincingly) רקיע functions as a footstool (Zimmerli 1969:122ff). However, Cooke (1936:111) thinks that the base of the throne rather than the throne itself is of lapis, against the wording of Ezk 10.1. Preuss (1991:I,260; ET I,226) interprets Ezk 1 and 10 as meaning that the Lord is enthroned 'in the region above the heavenly ocean', and links the passages with Is 6.1; 66.1, Ps 104.3. Keel points out that the form of the throne is not described at all (1977:255), and Haran believes that since the ark is not mentioned, the throne is taken to be composed of the cherubim's wings, and wanders about in the heavens (1978:250–51). Allen (1994:26ff) sees the throne vision as a theophany of judgement, which would certainly be one of the concepts associated with כִּסֵא. Tengström (1993:95) believes that the word כִּסֵא in passages describing initial prophetic visions indicates a literary structure, and links the beginning and end of books, as at Is 6.1; 9.6, Ezk 1.26; 43.7, Dan 2.44; 7.14 (in Aramaic).

In Is 6.1, it is unclear whether it is the Lord or his throne that is 'high and lifted up', and both are equally possible. Greenfield (1985) compares the Ugaritic text *KTU*[2] 1.6 I 39–45, where the gods try to replace Baal, the deposed head of the pantheon, but fail because none of them is big enough to occupy Baal's huge throne. In the Enuma Elish, too, Marduk is immensely tall. In the same way, Yahweh is depicted as king, sitting on a high, elevated throne, with the train of his robes, his lower limbs or genitals (see Driver 1971 and Eslinger 1995) filling the temple. This would imply that he is superhuman in size: Smith (1988:425) observes that the cherubim throne is 10 cubits in height, and therefore that Is 6.1 has a throne of the same dimensions in mind. 1Kg 8.22–61 denies the possibility of God being contained in the temple or even by the heavens. Is 66.1 may also have Is 6.1 in mind. Keel (1977:60) also stresses that the throne must be higher than the beholder, perhaps on a high podium or steps (ibid. 61, figure 22). Krebs (1974:5) points out that this is necessary in order to prevent the king or deity from the psychological disadvantage of having to look up to a standing petitioner. Either the suppliant was forced to kneel or prostrate him or herself, or the throne would be raised so that the petitioner would have to look up. To a prostrate or kneeling suppliant, the seated figure would seem abnormally large, hence the depiction of enthroned deities as huge.

7. Art and Archaeology

(See also the section on Solomon's throne in *Exegesis*.)
Thrones are very frequently represented in the Ancient Near East, especially in Egyptian and Assyrian art, and these represent the two main styles. For thrones of approximately biblical date and provenance, see Broshi 1962:219–20: an Egyptian-style round-backed throne flanked by sphinxes, found in Israel, and the similar one on the Ahiram sarcophagus (also *ANEP* 458). Metzger (1985:II, figure 271A) provides an drawing of a throne with lion figures on the arm rests, belonging to Rameses III. There is an Assyrian-style throne with cedar cone feet, scroll work on stretcher, and straight backrest on the Bar Rakab stele, *ANEP* 460. See also Keel (1977: figures 111, 113, 114, 115).

8. Conclusion

(For good general coverage of the concept of throne, see Brettler 1989:81–85).

A.1 כִּסֵּא is probably derived ultimately from Sum *gu-za*, via Akk *kussû*.

A.2 כִּסֵּא is intrinsic to the notion of kingship to a much greater degree than עֲטָרָה, נֵזֶר, כֶּתֶר or אֶצְעָדָה. 'Throne' stands for 'regal power' in Gn 41.40. 'To sit on the throne' means 'to be king', and is synonymous with מָלַךְ and מָשַׁל. It is an expression used of both human kings and God, and is absolutely central to the concept of kingship both symbolically and literally, with a significance similar to that of 'crown' and 'coronation' in English.

A.3 God's throne is located in the sanctuary, and at a later period in the heavens. However, although he is often described as sitting upon the cherubim, the term כִּסֵּא does not appear in this exact context, cf. Ps 61.8, Is 10.13 of kings where כִּסֵּא is not mentioned.

A.4 Only Solomon's כִּסֵּא is described in detail, and we can only speculate about the form of other thrones and seats, though there are plenty of Ancient Near Eastern representations of 'Sitzmöbel'.

A.5 כִּסֵּא in the sense of an ordinary seat exists, but does not often occur. It appears to be understood in 1Kg 13.20, Est 6.10, Jdg 4.5, but יָשַׁב in the sense of sitting could mean that the subject sat on the floor or ground (as implied in Jdg 13.9, and stated in Jr 25.5; 35.15: possibly at 2Kg 6.32) or on a bed. When a chair is mentioned it may be a significant detail, indicating the honour due to and possibly the function and age of the sitter, as with Eli and Bathsheba.

BIBLIOGRAPHY

Allen, L.C. 1994. Commentary on *Ezekiel* 1–19 (WBC).

Baker, H.S. 1966. *Furniture in the Ancient World. Origins and Evolution 3100–475 BC.* London.

Bernhardt, K-H. 1961. *Das Problem der altorientalischen Königsideologie im Alten Testament unter besonder Berücksichtigung der Geschichte der Psalmenexegese dargestellt und kritisch gewürdigt.* VTS 8. Leiden.

Bertholet, A. 1936. Commentary on *Esekiel* (HAT).

Brettler, M.Z. 1989. *God is King.* JSOTSS 76. Sheffield.

_____. 1995. *The Creation of History in Ancient Israel.* London and New York.

Broshi, M. 1962. Article כִּסֵּא in *EM* IV:216–20.

Brunner, H. 1958. Gerechtigkeit als Fundament des Thrones. *VT* 8:426–28.

Budde, K. 1902. Commentary on *Samuel* (KHAT).

Canciani, F. and G. Pettinato. 1965. Salomos Thron, philologische und archäologische Erwähgungen. *ZDPV* 81:88–108.

Caquot, A. 1956. Remarques sur le Psaume CX. *Semitica* 6:33–52.

Carlson, R.A. 1964. *David the Chosen King. A Traditio-Historical Approach to the Second Book of Samuel.* Stockholm.

Childs, B.S. 1974. Commentary on *Exodus* (OTL).

Clements, R.E. 1965. *God and Temple.* Oxford.

Cody, A. 1969. *A History of the Old Testament Priesthood.* Analecta Biblica. Rome.

Cooke, G.A. 1936. Commentary on *Ezekiel* (ICC).

Curtis, E.L. 1910. Commentary on *Chronicles* (ICC).

Dahood, M. 1965, 1968, 1970. Commentary on *Psalms* I, II, III (AB).

Dhorme, E. 1926. *Le Livre de Job.* Paris. ET 1967, London.

Driver, G.R. 1971. Isaiah 6:1 'his train filled the temple'. 87–96 in *Near Eastern Studies in Honour of William Foxwell Albright* , ed. H. Goedicke. Baltimore and London.

Driver, S.R. 1918. Commentary on *Exodus* (CBC).

Driver, S.R. and G.B. Gray. 1921. Commentary on *Job* (ICC).

Ellenbogen, M. 1962. *Foreign Words in the Old Testament. Their Origin and Etymology.* London.

Eslinger, L. 1995. The infinite in a finite organical perception (Isaiah VI 1-5). *VT* 45:145–73.

Fabry, H-J. 1984. Article כִּסֵּא in *TWAT* IV:247–72: ET *Theological Dictionary of the Old Testament* VII:232–59.

Feldmann, F. 1925. Commentary on *Isaiah* 1-39 (EHAT).

Fischer, J. 1937. *Das Buch Isaias I (1-39).* Bonn.

Fohrer, G. 1969. *Geschichte der israelitischen Religion.* Berlin. ET 1973, *History of Israelite Religion.* London.

Fraenkel, M. 1960. Bemerkungen zum hebräichen Wortschatz. *HUCA* 31:55–102.

Fritz, V. 1977. *Tempel und Zeit. Studien zum Tempelbau in Israel zu dem Zeltheiligtum der Priesterschaft.* WMANT 47. Neukirchen-Vluyn.

Geiger, A. 1857. *Urschrift and Übersetzung der Bibel.* Breslau.

Gordon, R.P. 1986. *1 and 2 Samuel: A Commentary.* Exeter.

Gray, G. B. 1912. Commentary on *Isaiah* 1-39 (ICC).

Gray, J. 1964. Commentary on *Kings* (OTL).

Greenfield, J.C. 1985. Ba'al's throne and Isaiah 6.1. 193–98 in *Mélanges bibliques et orientaux en l'honneur de M. Mathias Delcor,* ed. A. Caquot, S. Légasse, M. Tardieu. AOAT 215. Neukirchen-Vluyn.

Grimme, H. 1902. *Psalmenprobleme. Untersuchungen über Metrik, Strophik und Paseq des psalmenbuches.* Freiburg.

Gunkel, H. 1926. Commentary on *Psalms* (HAT).

Halpern, B. 1988. *The First Historians. The Hebrew Bible and History.* San Francisco.

Handy, L.K. 1992. Article 'Sedheq (Deity)' in *ABD* V:1065–66.

Haran, M. 1959. The Ark and the cherubim: their symbolic significance in the Biblical ritual. *IEJ* 9:30–38, 89–97.

____. 1978. *Temples and Temple Service in Ancient Israel. An Inquiry into the Character of Cult Phenomena and the Historical Setting of the Priestly School.* Oxford.

Holladay, W.L. 1986. Commentary on *Jeremiah* 1–25 (Herm).

____. 1989. Commentary on *Jeremiah.* 26–52 (Herm).

Japhet, S. 1989.*The Ideology of the Book of Chronicles and its Place in Biblical Thought.* Beiträge zur Erforschung des Alten Testaments und des antiken Judentums 9. Frankfurt am Main.

____. 1993. Commentary on *I and II Chronicles* (OTL).

Johnson, A.R. [2]1967. *Sacral Kingship in Ancient Israel.* Cardiff.

Kaufman, S. 1974. *The Akkadian Influences on Aramaic.* Chicago.

Keel, O. 1977. *Jahwe-Visionen und Siegelkunst. Eine neue Deutung der Majestätsschilderung in Jes 6, Ez 1 and 10 und Sach 4.* Stuttgarter Bibelstudien 84/85; Stuttgart.

Kissane, E.J. 1941. *The Book of Isaiah* I. Dublin.

Kittel, R. 1900. Commentary on *Kings* (HKAT).

Klein, R. W. 1983. Commentary on *1 Samuel* (WBC).

Knierim, R. 1968. The vocation of Isaiah. *VT* 18: 47–68.

Komlosh, Y. 1973. המקרא באור התרגום [*The Bible in the light of the Targum*]. Tel Aviv.

Kraus, H.J. [3]1966. Commentary on *Psalms* I–II (BK). ET 1989, *The Psalms.* Minneapolis.

Krebs, W. 1974. Der sitzende Gott. *TZ* 30:1-10.

Kuntzmann, R. 1993. Le trône de Dieu dans l'oeuvre du Chroniste. 19–27 in *Le Trône de Dieu,* ed. M. Philonenko. WUNT 69. Tübingen.

Leslau, W. 1958. *Ethiopic and South Arabic Contributions to the Hebrew Lexicon.* University of California Publications in Semitic Philology 20. Berkeley.

Levenson, J.D. 1985. The Jerusalem Temple in devotional and visionary experience. 32–61 in *Jewish Spirituality: From the Bible through the Middle Ages,* ed. A. Green. London.

Lindars, B. 1995. *Judges 1–5.* Edinburgh.

Lipiński, E. 1963. *Yahweh malak. Bibl* 44:405–60.

____. 1988. Emprunts suméro-akkadiens en hébreu biblique. *ZAH* 1:61–73.

Loretz, O. 1979. *Die Psalmen II. Beitrag der Ugarit-Texte zum Verständnis von Kolometrie und Textologie der Psalmen 90–150.* AOAT. Neukirchen-Vluyn.

____. 1994a. Zur Zitat-Vernetzung zwischen Ugarit-texten und Psalmen. *UF* 26:225–43.

____. 1994b. Gottes Thron in Tempel und Himmel nach Psalm 11. *UF* 26:245–70.

Mastin, B.A. 1976. A note on Zechariah vi 13. *VT* 26:113–16.

McCarter, K. 1980. Commentary on *I Samuel* (AB).

McCullough, W.S. 1956. 'The enthronement of Yahweh' Psalms. 53–61 in *A Stubborn Faith. Papers on Old Testament and Related Subjects Presented to Honour William Andrew Irwin*, ed. E.C. Hobbs. Dallas.

McKane, W. 1986. Commentary on *Jeremiah 1–25* (ICC).

Mettinger, T.W.D. 1976. *King and Messiah: the Civil and Sacral Legitimation of the Israelite Kings*. CBOT 8. Lund.

____. 1982. *The Dethronement of Sabaoth. Studies in the Shem and Kabod Theologies*. CBOT 18. Lund.

Metzger, M. 1970. Himmlische und irdische Wohnstatt Jahwes. *UF* 2:139–58.

____. 1985. *Königsthron und Gottesthron. Thronformen und Thron-darstellungen in Ägypten und im vorderen Orient im dritten und zweiten Jahrtausend vor Christus und deren Bedeutung für das Verständnis von Aussagen über den Thron im Alten Testament*. AOAT 15. Neukirchen-Vluyn.

Meyers, C.L. and E.M. Meyers. 1987. Commentary on *Haggai, Zechariah 1–8* (AB).

Michel, D. 1956. Studien zu den sogennanten Thronbesteigungspsalmen. *VT* 6:40–68.

Mitchell, H.G., J.M. Powis Smith, J.A. Bewer. 1912. *Haggai, Zechariah, Malachi, Jonah* (ICC).

Montgomery, J.A. and H.S. Gehman. 1951. Commentary on *Kings* (ICC).

Murtonen, A. 1988, 1989. *Hebrew in its West Semitic Setting. A Comparative Survey of Non-Masoretic Hebrew Dialects and Traditions. Part I. A Comparative lexicon: Section Ba: Root System: Hebrew Material,* and *Section Bb.Root System: Comparative Material and Discussion*. Studies in Semitic Languages and Linguistics 13. Leiden.

Newsom, C. 1985. *Songs of the Sabbath Sacrifice*. Atlanta, GA.

North, C.R. 1932. The religious aspects of Hebrew kingship. *ZAW* 50:8–38.

Noth, M. 1968. Commentary on *Kings* (BK).

____. 1960. *Gesammelte Studien zum Alten Testament*. TBü 11. Munich.

Ollenburger, B.C. 1987. *Zion, the City of the Great King. A Theological Symbol of the Jerusalem Cult*. JSOTSS 41; Sheffield.

Paas, S. 1993. 'He Who builds His stairs into Heaven'... (Amos 9:6a). *UF* 25:319–25.

Perles, J. 1922. *Analekten zur Textkritik des Alten Testaments II*. Leipzig.

Petitjean, A. 1969. *Les Oracles du Proto-Zacharie*. Paris and Louvain.

Philonenko, M., ed. 1996. *Le Trône de Dieu*. WUNT 69. Tübingen.

Polzin, R. 1980. *Moses and the Deuteronomist. A Literary Study of the Deuteronomic History. Part I. Deuteronomy, Joshua, Judges*. New York.

____. 1989. *Samuel and the Deuteronomist. A Literary Study of the Deuteronomic History. Part II. 1 Samuel*. San Francisco.

Preuss, H.D. 1991. *Theologie des Alten Testaments I: JHWHs erwählendes und verpflichtendes Handeln*. Stuttgart. ET 1995, *Old Testament Theology* I.

Edinburgh.

Proksch, O. 1930. Commentary on *Isaiah* I (KAT).

Ridderbos, J. 1954. Jahwäh malak. *VT* 4:87–89.

Rignell, L.G. 1950. *Die Nachtgesichte des Sacharja*. Lund.

Ringgren, H. 1947.*Word and Wisdom. Studies in the Hypostatization of Divine Qualities and Functions in the Ancient Near East.* Lund.

____. 1963. *Israelitische Religion*. Stuttgart. ET 1966 *Israelite Religion*. London.

Rose, W. 1997. Zerubbabel and Zemah—Messianic expectations in the early post-exilic period. Doctoral thesis, Oxford.

Rosenberg, A. 1965. The god Sedeq. *HUCA* 36:161–77.

Rouillard, H. Royauté céleste et royauté terrestre en 1 R 22. 100–107 in *Le Trône de Dieu*, ed. M. Philonenko. WUNT 69. Tübingen.

Salonen, A. 1963. *Die Möbel des Alten Mesopotamien nach sumerisch-akkadischen Quellen. Eine lexicalische und kulturgeschichtliche Untersuchung.* Helsinki.

Schmid, H. 1968. *Gerechtigkeit als Weltordnung. Hintergrund und Geschichte des alttestamentlichen Gerechtigkeitsbegriffes.* Beiträge zur historischen Theologie 40; Tübingen.

Schmidt, W.H. [2]1966. *Königtum Gottes in Ugarit und Israel.* BZAW 80. Berlin.

Schreiner, J. 1963. *Sion-Jerusalem: Jahwes Königssitz. Theologie der heiligen Stadt im Alten Testament.* SANT 7. Munich.

Sellin, E. 1922. Commentary on *Twelve Prophets* (KAT).

Smith, M.S. 1988. Divine form and size in Ugaritic and pre-exilic Israelite religion. *ZAW* 100:424–27.

Spina, F.A. 1994. Eli's seat: the transition from priest to prophet in 1 Sam 1–4. *JSOT* 62:67–75.

Stoebe, H.J. 1973. Commentary on *I Samuel* (KAT).

Tengström, S. 1996. Les visions prophétiques du trône de Dieu. 28–99 in *Le Trône de Dieu*, ed. M. Philonenko. WUNT 69. Tübingen.

Uehlinger, C. 1992. Audienz in der Götterwelt. Anthropomorphismus und Soziomorphismus in der Ikonographie eines altsyrischen Zylindersiegels. *UF* 24:339–59.

Vaux, R. de. 1960–61. Les chérubins et l'arche d'alliance, les sphinx gardiens et les trones divins dans l'ancient Orient. *Mélanges de l'Université S. Joseph* 37:93–124.

____. 1967. Le lieu que Yahvé a choisi pour établir son nom. 219–28 in *Das ferne und nahe Wort. FS Leonhard Rost zur Vollendung seines 70. Lebensjahres.* Ed. F. Maass. BZAW 105. Berlin.

Weippert, H. 1977. Article 'Möbel' in *BRL*[2] 228–32, esp. 231–32.

Williamson, H.G.M. 1985. Commentary on *Ezra* and *Nehemiah* (WBC).

____. 1982. Commentary on *1* and *2 Chronicles* (NCBC).

Weinfeld, M. 1972. *Deuteronomy and the Deuteronomic School* . Oxford.

Willis, J.T. 1979. Samuel versus Eli. *TZ* 35:201–12.

Wilson, G.H. 1985. *The Editing of the Hebrew Psalter.* SBLDS 76. Chico, CA.

Zimmerli, W. 1969. *Ezechiel I* (BK). ET 1979, *Ezekiel* (Herm).

Alison Salvesen
University of Oxford

כֶּתֶר

Introduction
Grammatical type: n m.
Occurrences: 3 occurrences BH (Est 1.11; 2.17; 6.8); 1 occurrence Q (4QPrFêtes [4Q509] 97-8 ii 3). No occurrences in Sir, Ep.

Text doubtful:
Est 6.8: The wording is often disputed on the grounds that it is not likely that a horse would wear a crown or turban and that it must be Mordecai who is to wear the כֶּתֶר מַלְכוּת. Emendation of the text is therefore suggested by most commentators (Bertheau/Ryssel 1887:427–28, Haupt 1907–8:48, Bardtke 1963:348 n.13, Moore 1971:65, Gerleman 1973:116–18, Wernberg-Møller 1975:242, Berg 1979:61, Clines 1984:192 n.8).

1. Root and Comparative Material
A.1 The BH verb כתר, 'surround', may be related if כֶּתֶר refers to a fabric turban or a metal fillet around the head. There would be an obvious connection with the similar word כֹּתֶרֶת, a capital surrounding the top of a pillar. However, the form כֶּתֶר is 'primitive', and one might expect a form such as the active participle masculine, or a more complex form with a prefix, cf. מִצְנֶפֶת and מִגְבָּעָה, words for native Israelite turbans from the roots צנף and נבע. Against that we have the example of נֵזֶר, used of the gold plate on the headdress of the Israelite high priest and also of the king's diadem. But a 'simple' Hebrew word in a later biblical book for what is essentially a foreign item of dress is problematic.

A.2 The word appears frequently in RH (bMen 29b = bShabb 29a; bShabb 29b), notably to describe Taggin, 'crownlets' on some letter shapes, and also in later JArm (כִּתְרָא), especially in the Zohar.

A.3 כֶּתֶר is generally considered to be related in some way to Greek κίδαρις/κίταρις, a word used by classical authors to describe the distinctive headgear of the Persian kings in the Achaemenid period and which Alexander also assumed.

Chantraine (1970) states: "emprunt oriental quasi certain. Hypothèse sémitique chez Lewy, *Fremdwörter* 90". Szemérenyi's review of Chantraine (1971:673) refines this by stating that 'Near Eastern provenance is not almost but quite certain', and cites Hebrew Est and Arm *kitra*: "The connection was already stated by Grimme, *Glotta* 14 (1925) p. 16".

The classical evidence is conflicting on the exact definition of the word κίδαρις. The earliest recorded use is in Herodotus, where ordinary Cypriot soldiers wear the κίδαρις while their kings wore μίτραι (7.90). κίτταρις is glossed by Hesychius as διάδημα, i.e. a cloth fillet bound around (διαδέω) the head and tied by a knot at the back: the διάδημα became the symbol *par excellence* of Hellenistic rulers and the word was used in a metaphorical sense then as the English word diadem is now. Philo too regards κίδαρις as the eastern equivalent of, or alternative to, a διάδημα (*De Vita Mosis* 2.116.2). However, other Greco-Roman authors, e.g. Arrian and Plutarch, often treat κίδαρις as synonymous with the king's upright *tiara*, which appears to have been a kind of hat or cap rather than a headband, or they speak of the κίδαρις itself as upright. Lexicographers including Hesychius suggest that τιάρα is the same as κίδαρις, though there is a tendency to lump all exotic hats under the same heading, especially in the later period.

All this has caused some scholars in the field of Ancient Iran to regard the κίταρις as a term for the upright *tiara* of the king, though this places undue weight on the confused testimony of later Greek writers. Even so, some sources still speak of the *tiara* and *kitaris* as distinct, for instance Plutarch, who elsewhere implies that they are synonymous. Strabo too lists the *tiara* and *kitaris* as separate items of royal Median dress. Curtius Rufus (mid-1st century CE) explains that the 'cidaris' was the distinctive headdress of the Persian kings: 'a blue turban/diadem with white spots, which went around the head'. Much earlier, Xenophon describes Cyrus the Great's apparel in some detail (*Cyropaedia* 8.3.13). He says that the king wore a διάδημα around the upright *tiara*, and that the king's 'relations' also wore this distinguishing mark even in the writer's own time. However, he does not give the oriental name for this διάδημα.

Since Gr κίταρις appears to be related to כֶּתֶר, in theory it should be possible to reconstruct the word that underlies them both, but so far no convincing reconstruction has been made. The variant Gr forms κίταρις - κίδαρις - κίτταρις are thought to reflect an attempt to capture non-Gr dentals in the underlying Sem or even Iranian words. The early reference to κίταρις in Herodotus could be explained by the strong Phoenician influence on Cyprus, especially through the colony of Kition, and the Semitic word may well have entered Greek via Cyprus.

B.1 Lagarde (1866:207) suggested that כֶּתֶר might be derived from Pers, and Marti (1896:Gloss. *67 under כרבלא) regarded Pers χ*audhā* as the source for κίταρις. However, the latter seems most unlikely on philological grounds, since the appearance of the /r/ in AH and Gr would be quite unexpected. Besides, χ*audhā* refers to a Scythian cap and not to a crown [Dr. Elizabeth Tucker, personal communication].

B.2 Another Persian etymology offered was the Old Iranian word for power, χ*šaθra*, originally suggested by G. Rawlinson (see Bertheau/Ryssel 1887:390), and Driver (1951:55 n. 3), but this was rejected by Eilers (1954–56:331) and corrected in Driver's second edition (1957:98).

B.3 None of the known native Iranian words for headdresses appears to be connected with כֶּתֶר, and there is no obvious Old Iranian original that can be easily reconstructed from κίδαρις and כֶּתֶר. [E. Tucker, personal communication] Eilers surveys words for crowns in Persia and the Ancient Near East, but gives nothing that corresponds to כֶּתֶר. He believes that כֶּתֶר is the origin of 'Iranian' κίδαρις/κίτ(τ)αρις (1977:164).

B.4 Several of the terms for royal symbols in Est are Aramaic in origin e.g. שַׁרְבִיט, יְקָר, תַּכְרִיךְ, גְּנָזִים, and כֶּתֶר may also belong with them. However, the native Aramaic root כתר means 'to remain', which cannot be related to כֶּתֶר. Eilers (1954:331) suggests an Arm etymology for κίταρις, < *kitrā'iṯ, 'surroundingly'(?), an adverb, but no such word is attested.

B.5 *HAL* 482 suggests that the word כֶּתֶר is cognate to Arb *katara*, which means 'to have a big hump', and is used of a camel. Related Arb words refer to a cupola or vaulted dome, and by extension, to dignity or honour: e.g. Kazimirski, KTR 'to have a large hump (of a camel)', also 'rank, dignity', 'vaulted structure, cupola, 'bosse d'un chameau, surtout très élevée.' Steingass, *katr* 'quantity, quality, dignity, small camel-litter': *katr, kitr, katar* etc., 'large camel-hump', *kitr* 'vault, arch, cupola', IV *aktar* 'to have a large hump'. However, the most recent dictionary of classical Arabic, *WKAS* (1970:I:46, 544), gives only a noun, *ka/itrun*, 'Höcker/hump', which can be used metaphorically of a pile of stones or dates or heaped-up foam, but the lexicon does not mention a meaning 'dignity, honour' etc. A connection between כֶּתֶר and *ka/itrun* presumes PS *ktr* underlying both words. On the semantic level, כֶּתֶר could then refer to a high or domed hat resembling a camel's hump, as the upright *tiara* of the Persian kings was. But it is doubtful that Esther and Vashti could have worn this, given its military associations and the unanimous testimony of classical sources that only the king wore it.

B.6 Mayer (1960:329) mentions the possibility of a connection with *kudurru*, 'tiara', following Hommel cited in Lewy (1895:90). In fact, this Neo-Bab word refers to an ornament worn on the neck. The word *kudurrānu* may refer to a crested bird if there is a connection with *kudurru*, but this is not proven (CAD 8:494, 497).

2. Formal Characteristics

A.1 *qitl*

A.2 All occurrences are in cons sg.

3. Syntagmatics

A.1 כֶּתֶר always appears in the construct in AH: as the *nomen regens* of מַלְכוּת in the 3 occurrences in Est, and probably of צֶדֶק in 4Q509 97-8 ii 3

A.2 Each time in Est it is used with the prep בְּ: in 1.11 it precedes כֶּתֶר מַלְכוּת, in 2.17 and 6.8 it indicates the placing of the כֶּתֶר מַלְכוּת on someone's head.

A.3 מַלְכוּת is used a number of times in Est, particularly as the *nomen rectum* governed by another noun: Est 1.7 (wine), 1.19 (word), 6.8, 8.15 (clothes): also with def art 1.2,9, 5.1 (palace): with m suf (1.2, 5.1 (throne), 1.2, 2.16, 5.1 (palace), 1.4 (glory). (There are similar phrases in Arm Dan e.g. 4.15, 26, 27, 33, 6.8,27, but these have less of an adjectival nuance and apart from 4.27 [בֵּית מַלְכוּ] can be translated more readily as 'of the kingdom'.) The use in Est of מַלְכוּת with other nouns such as כִּסֵּא, בַּיִת and שַׁרְבִיט suggests that it is used to differentiate royal from ordinary objects and is not mere tautology. A royal כֶּתֶר may have differed from an ordinary one in the style, fabric or colour used.

A.4 It is the obj of the act vb שִׂים (qal) in Est 2.17, and the subj of the pass vb נתן (niph) in Est 6.8.

A.5 The subj of the verb in 2.17 is the king.

4. Versions
LXX:

A.1 The dating of Greek Est, which exists in two versions, the LXX and Alpha texts, is very uncertain. See Fox (1990), Jobes (1995), de Troyer (1995:70). In both texts כֶּתֶר is translated by διάδημα, not by κίδαρις which appears in LXX Ex 28 for the headgear of priests: Ex 28.4,35 for מִצְנֶפֶת, 28.36 and 29.9, Lv 8.13 for מִגְבָּעָה; and in Sym Is 28.5 for צְפִירָה, Aq Sym Is 62.3 for צָנִיף. These Hebrew words are generally thought to refer to types of turban. Other uses of κίδαρις are at Ezk 21.31 for מִצְנֶפֶת (parallel to στέφανος, עֲטָרָה), Zc 3.6(5) for צָנִיף. At Is 62.3 LXX renders צְנִיף מְלוּכָה by διάδημα βασιλείας.

Perhaps the translators of Est wished to avoid the suggestion that the Persian king wore a headdress similar to that of the Jewish high priest. Alternatively, the translations of Esther may have originated in a Hellenistic milieu no longer familiar with Achamenid royal accoutrements, and the word διάδημα was used because it was the obvious symbol of Hellenistic and Parthian royalty, especially through the influence of coins bearing the ruler's head.

Tg (ed. Sperber):
A.1

תָּגָא דְדַהֲבָא 'golden crown' Est 1.11
תָּגָא דְמַלְכוּתָא 'royal crown' Est 2.17
כִּתְרָא דְמַלְכוּתָא 'royal crown' Est 6.8.

tāgā and *kitrā* are used almost interchangeably in JArm, but the former is Pers, and the latter probably Sem in origin.

Pesh:
A.1 *tāgā (d-malkutā)* : 1.11 with suf: 'her royal diadem', *tāgā d-malkutā*.

Vg:
A.1 *diadema*
(Est 2.17 *diadema regni:*, Est 6.8 *regium diadema*)

5. Lexical/Semantic Field
A.1 In Est 6.8 כֶּתֶר מַלְכוּת is listed with royal clothing and a horse ridden by the king.

A.2 The Qumran occurrence is apparently in parallelism with the phrase '*nēzer* of beauty'.

6. Exegesis
A.1 Vashti is to wear the כֶּתֶר מַלְכוּת when she appears in public before the king and his guests (1.11). The placing of the כֶּתֶר מַלְכוּת on Esther's head by the king symbolises her becoming queen, וַיַּמְלִיכֶהָ. Mordecai, or the horse, wears the כֶּתֶר מַלְכוּת as a sign of royal favour. Thus in each case in Est the כֶּתֶר מַלְכוּת symbolises royal favour and public recognition by the king.

A.2 From the contexts it is clear that כֶּתֶר מַלְכוּת refers to something worn on the head. The fact that the only other occurrence of כֶּתֶר in AH is a late one, at Qumran, suggests that it was originally an item associated with the Persian royal court rather than a Israelite/Judahite or Hellenistic setting where נֵזֶר, עֲטָרָה, צָנִיף or מִצְנֶפֶת tend to be used of royal headdresses. But this may be an argument from silence.

A.3 Moore (1972:81), no doubt depending on Xenophon etc., suggests that a כֶּתֶר מַלְכוּת should be understood as 'royal turban': 'made of blue and white cloth, it probably contained a tiara'.

B.1 It has been suggested that a כֶּתֶר is to be identified with the upright *tiara* of the Persian kings, but there are problems with this if we assume that the writer of Est was in any way accurately acquainted with the customs of the Persian court. It was well known that the king alone wore it — to assume the upright *tiara* was to declare oneself king — and there is no suggestion in literature that a woman, even a queen, could wear it. It was also an item of Median battledress, and not appropriate attire within the royal palace of Susa.

Art and Archaeology

There are many different types of royal headdress depicted in Pers art, though only a few from the Achaemenid period resemble a fabric diadem.

In Roaf (1983:Plates XII a-e) there are reliefs of horses with bound-up manes from Persepolis. These may be of relevance to Est 6.8. Roaf (ibid. 132 and figure 132) also has sketches of Persian headdresses.

From an earlier period, Dalley (1991:125 figure 8) shows Assurnasipal II with ribbons hanging down his back from an ornamental headband, and tasselled/fringed ends.

Calmeyer (1976, 1977, 1988) and von Gall (1974, 1975) have the most detailed discussions and ample illustrations of Persian crowns, but Jacobs (1994:135–36) disagrees with von Gall's identification of the *kidaris* with the upright tiara, and believes that Curtius Rufus was referring to a fabric diadem in *Hist. Alex.* 3.3.19 in speaking of the special headdress of the Persian kings.

7. Conclusion

A.1 Since Vashti, then Esther, wears it as queen and consort, a כֶּתֶר מַלְכוּת must be a mark of high royal rank. There is no way of knowing from the biblical occurrences whether the king also wore it. The interpretation of the occurrence in Est 6.8 depends on whether the horse or Mordecai is supposed to wear the כֶּתֶר מַלְכוּת. If the former, it could denote something belonging to the king. If the latter, it would be a sign of the highest favour and honour from the king. The occurrence of כֶּתֶר in 4QPrFêtes is difficult to interpret since the context is so fragmentary, but it does appear close to נֵזֶר, which in BH is the headdress of a high priest or king.

A.2 The use of the construction כֶּתֶר מַלְכוּת suggests that an ordinary form of כֶּתֶר existed. There are no clues in Est as to what the כֶּתֶר מַלְכוּת consisted of, but if the king's horse wore it, it is likely to have been not a crown in the sense of a heavy circular metal ring, but something that could have been tied on: a metal strip with ties, or a fabric fillet?

A.3 It is possible that the כֶּתֶר/*kitaris* was a Greek-type diadem, a special fabric fillet worn alone or around the crown or *tiara* worn by the king, but not itself restricted to the king, as Xenophon's account states. Such headbands were found in Mesopotamia from Assyrian and Babylonian times through the Achaemenid period to the Seleucid, Parthian and even Sassanid dynasties. It appears especially frequently on Parthian coins, where under Greek influence it is worn alone.

A.4 The matter of the root and its derivation must be left open. AH כתר 'surround' is possible and the easiest and least controversial solution. A connection with Arb *katara* is less likely because it would seem to imply a high domed headdress, and this sort of headgear, the upright *tiara*, was only worn by the Persian kings themselves.

BIBLIOGRAPHY

Bardtke, H. 1963. Commentary on *Esther* (KAT).

Berg, S.B. 1979. *The Book of Esther*. SBLDS 44. Missoula, MT.

Bertheau, E., rev. V. Ryssel. 1887. *Die Bücher Esra, Nechemia und Ester*. Leipzig.

Calmeyer, P. 1976. Zur Genese altiranischer Motive IV. Persönliche Krone und Diadem. *AMI* n.F. 9:45–95.

_____. 1977. Von Reisehut zur Kaiserkrone. B. Stand der archäologischen Forschung zu den iranischen Kronen. *AMI* n.F. 10:168–90.

_____. 1988. Zur Genese altiranischer Motive X. Die elamisch-persische Tracht. *AMI* 21:27–51.

Chantraine, P. 1970. *Dictionnaire étymologique de la langue grecque*.

Clines, D.J.A. 1984. *The Story of Esther*. Sheffield.

Cresci Marrone, G. 1978. Techniche di trasposizione della terminologia greco-orientale nell'opera di Curzio Rufo. *Istituto Lombrado accademia di scienze e Lettere, Rendiconti. Classe di Lettere e Scienze Morali e Storiche* 112:51–60.

Dalley, S. 1991. Ancient Assyrian textiles and the origins of carpet design. *Iran* 29:117–36.

Driver, G.R. [1]1951, [2]1957. *Aramaic Documents of the Fifth Century B.C.* etc. Oxford.

Eilers, W. 1954–56. Neue aramäische Urkunden aus Ägypten. *Af O* 17:31.

_____. 1977. Vom Reisehut zur Kaiserkrone. A. Das Wortfeld. *AMI* N.F. 10:153–68.

Fox, M.V. 1990. *The Redaction of the Book of Esther*. Atlanta, GA.

von Gall, H. 1974. Die Kopfbedeckung des persischen Ornats bei den Achämeniden. *AMI* n.F. 7:145-61 and pls 31–36.

_____. 1975. Die Grosskönigliche Kopfbedeckung bei den Achämeniden. 219–32 in *Proceedings of IIIrd Annual Symposium on Archaeological Research in Iran*. Ed. F. Bagherzadeh. Tehran.

Gerleman, G. 1973. Commentary on *Esther* (BK).

Haller, M. 1940. Commentary on *Esther* (HAT).

Haupt, P. 1907–8. Critical notes on Esther. *AJSL* 24:97–186, repr. 1–90 in *Studies in the Book of Esther*, ed. C.A. Moore. New York 1982.

Hintze, A. 1994. The Greek and Hebrew versions of the Book of Esther and its Iranian background. *Irano-Judaica* III:34–39.

Jacobs, B. 1994. Drei Beiträge zu Fragen der Rüstung und Bekleidung in Persien zur Achämenidenzeit. *Iranica Antiqua* 29:125–67.

Jobes, K. 1996. *The Alpha-Text of Esther: its Character and Relationship to the Masoretic Text.* SBLDS 153. Atlanta, GA.

Kazimirski, A. de Biberstein. 1860. *Dictionnaire arabe-français* II. Paris.

de Lagarde, P. 1866. *Gesammelte Abhandlungen.* Leipzig.

Lewy, H. 1895. *Die semitischen Fremdwörter im Griechischen.* Berlin.

Marti, K. 1896. *Kurzgefasste Grammatik der biblisch-aramäischen Sprache.* Berlin.

Mayer, M.L. 1960. Gli imprestiti semitici in greco. *Istituto Lombrado accademia di scienze e Lettere, Rendiconti. Classe di Lettere e Scienze Morali e Storiche* 94:311–51.

Roaf, M. 1983. Sculptures and sculptors at Persepolis. *Iran* 21. Plates XII a-e.

Root, M.C. 1979. *King and Kingship in Achaemenid Art.* Acta Iranica 3e Série IX. Leiden.

Thompson, G. 1965. Iranian dress in the Achaemenid period. *Iran* 3:121–26.

Steingass, F.J. 1884. *The Student's Arabic-English Dictionary.* London.

Szemérenyi, O. 1971. Review of Chantraine in *Gnomon* 43:673.

de Troyer, K. 1995. An oriental beauty parlour: an analysis of Esther 2.8–18 in the Hebrew, the Septuagint and the Second Greek Text. 47–70 in *A Feminist Companion to the Bible,* ed. A. Brenner. Sheffield.

Wernberg-Møller, P. 1975. Review of Gerleman in *JSS* 20:241–43.

WKAS = Wörterbuch der klassischen arabischen Sprache. Eds. A. Fischer et al. Wiesbaden 1970. I:46, 544.

Alison Salvesen
University of Oxford

מְאֵרָה

Introduction
Grammatical Type: n f.
Occurrences: Total 5x OT, 0x Sir, 0x Qum, 0x inscr.

Text doubtful:
A.1 The LXX of Ml 3.9 implies a reading of the vb (perhaps the inf abs) רָאָה (see Versions **A.3**). Kruse-Blinkenberg suggests that the LXX translator was confused by the niphʿal of אָרַר, which only occurs here (1966:112, n. 94). The MT is difficult to interpret in this passage and the LXX diverges from it considerably in verses 9–11 (see Brichto 1963:104–05).

B.1 The Sam text at Dt 28.20 reads המרה ("grief") in place of the MT הַמְּאֵרָה.
Qere/Ketiv: none.

1. Root and Comparative Material
A.1 In BH the cognate vb אָרַר occurs 64 times. There are possibly two occurrences of the n [אֲרָרָה] in Qum.

A.2 In RH the form מארת often occurs, sometimes with the meaning "curse" (e.g. Tan Gen 11). On some occasions (e.g. pSanh 28b, 29d; bBer 20b) it denotes "poverty", and the expression בעל מארה (bBeṣah 15b) denotes a "poor man". It may also be used of something that has been "spoiled" (tBB 6.2).

A.3 Albright in his edition of Proto-Sinaitic inscrs identifies the form *mʾr[t]* in an inscr from Shechem (dated by him to c. 1450–1400). It is an incantatory plaque that calls for the operation of the "words of [this] curse", *rǧm mʾr[t]* (Albright 1969:10). He suggests that this is cognate with Heb מְאֵרָה (ibid.:11).

A.4 The Arm מאירה, which occurs twice in the Tg as a translation of Heb מְאֵרָה (Dt 28.20 [TgO, PsJ, Neo], Ml 2.2), is probably to be seen as a loan-word from Heb (Sokoloff:288). Ges.-18 (103) cites without elucidation the JAram ארר, but Cohen (34) distinguishes this from the root of the Heb אָרַר and renders it as "oiseleur". There is also the Syr lexeme ʾarrā, "appât pour oiseaux(?), oiseleur(?)" (Cohen:34), which is probably cognate to the JAram.

A.5 The root is attested in Akk arāru, appearing both as a noun and a verb. It is necessary to differentiate between this root and two other roots. arāru I has the primary meaning of "to bind (by an incantation), to ban". It frequently occurs with a negation of its antonym pašāru, "to loosen". Thus, a standard expression was arrat la napšuri lirur(ū), "may the god(s) ban with an unlooseable ban" (Brichto 1963:115–116). The term pašāru is itself used with other terms for magic, offences and retributive punishments (ibid.:116, n. 82). arāru I came to be used of both gods and humans uttering a curse (CAD

1-a:234–36; *AHw*:65). It could also be used more generally of the action of humans: "to treat with disrespect, to insult, to disown, disavow".

Derivatives from the root of *arāru* I are *arru*, "cursed" (CAD 1-a:305; *AHw*:65), *ariru*, a noun possibly denoting "a priest that denounces a curse" ("Verfluchungs-priester (?)", *AHw*:68), and the nouns *arratu* and *erretu*, "curse" (CAD 1-a:304–05; *AHw*:70) or an "accursed person" (CAD 1-a:305), corresponding to the Heb מְאֵרָה (Scharbert 1973:437).

arāru II (*harāru* II) has the meaning "to fear, become agitated, panic-stricken" (CAD 1-a:236–37) and "aufstören" (*AHw*:65).

arāru III, classed by *AHw* under *erēru* (238), means "to rot", "to discharge a putrid liquid", or "to defecate" (CAD 1-a:237–38).

A.6 Leslau notes the form in Socr of *ʾerer*, "to get angry, to curse" (1958:11). There is also in Tigre the vb *ʾarar*, "to shame".

A.7 There are no other cognates in Semitic languages, and, therefore, it is only Akk that is a close parallel. The other languages with possible cognates (Socr, Tigre) are tentative proposals, and their meanings diverge from that of the Heb אָרַר.

B.1 The Arb *ʾarra*, "to stimulate (sexually), to drive away" is unlikely to be cognate with אָרַר. It is probable that it is cognate with Akk *arāru* II (CAD 1-a:236–37), "to tremble, to flicker, to burn, to be excited, stimulated" (Cohen:34; Scharbert 1973:437).

2. Formal Characteristics
A.1 *maqtil-h* (BL: 492 *wζ*).
A.2 *HAL* (513), as BL (492 *wζ*), suggest that מְאֵרָה is derived from *maʾirrat*, though their reference to BL: 431 *w* is due to their misunderstanding of BL.

B.1 [nil]

3. Syntagmatics
A.1 The מְאֵרָה is sent (שָׁלַח) by God against (בְּ) someone (Dt 28.20; Ml 2.2).
A.2 In a cognate phrase the nations are cursed (אָרַר) with (בְּ) a מְאֵרָה (Ml 3.9).
A.3 In Pr the מְאֵרָה is said to be of the Lord (3.33), and he who hides his eyes from the poor is a רַב־מְאֵרוֹת (28.27).
A.4 The מְאֵרַת יהוה is contrasted with his action of blessing, יְבָרֵךְ (Pr 3.33).
A.5 The Lord sending the מְאֵרָה is joined by waw consecutive to the expression וְאָרוֹתִי אֶת־בִּרְכוֹתֵיכֶם (Ml 2.2).

B.1 [nil]

4. Versions
a. LXX: ἔνδεια (Dt 28.20); ἀπορία (Pr 28.27); κατάρα (Pr 3.33, Ml 2.2); ἀποβλέπω (Ml 3.9); σπάνις (Thd and Aq on Dt 28.20); ἀχορτασία (Sym on Dt 28.20).

b. Pesh: *lawṭṭā᾽* (Pr 3.33; Ml 2.2, 3.9); *ḥusrānā᾽* (Dt 28.20); [no text] (Pr 28.27).

c. Targum: מְאֵירְתָא (Dt 28.20 [TgO, PsJ, Neo], Ml 2.2); לוֹט (Pr 3.33, 28.27, Ml 3.9).

d. Vulgate: *egestas* (Pr 3.33, Ml 2.2); *penuria* (Pr 28.27, Ml 3.9); *fames* (Dt 28.20).

A.1 The Vg of Dt 28.20, Pr and Ml 2.2 (*fames, egestas, penuria*), the LXX of Dt 28.20 and Pr 28.27 (ἔνδεια, ἀπορία), and the Pesh of Dt 28.20 (*ḥwsrn᾽*), all understand מְאֵרָה to denote "want, poverty". There is already in the OT an association between curse and poverty at Pr 28.27 where the curse connoted poverty (see Exegesis **A.4**), as also indicated by the LXX translation there of ἀπορία, "loss" (Gordon 1997:526). In Ha 1.6 the Tg translates צְרוֹר נָקוּב, "a bag with holes", as מאירתא, "curse", also suggesting an association between curse and poverty. This seems more likely than understanding the Tg to be treating נָקוּב as if it is derived from נָקַב II (Lv 24.11, 16) (see Cathcart & Gordon 1989:177). Likewise, Sir cautions his readers to avoid being cursed by the poor, to whose curse God will listen (Sir 4.5–6). It is possible that the Versions have been influenced by the use of מארה in RH.

A.2 Rashi on Dt 28.20 refers to the rare word ממארת at Lv 13.51 and adds the gloss חסרון, "lack". This corresponds both to the LXX and the Pesh, the latter using a lexeme cognate with Rashi's gloss.

A.3 The LXX of Ml 3.9 renders the Heb בַּמְּאֵרָה אַתֶּם נֵאָרִים as καὶ ἀποβλέποντες ὑμεῖς ἀποβλέπετε, which suggests the root ראה rather than ארר. Brichto (1963:104–106) argues that the Heb is intelligible, but that other parts of the LXX assist in explaining the meaning of the Heb מְאֵרָה in this passage (see IA. Introduction, Text Doubtful). It is possible that the translators of the LXX were misled since this is the only occasion in which we find אָרַר in the niphʻal (Kruse-Blinkenberg 1966:112, n. 94). A variant reading attempts to clarify the Greek translation. Muraoka (1993:23–24) notes that the variant εἰς αὐτά, referring back to the tithes, is intended to render ἀποβλέπω in its meaning "to turn attention [to]" (cf. LXX at Ho 3.1). He also notes that the Geez use of *taʻawwara*, "to be neglected, despised" attests to the sense of the passage (Muraoka 1993:24).

A.4 Kruse-Blinkenberg also notes that the Pesh translates Ml 3.9 more accurately than the Syro-Hexapla (1967:69).

B.1 It has been suggested that at Dt 28.20 the LXX translator expresses an aspect of a curse, in contrast to the abundance of goods bestowed in 28.3–5 (Dogniez & Harl 1992:288; cf. Wevers 1995:434). Wevers (1995:434) proposes that the "curse is understood in terms of the result of the curse", and notes that this is seen in all the Greek translations of the verse. The other Heb nouns in the passage have caused the ancient translators difficulties so that the translators concretized them. Theodotion translates מְהוּמָה, "panic", as ἐκλιμία, "famine", which is really the cause of the panic (cf. Aquila and Symmachus). Likewise, מִגְעֶרֶת is rendered by Theodotion as ἀνάλυσις ("destruction"), and by Aquila as ἐπιτίμησις ("censure"), which is possibly what the Heb noun means. In the case of מְאֵרָה the wider use of the translation "poverty" throughout the Versions militates against viewing the translation here as only part of the translators' difficulties with the nouns in the verse.

5. Lexical/Semantic Field(s)

A.1 [see אָרַר]

B.1 [nil]

6. Exegesis

A.1 This lexeme is commonly understood to mean "curse". *HAL* (513) render it as "Verfluchung", BDB (76) as "curse", Zorell (405) as "maledictio", and Alonso Schoekel as "maldición" (376).

A.2 In Dt 28.20 מְאֵרָה follows the series of curses beginning with אָרוּר (see אָרַר). The lexeme is in this verse followed by two nouns that are more general in nature: הַמְּהוּמָה, "panic", and הַמִּגְעֶרֶת, "rebuke". Brichto (1963:113) suggests that we have here a case of hendiadys, the curse being sent to "chastise and confound". The verse implies that the מְאֵרָה is a troublesome state caused by God.

A.3 As in Dt 28.20, forceful verbs are also used in Ml 2.2 and 3.9, from which Brichto (1963:113) infers that the operative sense is to be understood (see **B.1** below). The context offers little for determining its meaning here. In Ml 2.3 it appears that part of the curse involves banishment from God's presence.

A.4 In Pr 3.33 and 28.27 there is also no hint of anything being spoken as integral to the מְאֵרָה. In 3.33 the מְאֵרָה of the Lord is on the house of the wicked, which suggests that they are in a particular state, and this is contrasted with receiving the Lord's blessing. In Pr 28.27 an "abundance of curses" (רַב־מְאֵרוֹת) is contrasted with a lack of want (אֵין מַחְסוֹר).

B.1 Brichto finds in the occurrences of מְאֵרָה that there is no indication of anything spoken, but that the curse is "in the material, operative sense", or, in other words, a "spell" (1963:113–114). Scharbert, by contrast, finds it necessary to tie the curse to an imprecation (Scharbert 1958:7). In speaking of an operative curse, Brichto is drawing upon the language of Gevirtz (1959), who understood the very utterance of the curse word itself to be effective for the power of the curse. Thiselton (1974:283–99), who draws upon the linguistic studies of Austin (1962), has shown that words do not have inherent power, but that words such as blessing and cursing are examples of "performative language", whose effectiveness is dependent upon their being uttered by the appropriate person in the appropriate situation.

7. Conclusion

The occurrences of מְאֵרָה are too few to make any confident assertion on its meaning. It seems to express a state of discomfort, sometimes directly ordained by God (e.g. Dt 28.20; Ml 2.2) or as the result of not acting righteously (Pr 28.27). It has an association with the state of poverty in Pr 28.27, as well as in the Versions and RH. There may, therefore, be an ironic twist in Ml 3.9 that God sends a מְאֵרָה on those who are robbing him. The instance in Pr 28.27 is the only case where God is not said to be acting.

BIBLIOGRAPHY

Albright, W.F. 1969. *The Proto-Sinaitic Inscriptions and their Decipherment*. Harvard Theological Studies, 22; Cambridge, MT.

Austin, J.L. 1962. *How to do Things with Words*. Oxford.

Brichto, H.C. 1963. *The Problem of "Curse" in the Hebrew Bible*. *JBL* Monograph Series, xiii. Philadelphia.

Cathcart, K.J. & R.P. Gordon. 1989. *The Targum of the Minor Prophets, translated with a critical introduction, appendix and notes*. The Aramaic Bible, 14. Edinburgh.

Dogniez, C. & M. Harl. 1992. *Le Deutéronome*. La Bible d'Alexandrie. Paris.

Gevirtz, S. 1959. Curse Motifs in the Old Testament and in the Ancient Near East. Unpublished PhD dissertation. University of Chicago.

Gordon, R.P. 1997. Article ארר in W.A. VanGemeren (ed.). *The New International Dictionary of Old Testament Theology and Exegesis*. Carlisle: vol. 1, 524–26.

Kruse-Blinkenberg, L. 1966. The Pesitta of the Book of Malachi. *ST* 20: 95–119.

Kruse-Blinkenberg, L. 1967. The Book of Malachi according to Codex Syro-Hexaplaris Ambrosianus. *ST* 21:62–82.

Muraoka, T. 1993. *A Greek-English Lexicon of the Septuagint (Twelve Prophets)*. Leuven.

Scharbert, J. 1958. " Fluchen" und "Segnen" im Alten Testament. *Bib* 39: 1–26.

Scharbert, J. 1973. Article ארר in *TW* 1:437–52.

Thiselton, A.C. 1974. The supposed power of words in the Biblical writings. *JTS* 25:283–99.

Wevers, J.W. 1995. *Notes on the Greek Text of Deuteronomy*. SBLSCS 39. Atlanta, GA.

James K. Aitken
University of Cambridge

מַעְגָּל II

Introduction

Grammatical Type: n m/f.

Occurrences: Total 13x OT, 0x Sir, 2x Qum (4Q184 1.9, 17), 0x inscr.

Text doubtful: An alternative reading for מַעְגְּלֶיךָ in Ps 65.12 of מַעֲלוֹתֶיךָ, "your chambers", has been noted by Held (1974:108, n. 11) at the suggestion of Ginsberg (cf. Ps 104.3, 13; and Ginsberg 1950–1951:102). This may be reflected in some of the medieval commentators (e.g. Qimḥi), who take the word here to denote "clouds" (Held 1974:108, n. 11). Some difficulty with the word may also be reflected in the Tg (see Versions **A.4**). Graetz (1883:403) would eliminate מַעְגָּל from the verse.

Qere/Ketiv: none.

1. Root and Comparative Material

A.1 מַעְגָּל II is to be distinguished from מַעְגָּל I (1Sm 17.20, 26.5, 7), which means a "military camp". מַעְגָּל II is often said to be derived from עֲגָלָה, a "waggon", and therefore rendered "waggon-track, rut" (cf. NRSV on Ps 65.12[11]) and said to be used figuratively in the OT (BDB:722; *HAL*:576; Sauer 1971:459). *HAL*, for example, glosses מַעְגָּל as "Wagenspur, Geleise" in Ps 65.12, and then classes all the other uses as metaphorical. Whether this is the etymology (see **B.1**) or that in **A.2** below, is a matter of conjecture. מַעְגָּל II does not appear in RH, but can be found in Modern Hebrew, perhaps through the influence of the OT .

A.2 Gesenius (1829:989) suggests an alternative derivation, from the root עגל, "to roll" (from which עֲגָלָה is presumed to derive ultimately), since the word referred to a "track" or "rut" in which the wheels revolved ("*orbita* in qua rotae *volvuntur*"), and he cites Ps 65.12. From this it came to be used for a way ("*via*"), he argues. מַעְגָּל may also be derived from עֵגֶל, "calf", or עֶגְלָה,"heifer", both also thought to be from the root עגל, "to roll". In that case a מַעְגָּל would be a path on which a calf travels.

A.3 In Ug the words possibly derived from a similar root are ʿgl, "calf", or ʿglt, "heifer" (see *UT*:1811).

A.4 Pun has the form ʿgl I, "calf", and in both Pun and Phoen the lexeme ʿglh I denotes a "chariot" (*DNWSI*:824).

A.5 The lexeme עגל, "a calf", is found in OAram (*DNWSI*:824) and in Arm of other periods. In Hatr עגלה II and perhaps עגל II denote a "crushing roller" (*DNWSI*:824).

A.6 Syr has a similar range of possible cognates as Heb (Brockelmann: 509–10).

A.7 In Akk *agalu* is a horse, and then came to be used of any traction animal (I-a:141).

A.8 Arb has the forms ʿajila ("to hurry"), ʿijl ("calf") and ʿajala ("wheel")

(Wehr 1979:693), but these are no more helpful than the Heb forms for determining the etymology of מַעְגָּל.

B.1 Koch (1977:297) and Dorsey (1991:235–36) doubt that our lexeme is derived from the word for "waggon" since there is no example of its "foreground spatial use" (Koch 1977:297). Since, however, our corpus is limited, it is possible that a lexeme had an original literal meaning that is no longer extant in our sources (see Exegesis **A.2**).

2. Formal Characteristics

A.1 *maqtal* (BL:490 *ze*)

A.2 The gender is ambiguous. A f pl form, מַעְגְּלוֹת, appears 4 times (e.g. Pr 2.15: מַעְגְּלֹתָם; 4Q184 1.9) and a m pl form, always in cstr, 4 times (e.g. Ps 23.3, 4Q184 1.17). The gender is only made apparent at Ps 65.12, where מַעְגָּלֶיךָ is used with the m pl form of the vb (Dorsey 1991:234), and at 4Q184 1.9 where מעגלותיה is used with the f pl ptc. Little can be said of the gender variation on the basis of so few occurrences. Nonetheless, one may note a tendency for nouns having to do with places to have a double gender, and that other words for road (דֶּרֶךְ, and perhaps אֹרַח and נָתִיב) also exhibit this aspect.

3. Syntagmatics

A.1 A מַעְגָּל in cst may be a course taken or approved of by the Lord (Ps 17.5, 65.12).

A.2 A מַעְגָּל in cst may refer to the way of man in general (Pr 5.21).

A.3 A מַעְגָּל in cst may be the course taken by the evil person (Is 59.8, Pr 2.15) or by the "righteous" (צַדִּיק, Is 26.7, Pr 4.26), by one's "feet" (רֶגֶל, Pr 4.26) or that set by a "strange" woman (Pr 2.18, 5.6). The paths of the "strange woman" may lead to the "shades" (אֶל־רְפָאִים, Pr 2.18).

A.4 A מַעְגָּל may be "good" (טוֹב, Pr 2.9), "righteous" (צֶדֶק, Ps 23.3) or "upright" (יָשָׁר, Pr 4.11, 4Q184 1.17). A good path (Pr 2.9) is akin to "righteousness, justice and equity" (צֶדֶק וּמִשְׁפָּט וּמֵישָׁרִים) (but see Held 1974:109–110; Exegesis **A.4**).

A.5 מַעְגָּל is the direct object of the vb פִּלֵּס, "to align" (Is 26.7, Pr 4.26, 5.21). The vb פִּלֵּס occurs only six times in the OT, three of which appearances are in connection with מַעְגָּל. It is also used of a נָתִיב (Ps 78.50) and of an אֹרַח (Pr 5.6) (see Exegesis **B.1**).

A.6 One is "led" (hiph of נחה) in or "made to walk" (hif of דרך) in a מַעְגָּל (-בְּ, Ps 23.3, Pr 4.11). "Steps" (אָשׁוּר) may "hold fast" (תָּמַךְ) to a מַעְגָּל (Ps 17.5).

A.7 A net is stretched "beside" (לְיַד) a מַעְגָּל (Ps 140.6).

A.8 The מַעְגְּלוֹת themselves of a "loose woman" may "wander" (נוּעַ, Pr 5.6) or "lead astray" (hiph of שגה, 4Q184 1.9). They may "overflow" (רָעַף) with "richness" (דֶּשֶׁן, Ps 65.12).

A.9 מַעְגָּל (as the B word) is found in parallelism with דֶּרֶךְ (Is 59.8, Pr 4.11, 26, 5.21) and with אֹרַח (Is 26.7, Ps 17.4–5, Pr 2.15, 5.6), and (as the A word) with נְתִיבָה (4Q184 1.9). In Is 59.7–8 מַעְגָּל, as well as being parallel to דֶּרֶךְ, is in a context that includes the lexemes מְסִלָּה and נְתִיבָה. At Pr 2.18 מַעְגָּל is parallel to בֵּיתָהּ (see Exegesis **A.3**), and at Ps 65.12 to שָׁנָה (see Exegesis **B.3**).

B.1 [nil]

4. Versions

a. LXX: τροχιά (Pr 2.15, 4.11, 26, 5.6, 21); τρίβος (Ps 17.5 [=LXX 16.5], 23.3 [=LXX 22.3], 140.6 [=LXX 139.6]); ὁδός (Is 26.7, 59.8); ἄξων (Pr 2.9, 18); πεδίον (Ps 65.12 [=LXX 64.12]);

b. Peshitta: *šḇilā'* (Ps 17.5, 23.3, 140.6, Pr 2.9, 15, 18, 4.11, 26, 5.6, 21); *'urḥā'* (Is 26.7); *hlaḵtā'* (Is 59.8); *'aḡaltā'* (Ps 65.12);

c. Targum: שְׁבִילָא (Pr 2.9, 15, 18, 4.11, 26, 5.6, 21); אָרְחָא (Ps 140.6, Is 26.7); כִּיבְשֵׁי אֹרַח (Ps 65.12); הִלְכְתָא (Ps 23.3); הֲלִכְתָא (Ps 17.5); הַךְ (Is 59.8);

d. Vulgate: *semita* (Ps 23.3 [=Vg 22.2], Ps 140.6 iuxta Heb [=139.6], Pr 2.9, 18, 4.11, 26); *gressus* (Is 59.8, Ps 17.5, Pr 2.15, 5.6, 21); *callis* (Is 26.7); *campus* (Ps 65.12 iuxta LXX [=64.12]); *iter* (Ps 140.6 iuxta LXX [=139.6]); *vestigium* (Ps 65.12 iuxta Heb [=64.12]).

A.1 The LXX to Pr is the only text that uses the word τροχιά for מַעְגָּל (Tidwell 1980:65), although it also is the only text that uses the word ἄξων for the same lexeme (2.9, 18). Pr never renders מַעְגָּל by the more common translations for "road" of ὁδός or τρίβος. One of the two other occurrences of τροχιά in the LXX is again in Pr (4.27b), where it forms part of a free rendering of the verse under the influence of the vocabulary of the previous verse. The other occurrence of the Greek lexeme is in the Vaticanus manuscript at Ezk 27.19 (and preferred by Ziegler 1952:217) to translate קָנֶה, where other Greek versions have τροχός. The author of the Epistle to the Hebrews (12.13) also uses this word when quoting Pr 4.26. Lust glosses τροχιά as "wheel-track, course, path" (1996:482). Although the Greek lexeme may have the meaning "wheel-track", it seems unlikely that this is what it means in any of its occurrences in the LXX, where it appears to be the translation of the metaphorical use of "way, path". The LXX's rendering may indicate that the translator was trying to render a possible etymology of מַעְגָּל as deriving from the root עֲגָלָה, a "waggon", or עָגַל, "to roll" (see also **A.2** below).

A.2 It is of interest that the LXX translator of Pr twice renders מַעְגָּל by the Greek word ἄξων, "axle" (Pr 2.9, 18). This would seem to suggest that the translator recognized the derivation from עֲגָלָה, a "waggon", or עָגַל, "to roll", or even had in mind a root now preserved in the Arb "wheel" (see Root and Comparative Material A.8). That the LXX translator of Pr uses two words to render מַעְגָּל (τροχιά and ἄξων), both peculiar to that translation, and that both renderings suggest a similar etymology, make it highly probable that the translator aimed at an etymological translation. Lust (1992:43) translates ἄξων firstly as "axle" and then explains that at Pr 2.9 it is used *metaphorically* for "course" or "path". While it is correct that it should be translated "path", the whole explanation is that the translation of ἄξων as "path" is metaphorical, but that its use here should be deemed etymological.

A.3 The Pesh to Ps 65.12, *'aḡaltā'*, "waggon", also suggests an etymological rendering.

A.4 The rendering of the Tg (Lagarde 1873) at Ps 65.12, כִּיבְשֵׁי אֹורַח ("ways of the path") may represent some difficulty experienced by the translator with this verse. The appearance of כיבש in the verse implies that alongside מַעְגָּל the lexeme מְסִלָּה may once have appeared (at least in the translator's Vorlage), since כיבש regularly translates that lexeme (Held 1974:108, n. 11).

5. Lexical/Semantic Field(s)

A.1 [see דֶּרֶךְ]

A.2 מַעְגָּל is confined solely to poetic texts, and 7 of its 13 appearances in the MT are in the opening chapters of Pr.

A.3 מַעְגָּל is found most frequently in sapiential contexts, appearing most often in Pr and Ps, and in the sapiential literature of Qum (4Q184 1.9). Its only other occurrences are in two passages in Is (26.7; 59.8).

A.4 In 8 of its appearances in the MT מַעְגָּל forms a word-pair with other words (דֶּרֶךְ at Is 59.8, Pr 4.11, 26, 5.21, and אֹרַח at Is 26.7, Ps 17.4–5, Pr 2.15, 5.6) in the semantic field of "road", as well as in 1 of its 2 appearances at Qum (with נתיבה at 4Q184 1.9).

6. Exegesis

A.1 מַעְגָּל appears four times as a poetic synonym for אֹרַח, and four times for דֶּרֶךְ. The most frequent meaning of מַעְגָּל is that of the moral path of life, whether of the good man (guided by God or wisdom), or of the evil man.

A.2 The most frequent meaning of מַעְגָּל is that of a course of travel or the course of life (Dorsey 1991:235). The one likely exception to this metaphorical/sapiential tenor of מַעְגָּל is at Ps 140.6, where it may refer to a literal road. Although it is in a metaphorical context of laying traps for one's enemy, it forms part of an expression that derives from the literal act of spreading a net by the "wayside". *HAL* (576) seem to understand מַעְגָּל in Ps 65.17 also as a physical road. Dorsey (1991:235) notes that מַעְגָּל is "regularly in parallel" with אֹרַח and דֶּרֶךְ, both of which can mean "course of travel", but never in parallelism with מְסִלָּה or נָתִיב, which, he says, are more restricted to the meaning "road". Although he is correct that מַעְגָּל in the OT is never in parallelism with these latter lexemes, it does occur in a passage with them in neighbouring verses (Is 59.7–8). Furthermore, in 4Q184 מַעְגָּל is found in parallelism with נְתִיבָה (4Q184 1.9), suggesting there is not so sharp a distinction between the lexemes. Both 4Q184 and Is 59 are late passages, and so it could be surmised that it is a later tendency to present the words as synonymous. Nevertheless, the lexemes for road are mostly confined to poetry, and often found in sapiential literature, with no discernible distinction in meaning or use.

A.3 The pairing at Pr 2.18 of מַעְגְּלֹתֶיהָ אֶל־רְפָאִים with אֶל־מָוֶת בֵּיתָהּ, "her road to the shades", has induced some scholars to emend the text (noted by Held 1973:179). Held (1973:179–180), however, has shown that the pairing of בַּיִת with מַעְגָּל corresponds to that of בַּיִת with דֶּרֶךְ (Pr 5.8, 7.19; cf. 7.27). Furthermore, one may find the comparable pairing in the Akk words *bītu* and *ḫarrānu* (CT 15, 45:3–6) and there is a tradition in Akk of the netherworld being associated with the road leading to it (e.g. *ḫarrān lā tāri*, "road of no return", appears alongside *erṣet lā tāri*, "land of no return", in STT 73:35–38). Further evidence may be noted in 4Q184, which speaks of the דרכי שוחה, "the roads of the pit" (1.17).

A.4 The sequence "righteousness, justice and equity" (צֶדֶק וּמִשְׁפָּט וּמֵישָׁרִים) in parallelism with מַעְגָּל at Pr 2.9 seems to be the result of contamination from Pr 1.3. Some would emend מֵישָׁרִים to תִּשְׁמֹר, "you will keep" (e.g. Toy 1899:38, 50) or delete it altogether (Ehrlich 1913:vol. 6, 17). The LXX κατορθώσεις suggests the vb תְּיַשֵּׁר in place of מֵישָׁרִים, but this is not a suitable parallel to תָּבִין earlier in the verse (Held 1974:110). Held proposes that there has been a conflation of two versions. In that case מַעְגָּל will be the object of the verb יַשֵּׁר, which is also used with the nouns דֶּרֶךְ (Is 45.13, Ps 5.9, Pr 11.5) and אֹרַח (Pr 3.6, 9.15). In parallel to מַעְגָּל will be simply צֶדֶק וּמִשְׁפָּט, which will be the object themselves of the verb תָּכִין. An alternation between תָּבִין and תָּכִין can easily be seen as a scribal error, and it is known from other parts of the OT (e.g. the Qere/Ketiv at Pr 21.29 and 2Ch 33.16).

B.1 The vb פִּלֵּס in three instances governs מַעְגָּל (Is 26.7; Pr 4.26; 5. 21), as well as governing the nouns נְתִיב (Ps 78.50) and אֹרַח (Pr 5.6). It appears to be cognate with the noun פֶּלֶס, often understood to be a balance or scale (BDB:813), since in its two appearances in the OT (Pr 16.11; Is 40.12) and in its one appearance in Sir (42.4) it is parallel to מֹאזְנַיִם, "scales". The verb is consequently understood to mean "to make level, smooth" (e.g. BDB:814). This might suggest that a מַעְגָּל was a graded road (Dorsey 1991:234). In addition to the implications this meaning may have for ancient road construction, it may be determinative for the meaning of מַעְגָּל. Does it refer to a physical road or a course of travel?

Dorsey notes that the פֶּלֶס, rather than being the scale itself, has been identified as the pointer on the scales, which stands at right angles to the beam when the scales are balanced (Sellers 1962:830). He supports this interpretation by reference to the Akk vb *naplusu/palāsu* "to look at, observe" (*AHw*:814), since the pointer allowed one to see when the scales were balanced (Dorsey 1991:235; cf. *HAL*:883). In that case, he argues, if the verb פִּלֵּס is a denominative of the indicator arm, the verb would denote "to align, make straight" (Dorsey 1991:235). Dorsey here produces a meaning that is an extension of the use of פֶּלֶס and not of the Akk etymology that he cites, but nonetheless his contextual analysis is helpful. In Is 26.7 the term is parallel to יָשָׁר, and in the verse before and after Pr 4.26 there are warnings to keep looking forward (4.25) and not to turn aside (4.27). Likewise in Pr 5.6 the verb is in contrast to נוּעַ, "to wander". For Pr 5.21 Dorsey suggests an alternative, that the verb might be better understood to mean "to weigh by aligning the pointer", portraying the concept of God judging man's moral course (Dorsey 1991:235). As a result Dorsey derives two different meanings on the basis of the same etymology, which is extremely suspect in the light of the limited evidence. A recent solution offered by *HAL* is to see it as a case of homonymy. פִּלֵּס I is cognate with Akk *palāšu*, "durchbohren, einbrechen" (*AHw*: 815), and can be found in Is 26.7, Ps 58.3, 78.50, and possibly Pr 4.26 (*HAL*:882–883). פִּלֵּס II, on the other hand, is the one cognate with Akk *palāsu* (*AHw*:814), and can be found in Pr 5.6, 21, and possibly in Pr 4.26 and Ps 56.8 (*HAL*:883). The evidence, however, is too limited to allow us to determine anything for certain about the nature of a מַעְגָּל from its collocation with פֶּלֶס.

B.2 Dahood (1965:146; 1967:429) argues that the m pl of מַעְגָּל at Ps 23.3

and Ps 65.12 means "pastures". In Ps 23.3, he says, it is parallel to נְאוֹת דֶּשֶׁא, "green meadows" (23.2), and in 65.12 to נְאוֹת מִדְבָּר, "meadows of the wilderness" (65.13), whilst the LXX of Ps 65.12 (= 64.12) renders מַעְגָּלֶיךָ as τὰ πεδία σου, "your fields" (see also **B.3**). To this Tidwell (1980:69, n. 27) adds Pr 4.11 in view of its wording, which is comparable to Ps 23.3. Dorsey (1991:253, n.12) notes two errors in Dahood's reasoning. First, in Ps 23.3 מַעְגָּל is not in parallelism with נְאוֹת, which is in fact parallel in the present division to מֵי מְנֻחוֹת (See also **B.4**). Second, it does not follow that, since two words are parallel, they must be synonymous. Furthermore, Held (1974:111) notes that never is מַעְגָּל or any of its synonyms in parallelism with נָוֶה, and that the verb נָחָה is never a synonym of the verb רָבַץ in verse 2a. In Ps 65.12 נְאוֹת מִדְבָּר is not the parallel of מַעְגָּל, but גְּבָעוֹת in 65.13 (Held 1974:111).

B.3 The problematic parallel of שָׁנָה, "year", with מַעְגָּל in Ps 65.12 led Dahood (1966:116) to interpret שָׁנָה as "(mountain) peaks", citing Arb and Ug in support. Held (1974:108–109) has shown the faults in Dahood's solution, and instead suggests one of his own. He proposes one read שָׂדֹת, "fields", for שְׁנַת, providing a parallelism analogous to דֶּרֶךְ // שָׂדֶה in Jr 6.25. He indicates that the context involves various concrete agricultural terms.

B.4 Held argues that Ps 23.3 is a metrically defective hemistich. As there is no appropriate synonym in parallel to מַעְגָּל in that verse (see **B.2**), he would supply a clause containing the lexemes אֹרַח or דֶּרֶךְ (1974:112).

B.5 The interpretation and metrical division of Ps 140.6 is also problematic. Kissane has proposed to emend חֲבָלִים to שְׁבִילִים and thereby to provide a parallel for מַעְגָּל (1954:619–20). שְׁבִיל, however, is a rare poetic word, appearing only twice in the OT (Jr 18.15, Ps 77.20), and then only as the B-word to דֶּרֶךְ (Held 1974:112, n. 56). Nonetheless, שְׁבִיל was used once by Sir (5.9) and twice in Qum (1QH XV[=formerly VII].15, 4Q184 I 1.9), and the LXX at Jr 18.15 translates שְׁבִיל by σχοῖνος, "rope, cord", suggesting a possible confusion between שְׁבִילִים and חֲבָלִים. If this is a correct interpretation of the LXX at Jr 18.15, it would lend support to Kissane's suggestion. Held's proposal is that a substantive such as אֹרַח or דֶּרֶךְ has been omitted from Ps 140.6a (1974:115). In verse 6b he sees no need to emend to אֹרַח, as the LXX's ποσίν μου implies the reading רַגְלַי or פְּעָמַי, an idiom that has parallels elsewhere (Ps 25.15, 57.7, Pr 29.5, Jb 18.8–9, La 1.13).

7. Conclusion

מַעְגָּל is a lexeme confined to poetic texts, and, apart from the possible exceptions of Ps 65.12 and 140.6 (see Exegesis **A.2**), is only used of a moral "course". Its frequent parallelism with other words in the semantic field of "road" may represent a tendency to pair a common word with a less common poetic word (a tendency noted by Boling 1960:223–224).

The etymology of מַעְגָּל cannot be conclusively determined, but the fact that the word may not be extant in the meaning of a literal road (although see Ps 65.12) does not mean that it never had that meaning or that its root could not lie in a word that implied that. As it is confined to poetry, and is most frequent in sapiential contexts, its meaning is that of a path or course to be followed. It cannot be distinguished from the other road words that are also only to be found, for the most part, in poetry (שְׁבִיל, נְתִיבָה/נָתִיב, אֹרַח).

BIBLIOGRAPHY

Aistleitner, J. 1974. *Wörterbuch der ugaritischen Sprache*. Berlin.

Boling, R.G. 1960. Synonymous Parallelism in the Psalms. *JSS* 5:221–55.

Dahood, M. 1966. Commentary on *Psalms* II (AB, 16). New York.

id. 1967. Hebrew-Ugaritic Lexicography V. *Bib* 48:421-38.

Dorsey, D.A. 1991. *The Roads and Highways of Ancient Israel*. Baltimore and London.

Ehrlich, A.B. 1908–14. *Randglossen zur hebräischen Bibel: textkritisches, sprachliches und sachliches*. 7 vols. Leipzig.

Fabry, H.-J. 1986. Article סלל in *TWAT* 5:867–72.

Gesenius, W. 1829–1842. *Thesaurus Philologicus Criticus Linguæ Hebrææ et Chaldææ Veteris Testamenti*. Leipzig.

Ginsberg, H.L. 1950–1951. Some Emendations in Psalms. *HUCA* 23:97–104.

Graetz, H. 1883. *Psalmen II*. Breslau.

Held, M. 1973. Pits and Pitfalls in Akkadian and Biblical Hebrew. *JANES* 5:173–90.

Held, M. 1974. Hebrew ma`gal: A Study in Lexical Parallelism. *JANES* 6:107–16.

Kissane, E.J. 1954. *The Book of Psalms, Translated from a Critically Revised Hebrew Text, with a Commentary*. Dublin.

Koch, K. 1977. Article דרך in *TWAT* 2:288–312.

Lagarde, P. de. 1873. *Hagiographa Chaldaice*. Leipzig.

Lust, J. et al. 1992. *A Greek–English Lexicon of the Septuagint*. Part I A–I. Stuttgart.

Lust, J. et al. 1996. *A Greek–English Lexicon of the Septuagint*. Part II K–W. Stuttgart.

Sauer, G. 1971. Article דרך in *THAT* 1:456–460.

Sellers, O.R. 1962. Weights and Measures. In G.A. Buttrick. *Interpreter's Dictionary of the Bible*. New York:vol. 4:829–39.

Tidwell, N. 1980. A Road and a Way. A Contribution to the Study of Word-Pairs. *Semitics* 7:50–80.

Toy, C.H. 1899. Commentary on *Proverbs* (ICC). Edinburgh.

Wehr, H. ⁴1979. *A Dictionary of Modern Written Arabic*. Edited by J.M. Cowan. Wiesbaden.

Ziegler, J. 1952. *Ezechiel*. Septuaginta: Vetus Testamentum Graecum 16, 1. Göttingen.

James K. Aitken
University of Cambridge

מִשְׁעוֹל

Introduction
Grammatical Type: noun m.
Occurrences: Total 1x OT, 0x Sir, 0x Qum, 0x inscr.
Text doubtful: none.
Qere/Ketiv: none.

1. Root and Comparative Material
A.1 The lexeme מִשְׁעוֹל (Nu 22.24) is probably derived from a root *šʿ*
(BDB:1043), which has left no vbs in the Semitic languages, but cognate nouns
such as BH שֹׁעַל, "hollow of the hand" (Is 40.12) or "handful" (e.g. 1Kg 20.10).
Hence a מִשְׁעוֹל, it is concluded, was a "hollow way", a path that had been worn
out, sunken, or cut out.

A.2 Alternatively, the word may be from שֹׁעַל in its meaning "hollow of
the sole, step", a meaning that Dorsey believes prevails at 1Kg 20.10 (1991:239).
This meaning of the word is preserved in the Arm שְׁעוּלָה (see **A.3**). Hence, a
מִשְׁעוֹל would be a place for a foot to tread.

A.3 Possible cognate words in other Semitic languages are all derived
from the meaning "to be hollow" (Dorsey 1991:238). Arm has שְׁעוּלָא and שְׁעָלָא,
"hollow of the hand, palm" or "hollow of the sole"; Syr has *šuʿlāʾ*, "hollow of
the hand, handful".

A.4 Akk has the lexeme *šīlu*, "hollow, cavity, depression of the liver"
(*AHw*:1237).

A.5 Although the lexeme does occur in Modern Hebrew, used for a path
or narrow lane (Even-Shoshan 1975:803), this meaning is probably under the
influence of TgO and the Rabbinic commentators.

B.1 Budd (1984:250) states that the root of the word means "to be deep".
This seems to be an unjustified extension of the meaning "to be hollow".

2. Formal Characteristics
A.1 *miqta:l* (BL:493 *e*η).

3. Syntagmatics
A.1 The angel of the Lord stands in (-בְּ עָמַד) the מִשְׁעוֹל (Nu 22.24).

A.2 The מִשְׁעוֹל is said to be "of the vineyards" (הַכְּרָמִים, Nu 22.24), meaning
either through or between the vineyards.

A.3 It is flanked on either side by a גָּדֵר (Nu 22.24).

4. Versions
a. LXX: αὖλαξ (in pl)
b. Peshitta: *šḇīlāʾ*

c. Targum:

       TgO – שְׁבִילָא

       TgPsJ – דוחקא דמיצע ביני

       TgNeo – ביני סייני

       TgNeoMg – אמצא

       TgFrg (Vatican Ebr 440) – אמצע

d. Vulgate: *angustia* (in pl)

A.1 The LXX αὖλαξ, a "furrow", suggests that the translator may have understood the root of מְשָׁעוֹל to be *šˁl*, implying the concept of hollowness (see Root and Comparative Material **A.1**). Alternatively, he may not have known what the word meant and suggested what one would be likely to find in a vineyard.

A.2 Both the Vg (*angustia*) and TgPsJ (דוחקא) imply that the word refers to a confined or restricted area. This is probably an interpretation from the context. PsJ proceeds to insert the story of Esau and Laban building a wall and towers to divide the two nations.

A.3 TgNeoMg has perhaps misread or was unable to understand the word and translated it as "in the midst of" (באמצא). This word is also preserved in the PsJ tradition. TgNeo repeats the mention of the fences from later in the verse, perhaps also from a failure to understand the word.

B.1 Lust (1992:70) provides the translation "*avenue* (in a vineyard)" for αὖλαξ at Nu 22.24, although in its other occurrences in the LXX, as indicated by Lust, it means "furrow". In LSJ, apart from metaphorical uses, the word is given only as "furrow" in both Classical and Hellenistic Greek. Dorival correctly renders it as "sillon" (1994:427). It appears that Lust has been swayed by the Hebrew text in Nu, although the translation of מְשָׁעוֹל as "furrows" is explicable (**A.2** above). Furthermore, the plural (ταῖς αὖλαξιν) makes better sense if the angel is standing in furrows, which is physically possible, than in the avenues.

5. Lexical/Semantic Field(s)

    A.1. [see דֶּרֶךְ]

6. Exegesis

A.1 This word is most commonly interpreted to be a "narrow lane", or, derived from the root *šˁl*, a "hollow way" (e.g. BDB:1043) or "Hohlweg" (*HAL*:614).

A.2 The RV preserves the idea of hollowness in its translation "hollow way", whilst the NEB combines both hollowness and the meaning "road" in its rendering "where the road ran through a hollow".

A.3 Since מְשָׁעוֹל refers to something enclosed between two walls, it is likely that a מְשָׁעוֹל was a narrow area. Gray (1903:336) describes it as "the confined place between walls". The role of a גָּדֵר, "wall", in a vineyard seems to have been for protection around the fields. In Is 5.5, Ps 80.13 and Sir 36.30 the destruction or removal of the גָּדֵר leads to damage being caused to the crops. The מְשָׁעוֹל was a path running through vineyards, with a wall to prevent harm to the crops by people or animals. It presumably was a simple dirt track, since it was in a vineyard and apparently so narrow.

B.1 Budd (1984:250) and Martin's translation of Noth (1968:167) are influenced perhaps by the context or by the Versions, which themselves may be trying to determine the meaning by the context (see Versions **A.2**). These scholars translate מִשְׁעוֹל respectively by "a narrow place" and "a narrow path". It is interesting that where Martin translates "a narrow path", Noth's text merely says "Pfad" (1966:146).

7. Conclusion

Although the מִשְׁעוֹל has been conventionally interpreted as a "narrow lane", there is little that can be said for sure of it. The etymology, understood to be derived from the root "to be hollow", is strained in order to explain how it came to mean "lane". It could imply that a מִשְׁעוֹל was any hollow depression, such as a conduit or furrow (cf. LXX, Versions **A.1**, **B.1**).

One of the few things that can be said of the מִשְׁעוֹל is that, in this case at least, it forms part of a vineyard. The Versions witness to a variety of meanings, few of them (i.e. Pesh and TgO) pointing to the meaning "lane".

The only connection with the semantic field "road" is that the angel of the Lord previously stands in a דֶּרֶךְ. But the ass moves off the road into a field to avoid the angel (v. 23), who then stands in the מִשְׁעוֹל in the vineyard. Balaam strikes the ass to turn it back into the road, but there is no indication that he succeeds in this. The מִשְׁעוֹל is the second of three places in which the angel impedes the ass, and there is no indication that these places are all of the same nature. The presence on either side of a גָּדֵר suggests that it may have been a path of some sort, but it is not conclusive. A path is certainly feasible in the context, but renderings such as "hollow path" or "Hohlweg" represent excessive emphasis on etymology and would not be intelligible as glosses without knowledge of the etymology.

BIBLIOGRAPHY

Budd, P.J. 1984. Commentary on *Numbers* (WBC). Waco, Texas.

Dorival, G. 1994. *La Bible d'Alexandrie: Les Nombres*. Paris.

Dorsey, D.A. 1991. *The Roads and Highways of Ancient Israel*. Baltimore and London.

Gray, G.B. 1903. Commentary on *Numbers* (ICC). Edinburgh.

Lust, J. et al. 1992. *A Greek–English Lexicon of the Septuagint*. Part I A–I. Stuttgart.

Noth, M. 1966. *Das vierte Buch Mose. Numeri* (ATD). Göttingen.

Noth, M. 1968. Commentary on *Numbers* (OTL). Translated by J.D. Martin. London.

James K. Aitken
University of Cambridge

נֵזֶר

Introduction
Grammatical type: n m.
Occurrences: 28 total: 25 occurrences BH (Ex 29.6; 39.30, Lv 8.9; 21.12, Nu 6.4,5,8,9,12[2x],13,18[2x],19,21[2x], 2Sm 1.10, 2Kg 11.12, Jr 7.29, Zc 9.16, Pr 27.24, 2Ch 23.11, Ps 89.40; 132.18). No occurrences in Sir or Ep; 3 occurrences Q (4QpIsᵃ 8–10, 19; 1QSb4, 28; 4QPrFêtes[4Q509] 97-8 ii 3).

It is unclear whether נֵזֶר referring to the Nazirite's period of self-dedication and to his/her dedicated hair (Nu 6.4,5,8,9,12[2x],13, 18[2x],19,21[2x], Jr 7.29) is derived from the same root as נֵזֶר when it means something worn on the head of a king or priest (Ex 29.6; 39.30, Lv 8.9; 21.12, 2Sm 1.10, 2Kg 11.12, Zc 9.16, Pr 27.24, 2Ch 23.11, Ps 89.40; 132.18).

Text doubtful

A.1 Pr 27.24: Gemser (1937:76), Scott (1965:162) and Plöger (1983:327) suggest reading *אוֹצָר as a better parallel to חֹסֶן; Plöger also gives an alternative, *עֹשֶׁר.

A.2 Nu 6.2: It is possible that כִּי יַפְלִא לִנְדֹּר נֶדֶר נָזִיר לְהַזִּיר לֵיהוה should read *כִּי יַפְלִא לִנְדֹּר נֶדֶר נֶזֶר לְהַזִּיר לֵיהוה, on the basis of the Versions.

1. Root and Comparative Material

A.1 The AH noun נֵזֶר is used in two different contexts, as mentioned above in the Introduction:
1) to describe a type of headdress worn by
   a) a king
   b) the high priest
2) in relation to the practices of a Nazirite.

Some have doubted whether the two words are derived from the same root, but the second usage is certainly related in some way to the verb נָזַר (niph, hiph, and denomv hiph) 'refrain, abstain, be a Nazirite' and noun נָזִיר 'Nazirite', which both exist in BH and were adopted into RH, JAram and Syr. נֵזֶר itself was taken into RH and 'Aramaised' into the form נְזְרָא in JAram, though נזירותא 'Naziriteship' is more common. The latter form only is found in Syr (*nziruṭā*), along with the verb *nzar*, noun *nzirā*, and the derived adverb *nzirā'iṯ*, and *nzuryā*. The Syr terms apply only to abstinence, and outside translations of Nu 6 etc., they are used of Christian ascetical practices: the root and derivatives are never used with the sense of a special headdress.

A.2 Besides the problem of the relationship between the two types of נֵזֶר there is the question of whether the connection with the root נדר, 'vow', made in Nu 6 is purely contextual and semantic, or whether a single PS root once lay behind both נזר and נדר. The more traditional view is that there is an etymological connection between the two at the ProtoNWSem or PS stage, both deriving from *n-ḏ-r*, and with one root as a variant of the other (e.g. BDB 623, and more recently Levine 1993:218f). An essential point in this discussion is the existence of a 9th century OldArm inscription, the stele dedicated to Melqart by Bar-Hadad and first published by Dunand in 1939 (now *KAI* 2014). In it appear the words *zy nzr lh wšmᶜ qlh*, interpreted by Dunand (1939:71, 73) as 'because he protected him and heard his voice', correcting *nzr* to *nṣr*, and taking Melqart as the subj. of the verb, but Dunand suggested that an alternative was 'he consecrated himself', referring to Bar-Hadad, and this is the reading he later adopted (1942:44): 'to whom he made a vow and who heard his voice'. Della Vida (1943:30 n.1) noted that in OldArm *z* was used for both PS **z* and **ḏ*, and that the relationship between Ph and AH *nzr* and *nḏr* was obscure. He cited Bauer's view that Canaanite forms with *d* where *z* would be expected are from Ug. Ginsberg (1945:161) extended the meaning of *nzr* in the inscription to mean 'he prayed', but understood it as connected with AH *ndr*, 'to vow'.

A.3 The most recent contribution on the matter of the relationship of the roots נָזַר and נָדַר appears in Berlinerblau (1996:4th appendix), who neatly summarises debate on this subject into three schools of thought:

i) *The Arabic Deviance hypothesis*, which goes back to the philologists of the late 19th century (Wellhausen, Robertson Smith, Pedersen et al.), who believed that the single root in Arabic (ESArab and Arb *nḏr*) against the two roots of AH (נזר and נדר) must indicate that the situation in AH was an aberration: נזר was the 'real' cognate from which נדר split off.

ii) *The Consonantal Shift Theory*: PS **nḏr* produced both נזר and נדר. This led to very complicated theories based on Albright's article (1942:26) on the Bar-Hadad inscription which argued that the Aramaeans used Ph/Can spelling wherever possible, and thus used ז for Arm ד. Therefore Arm נזר derived from PS **nḏr* 'to vow' and meant 'to vow' in the Bar-Hadad inscription, with the king as the subject. In contrast, Levi della Vida (1943:30 n. 1), following Bauer (1933:473), believed that Can forms with *d* where *z* would be expected (*ndr*) were influenced by Ug. Similarly, Priebatsch (1980:322 and n. 13) states that *nzr* was the original form of PS **nḏr*, and *ndr* was borrowed from Ug or a similar dialect into AH, just as Syr (which already had *ndr*) borrowed *nzr* from AH.

However, Ginsberg (1945:161 n. 8) rejected the idea that AH had borrowed from the peripheral Ugaritians such an important religious concept and theological term as vowing (*ndr*), and explained the existence of the anomalous *ndr* against the expected *nzr* as due to a blending or contamination of *nzr* with *ndb*, another important religious concept.

In brief, this school saw נדר as a variant of Can נזר, itself < ProtoCan **nzr* and ultimately < PS **nḏr*.

iii) The third theory, which Berlinerblau commends for using fresh philological evidence, is that of Boyd (1986:61–75). Boyd's objection to an etymology from a supposed PS **nḏr* 'vow' is that it would yield **nzr* in Ph/Pun and Tigre, but in fact these have *ndr* and *nädärä* respectively for the meaning 'to vow'. One resolution of this problem would be to say that these forms are loanwords from Arm into AH and Tigre (and נזר an AH loan to Arm), through religious influence, but Arm *ndr* is unlikely to have entered Ph/Pun in this way and thus presents a serious anomaly. Boyd cites Rabin's suggestion (1970:297) that the presence of a liquid, /r/ or labial in a root produces the example Arb $\underline{d}$ = AH d, and therefore it is possible that PS *$\underline{d}$ < d, not z, in the root ndr in Can languages. (Rabin assumed a connection between נדר, Arb $na\underline{d}ara$ 'to vow', and Arb $na\underline{d}ira$, 'to be on one's guard' [1970:294 § 21]). Blau (1977:81–110) also suggested that AH $\underline{d}$ > d, not > z, owing to dissimilation in the presence of /r/, or because of a dialect mixture. Boyd follows von Soden in connecting Akk $naz\bar{a}ru$ 'to blaspheme, insult, curse' with Arb nzr 'to despise, deem little' and Eth (Geez) nzr 'bite', but makes these cognate with AH נזר 'to consecrate'. 'The semantic change in AH may be understood as a shift in thought from "cursing, insulting" etc. to "cursing all 'worldly' things when taking the Nazirite vow", hence, "the setting aside of oneself to the service of the divinity" (Boyd 1986:66). Boyd then traces the root nzr back with the help of Ethiopic comparative material where the same root exists alongside ndr 'to vow' and means 'feel pain' in some dialects and 'bite' in others: Leslau (1956:220) sees the semantic development as 'biting' > 'expression of pain by the grinding of the teeth' > 'the feeling of pain itself'.

Boyd concludes that there were four separate roots in PS, *ndr / $n\underline{d}r$ 'to vow': *ndr A 'to roll/pour down', *ndr B 'be strange, odd', *nzr 'to bite'. AH נזר derives from the last of these, which developed from 'bite' (the meaning was retained in the Eth languages) to 'separate, consecrate', and to 'curse, insult' in Akk, 'despise: be little' in Arb. He sees Ug $mn\underline{d}r$, OArm nzr as dialectal aberrations (d > $\underline{d}$ __/r), and therefore irrelevant, and believes that OldBab $nad\bar{a}rum$ must be a WSem loan since it is preserved alongside Akk $naz\bar{a}ru$. Arb $na\underline{d}ir$ is irrelevant as the root covers concepts of both vowing and consecrating: he believes that the latter was absorbed into ndr by a loan translation from NWSem through theological influence. נזר and נדר in AH moved together semantically once the semantic shift 'biting' > 'cursing' > 'separating/consecrating' had taken place.

Boyd's arguments are moderately convincing on the philological level, but the semantic development ('bite' > 'consecrate') seems strained. He does not cover the noun נֵזֶר specifically, but his treatment would suggest that he regards the two usages of נֵזֶר ('hairgrowth' and 'diadem') as derived from the same root, and sharing the same meaning originally. Berlinerblau supports him, however, as Boyd's philological analysis matches Berlinerblau's distinction between נדר and נזר (on which the latter takes issue with Cartledge [1992:23]):

a) נדר is to vow positively, i.e. at some time in the future to make an offering to the deity in return for the granting of the vower's petition,

b) נזר is to vow negatively, to consecrate one's person to the Lord with no demands, and for a fixed time.

However, Berlinerblau does not comment on Boyd's idea that PS *nzr meant 'to bite', nor on the meaning of the noun נֵזֶר.

A.4 J. Huehnergard and J. Hackett (personal communication) take the more traditional view espoused by Keller (1976:39–43) and Gibson (1978:4; 1975:4). They comment that נזר is the expected form in OldArm, the spelling for [$n\underline{d}ar$], and that this form was also the original one in AH for vowing. It was later displaced by the borrowing (from Ug or Arm) נדר, which took over the general semantic field of positive vowing, 'devotion, commitment, pledge', while the older form נזר was left to cover the more restricted and specialised field of negative vowing, 'restriction, abstinence, self-denial > consecration'. In support of this they point out that the נֵזֶר or hair offering can be compared with Ph and Ug *mndr*, a 'votive offering' rather than a vow.

A.5 There is the possibility of a relationship of נֵזֶר with זֵר, 'circlet, border, band', a noun found very frequently in Ex (chapters 25, 30 and 37) to describe a feature added to the ark and altars in the Tabernacle, and perhaps derived from זרר, 'to press'. There also exist RH זֵיר, and Syr *zirā*, a crescent-shaped ornament worn by women and camels (Payne Smith 1119). This would provide quite a good semantic parallel to the נֵזֶר worn by priests and kings. In fact, Pesh Ex translates זֵר as *klilā*, the word used in Pesh for נֵזֶר (see § 4 *Versions*).

B.1 Milgrom (1991:511–13) follows the suggestion of Görg (1977) that the etymology is from Eg *nzr.t* 'snake goddess', or Eg *nśr.t* 'flame', both describing the Uraeus serpent projecting from Pharaoh's crown, an apotropaic device to which AH נֵזֶר in Lv 8.9, Ex 29.6; 39.30 could be compared because of the expiatory powers hinted at in Ex 28.38 for its synonym צִיץ, as interpreted in tPesah 6.5, mPesah 7.7: the צִיץ effects acceptance of the Passover offering in the event of its uncleanness. However, J. Baines (personal communcation) rejects an Eg etymology because the word is used in Eg only in a metaphorical sense. Moreover, Eg *z* disappeared around 2500 BCE. So at present it is safer to assume a NWSem etymology for נֵזֶר.

Milgrom's support of Görg's etymology would also imply that he sees no connection between נֵזֶר denoting a priestly or royal headdress and נֵזֶר of the Nazirite, but in fact his definition of the word נֵזֶר as 'dedication, consecration', with root meaning 'to keep apart (for sacred purposes)', suggests that he does see a connection between the two, at least on the synchronic level.

2. Formal characteristics

A.1 *qitl*-type segholate noun (Barth 1894: § 21; GK § 84; JM § 88C*h*).

Whatever the historical relation between the two roots נזר and נדר, each of them possesses a segholate noun in AH: נֵזֶר and נֵדֶר / נֶדֶר.

A.2 *נָזַר exists in BH only in the niph and hiph 'dedicate oneself' + לְ, or 'abstain from' + מִן (though the reading giving the hiph form in Lv 15.31 is sometimes said to be from זהר), as a denominative hiph in Nu 6 'be a Nazirite', and a noun נָזִיר. In contrast, נָדַר exists only in the qal. This may support the view that the two roots are related forms existing in the same general semantic field in AH, but occupying specific areas within that field.

A.3 The noun מִנְזָר may mean 'consecrated one', Na 3.17 (מִנְּזָרַיִךְ), though König (1895:II, 1, 90) revocalised as *מִנְזָרַיִךְ, 'crowned'.

3. Syntagmatics

A.1 a) A priestly or royal נֵזֶר can be the obj of נתן qal (Ex 29.6, 2Kg 11.12 //2Ch 23.11), עשׂה qal (Ex 39.30), שׂים qal (Lv 8.9), לקח qal (2Sm 1.10), חלל pi (Ps 89.40), and one of the objects of hiph בוא (2Sm 1.10)

b) A Nazirite נֵזֶר can be the obj of גלח hitp (Nu 6.19), גזז qal (Jr 7.29), and the presumed obj of שׁלח hiph (Jr 7.29).

A.2 A priestly or royal נֵזֶר is the subj of צִיץ hiph (Ps 132.18).

A.3 a) A priestly or royal נֵזֶר is the *nomen regens* of קֹדֶשׁ (Ex 29.6, 39.30; Lv 8.9), שֶׁמֶן (Lv 21.12). With suf: Ps 132.18, 89.40 (3 m sg, referring to 'your anointed one'/'your servant'): very frequent in Nu 6 (4,5,8,9,12[2x],13,18[2x], 19, 21[2x]). 2psf suf in Jr 7.29.

b) A Nazirite נֵזֶר is the *nomen regens* of אלהים + 3psm suf (Nu 6.7).

A.4 a) A priestly or royal נֵזֶר is the *nomen rectum* of צִיץ (Ex 39.30) (but cf. Lv 8.9), אֲבָנִים (Zc 9.16).

b) A Nazirite נֵזֶר is the *nomen rectum* of יָמִים (Nu 6.4,8,12,13), נֶדֶר (Nu 6.5), רֹאשׁ (Nu 6.9,18[2x]), תּוֹרָה (Nu 6.21).

A.5 a) The *preposition* עַל is often used with נֵזֶר and indicates position: Ex 29.6, Lv 8.9 on the מִצְנֶפֶת; Lv 21.12 on the priest; 2Sm 1.10 on Saul's head, 2Kg 11.12//2Ch 23.11 on king Joash's head, Ps 132.18 on the king, Nu 6.7 on the Nazirite's head.

b) In Nu 6.21 עַל governs נֵזֶר.

A.6 A Nazirite נֵזֶר can be טָמֵא (Nu 6.12). A נֵזֶר is not forever, Pr 27.24 (assuming MT to be correct: see Text doubtful).

B.1 The immediate grammatical context is lacking for the occurrences from Q, so they cannot be classified from a syntagmatic point of view.

4. Versions

LXX:

A.1 Ex 29.6 τὸ πέταλον (τὸ ἁγίασμα) i.e. identification of צִיץ with נֵזֶר, cf. Lv 8.9 (τὸ πέταλον τὸ χρυσοῦν) τὸ καθηγιασμένον (ἅγιον).

A.2 In Lv 21.12 also the idea of sanctity is prominent: τὸ ἅγιον (ἔλαιον τὸ χριστόν), and hence Zc 9.16 נֵזֶר (אַבְנֵי) as (λίθοι) ἅγιοι, Ps 89.40; τὸ ἁγίασμα Ps 132.18

A.3 In Nu 6, although the translator could distinguish between the roots נזר and נדר, as demonstrated in Nu 6.2, where εὔχομαι εὐχήν is used for נדר, and ἀφαγνίζομαι ἁγνείαν for נזר, he frequently treats the two as synonymous by using εὐχή for נזר (Nu 6.4,7,8,9,12[1],13,18[1],19, 21[1]), and even by conflating them: Nu 6.5, where ἁγνισμοῦ stands for נדר נזרו (assuming the translator had a text as MT). The verb נזר is also usually translated by εὔχομαι but in Nu 6.12[1] by ἁγιάζομαι, and the noun by ἁγνεία in Nu 6.21[2]. (See further on the similar treatment of נזיר in LXX in Mayer 1986:330). Jr 7.29 depends on the sense of Nu 6 for its rendering of זרך as τὴν κεφαλήν σου, and the connection is made explicit by Sym τὴν κόμην τῆς ναζιραιότητος σου.

A.4 Non-priestly, non-Nazirite occurrences are treated with less certainty by LXX translators. 2Sm 1.10 τὸ βασίλειον is suitably vague, and the rendering is taken up by 2Ch 23.11. However, the reading of the Lucianic recension for 2 Sm 1.10, also found in Sym and Thd, is διάδημα. Aq has ἀφόρισμα here, and τὸ ἀφωρισμένον at 2Kg 11.12, whereas Sym has τὸ ἅγιον and Luc τὸ ἁγίασμα (cf. section A.1).

A.5 The later Gr versions tend to link together the two types of נֵזֶר, Nazirite and headdress, by using similar terms for them. However, the revisers do not agree with one another, each preferring a particular nuance of the root:

Sym likes the word ἄθικτον, 'untouchable, not to be touched', for Lv 8.9; 21.12, but also uses τὸ ἅγιον (2Kg 11.12) and ὁ ἁγιασμός (Ps 132.18). For Jr 7.29 he has the expression τὴν τρίχα τὴν ἁγίαν τῆς ναζιραιότητός σου for נִזְרֶךָ. Aq prefers the notion of setting apart, ἀφόρισμα, at Lv 21.12, cf. his use of ὁ ἀφωρισμένος for 'Nazirite' (Nu 6.18), probably also at Ex 29.6 (under the siglum ὁ ἑβρ´), 2Kg 11.12, Ps 132.18. Other, anonymous Gr renderings mention the idea of abstinence (τῆς ἐγκρατείας, Nu 6.4, cf. the rendering of נָזִיר as ὁ ἐγκρατής in Nu 6.18.

B.1 Dorival (1995:93) questions whether the Heb Vorlage of LXX Numbers had נזר as often as MT, because of the relative frequency of εὐχή and derivatives which would tend to represent נדר. In contrast there is no obvious rendering of נָזִיר, even though נזר is rendered by ἁγνεία etc. He explains this phenomenon by postulating two different redactions of ch. 6, that underlying MT being more 'institutional', and that behind LXX less institutional and less juridical. There are a number of objections to this theory. First, it assumes that the translator would always have rendered word for word; second that he would not have confused נדר and נזר orthographically or semantically; third that a single Gr word existed which could satisfactorily sum up the concept of Naziriteship (and considering the number of terms that the later revisers of LXX employ, this is unlikely). A more probable explanation for the phenomenon is that the translator was fully conscious of the overlap in sense and sound of נזר and נדר, and opted for εὐχή etc. as having the best catch-all meaning in this passage where most occurrences of נזר are concerned with the period of Naziriteship and the dedication of hairgrowth. At the same time the LXX translator shows awareness of the abstract meaning "consecration" of the root נזר by using the rendering ἀφαγνίσασθαι ἁγνείαν at the beginning of the passage (v.2) and κατὰ νόμον ἁγνείας at the end (v.21). In short, it is unnecessary to posit a variant Heb Vorlage for LXX to explain the frequent rendering of נֵזֶר by εὐχή in Nu 6.

Vg
A.1 Jerome does not have much to add to our knowledge of the ancient understanding of נֵזֶר, since in keeping with his usual practice he follows LXX or the Three for the meaning of נֵזֶר according to its context. He translates each phrase *ad sensum*, not word-for-word, and in places describing the priestly and Nazirite נֵזֶר he brings out the sense of sanctity or consecration:
    Ex 29.6 *lamminam sanctam* אֶת־נֵזֶר־הַקֹּדֶשׁ (cf. LXX πέταλον)
    Ex 39.30 (29 Vg) *lamminam sacrae venerationis* צִיץ נֵזֶר־הַקֹּדֶשׁ
    Lv 8.9 *lamminam auream consecratam in sanctificationem* אֵת צִיץ הַזָּהָב נֵזֶר־הַקֹּדֶשׁ
    Lv 21.12 *oleum sanctae unctionis* נֵזֶר שֶׁמֶן מִשְׁחַת.
    A.2 Jerome varies the rendering of נֵזֶר in Nu 6, with nuances of 'consecration' (6.4,7,9,13,18,21), 'separation' (6.5,8,12, cf. Aq), 'sanctification' (12,21), which has the interesting translation of עַל תּוֹרַת נִזְרוֹ as *ad perfectionem sanctificationis suae*.
    A.3 He follows LXX for his rendering of Ps 132.18, *sanctificatio*, Zc 9.16 *(lapides) sancti*, Luc/Sym/Thd at 2Sm 1.10 for *diadema*, and extends the usage

to the headdresses in 2Kg 11.12, 2Ch 23.11, Ps 89.40. In Jr 7.29 he uses the rather ordinary word *capillum*, 'hair'.

B.1 LXX 2Kg 11.12 ιεζερ (without an article) is a transliteration, presumably a corruption of *νεζερ, as the rendering of Syh (*n*ᵓ*zr*) suggests. Such transliterations are the hallmark of the 'Theodotionic' recension, which covers this part of 4Kgdm, cf. Thd Lv 21.12 νάζερ.

B.2 נֵזֶר in Pr 27.24 is rendered by a verb in LXX, παραδίδωσιν. It is not clear how the translator arrived at this. Pesh Pr 27.24 *mšallem* must derive from LXX, and TgPr Pr 27.24 *šlm* is from Pesh (Tg Pr is based on Pesh Pr in its entirety).

Tg

A.1 Tg (Pentateuch): When used of a royal or priestly headdress, כְּלִילָא, 'crown', whereas in Nu 6 נִזְרָא is used throughout. TgO Lv 21.12 uses the expression נֵזֶר שֶׁמֶן מְשַׁח רְבוּתָא 'the crown of the oil of anointing' for נֵזֶר שֶׁמֶן מִשְׁחַת (אלהיו) TgPsJ and TgNeo use similar equivalents (TgNeo נִזְרוּתָא for נִזְרָא), except in Nu 6.7 where כְּלִילָא appears unexpectedly in both.

A.2 Tg (Prophets): Royal headdress: 2Sm 1.10, 2Kg 11.12 כְּלִילָא, cf. 2Ch 23.11 כְּלִילָא דְמַלְכוּתָא, 'crown of the kingdom'

A.3 Tg (Hagiographa): TgPs uses כְּלִילָא in the royal psalms Ps 89.40, 132.18.

B.1 Jr 7.29 רַבְרְבָךְ 'your nobles' (figurative, perhaps from nobles being the 'crown' or 'head' of the people?), Zc 9.16 אֵיפוֹדָא (identifying the stones as those of the high priest's breastplate).

Pesh

A.1 There are two main terms corresponding to the two main senses of נֵזֶר, *klilā* 'crown' and *nzirutā*, 'naziriteship', the latter a borrowing from BH via JAram. However, the distinction in Pesh is not clear-cut, and there is also some evidence of LXX influence. The similarities to the renderings of Tg are also apparent, and may go beyond what we might expect from the closeness of the two forms of Arm.

A.2 a) *klilā* 'crown' Ex 29.6, Lv 8.9; 21.12, Nu 6.7!, 2Sm 1.10, 2Kg 11.12, Ps 89.40. A variant similar in meaning is *tāgā* (2Ch 23.11) a borrowing from Pers referring to the monarch's crown.

b) *nzirutā* 'naziriteship' Ex 39.30! (where צִיץ is translated as *klilā*), Nu 6.4,5,8,9,12(2x),13,18(2x),19,21(2x).

A.3 *šaʿrā* 'hair' Jr 7.29 — contextual? Cf. Vg ad loc.

A.4 *qaddišātā* 'holy things' Zc 9.16, *quds̆(y)* 'my sanctuary' Ps 132.18 cf. LXX ad loc.

5. Lexical/Semantic Field

A.1 Taking all occurrences of נֵזֶר together, the words מִצְנֶפֶת / קֹדֶשׁ / טָמֵא : נֶדֶר / נָזִיר / רֹאשׁ; צִיץ often appear in the same contexts as נֵזֶר. These would suggest that נֵזֶר belongs in the realm of the cult and ritual, as an item to do with cultic and royal adornment. The term in some places means something sacred to the

Lord placed on the head, in others it refers to the hairgrowth of the head dedicated to God, so there is a semantic overlap as well as homonymity in the corpus of AH even if the two uses turn out to be derived ultimately from separate and unrelated roots.

A.2 In Ps 89 and 132 the word בְּרִית appears in synonymous parallelism to נֵזֶר, and בֹּשֶׁת in antithetical parallelism. These again suggest that נֵזֶר was symbolic of kingship and rank. חֹסֶן 'wealth' (Pr 27.24) also occurs in parallel, but the verse as a whole is difficult to interpret and emendation had been suggested (see Introduction, Text Doubtful). כסא, כבוד and בגדי רוקמות occur in a list with נזר ק[ודש] in 4QIsᵃ 8-10 1.19: all are royal accoutrements.

A.3 Milgrom (1991:511–13), in accordance also with ancient tradition (see Versions A), regards צִיץ and נֵזֶר as synonymous in Lv 8.9, from a comparison with Ex 28.36 צִיץ זָהָב טָהוֹר, Ex 29.6 וְנָתַתָּ אֶת־נֵזֶר הַקֹּדֶשׁ עַל־הַמִּצְנֶפֶת, Ex 39.30 צִיץ נֵזֶר־הַקֹּדֶשׁ זָהָב טָהוֹר: Lv has conflated Ex 28 and 29. Is Ps 132.18 (וְעָלָיו יָצִיץ נִזְרוֹ) an allusion to, or pun on, Lv 8.9? Dahood's rendering 'will sparkle' (cf. Ug ṣṣ 'salt mine' [1970:249]) suggests that there is an allusion to the appearance of the נֵזֶר.

6. Exegesis

A.1 Milgrom (1991:511–13) and Mayer (1986:329–34), along with most scholars, define נֵזֶר as meaning 'dedication, consecration', with the root meaning 'to keep apart (for sacred purposes)': Milgrom sees a Nazir as someone set apart by his abstentions or by his high rank (Nu 6, Gn 49.26, Dt 33.16). The king therefore wore a נֵזֶר on his head as a sign of consecration.

A.2 Licht (1962:399–408) takes the view that the Nazirite נֵזֶר and diadem נֵזֶר are unrelated. He provides a picture of a woman wearing a crown which is labelled as a נֵזֶר, but one should note that the available occurrences of the word do not mention נֵזֶר being worn by a woman, only by a priest or a king. In this it may differ from עֲטָרָה, which does seem to have been worn by women and non-royals. Licht also suggests that Nah 3.17 מִנְּזָרַיִךְ refers to administrators wearing the נֵזֶר.

A.3 Levine (1993:220) states that 'the Seghollate [sic] noun *nēzer* "Naziriteship, restriction" is probably unrelated to *nēzer*, "crown, diadem"'. נֵזֶר is a term covering the restrictions on his life that the Nazirite undertakes (abstention from vine products, shaving, and contact with the dead) in Nu 6.12, and also the hair which he allows to grow and dedicates to God in Nu 6.7,9,18,19.

A.4 *Ritual*   In the case of the Nazirite of Nu 6 the נֵזֶר of hair reserved uncut as an offering to the Lord can be defiled by the Nazirite's contact with a dead body. The high priest must not leave the sanctuary when he is on duty or pollute it in any way because the נֵזֶר of oil, the anointing of his God, is upon him (Lv 21.12), and vv.10–11 prohibit him from contracting uncleanness from corpses, tearing his clothes or letting his hair become unkempt, even for close relatives, because of his anointing and the priestly garments he wears. Mayer (1986:332) sees the prohibition on defilement as arising from the consecration to the Lord common to both high priest and Nazirite, and he notes that both Nu 6 and Lv 21 derive from the Priestly circle.

A.5 This sort of defilement apparently does not occur with the royal נֵזֶר, since it is taken from the body of the dead or dying Saul and offered to David without any qualm. However, the occurrence at Ps 89.40 speaks of the Lord himself defiling (חלל pi) the royal נֵזֶר 'to the ground', which could mean either 'utterly' (Dahood 1968:202, 318, following Winton Thomas 1953:210–19) or even that it is thrown to the ground and defiled by this means. So there do appear to be some similarities between all types of נֵזֶר regarding the importance of keeping them from becoming טָמֵא or suffering profanation, חלל.

A.6 *Form* Following ancient tradition, Milgrom (1991:511–13) regards the high priestly נֵזֶר in Lv 8.9 as = צִיץ, usually understood as 'flower', 'blossom'. This may mean that the נֵזֶר was either rosette-shaped (the change of rendering in NSRV from 'rosette' Ex 30.36 to 'ornament' Lv 8.9 is unwarranted since the Heb wording is virtually identical), or that it flashed and shone, boosting the apotropaic properties given by the engraving 'Holy to the Lord' on it. Similar remarks might be made about the occurrence in Ps 132.18, the verb יָצִיץ suggesting that the royal נֵזֶר resembled the priestly one in shape or reflective properties. Elliger (1966:112) sees the golden flower as a later form of the diadem. However, the traditional interpretation of the priestly נֵזֶר is as a plate, cf. LXX πέταλον; Vg *lammina*; bShabb 63b: a gold plate of two fingers' breadth, running from ear to ear; Josephus: a gold plate engraved with the name of God, τελαμὼν ... χρύσεος (*Ant.* 3.178). Mayer (1986:333) describes the נֵזֶר as a metal fillet with holes for ties, and some decoration, such as rosettes, imitation flowers or precious stones. Caspari (1926:396) takes it as a special headdress to hold the hair in the desired style.

The high priest wore his נֵזֶר over his turban in active service on the sanctuary or Temple. Licht (1962:399–408) suggests that the form of נֵזֶר was a strip of gold that went around the מִצְנֶפֶת: this idea has the advantage of making it possible for a king to wear it on the battlefield, as in the case of Saul, perhaps over a helmet. However, Caspari (1926:396) regards the נֵזֶר as a hairband, a traditional item that became an indicator of royalty and was worn by the king instead of a helmet. Conversely, Caquot and de Robert (1994:367) regard the reference to the נֵזֶר as an anachronism, devised by the writer to denote David as Saul's successor, since the נֵזֶר is later part of the royal insignia of the Jerusalemite royal dynasty, cf. 2Kg 11.12; Ps 89.40; 132.18.

A.7 Zc 9.16 mentions (precious) stones sparkling in the diadem (אַבְנֵי־נֵזֶר מִתְנוֹסְסוֹת), which may also refer to reflective properties of the נֵזֶר. Alternatively, the gem-studded נֵזֶר may represent a late development where נֵזֶר is more like a conventional crown in form. Pr 27.24, another later text, uses נֵזֶר in a non-ritual context in parallel to 'wealth' in the context of one's agricultural property. Without resorting to emendation immediately, perhaps this again shows that נֵזֶר developed to become almost synonymous with 'crown': on the other hand the Versions do not register any kind of crown here, so perhaps emendation is advisable.

A.8 Lv 21.12 appears to refer to the anointing of priests generally, and not to the high priest's golden נֵזֶר, but this leads us to the thought that perhaps both the priestly and royal forms of נֵזֶר were a permanent token of the bearer's original anointing at his appointment. However, there is no support for this in 2Kg 11.12//2Ch 23.11, unless 'putting the נֵזֶר upon him' (2Kg 11.12) refers to an act of anointing with oil followed by the placing of a gold נֵזֶר on the head as a perpetual reminder.

A.9   The two Q occurrences represent both royal and priestly נֵזֶר. 4QpIs^a 8-10 1.19 speaks of the scion of David, and it seems that he will receive a glorious throne, a holy diadem, and variegated garments. This indicates some sort of enthronement ceremony. 1QSb 4 1.28 is part of the blessing of the Zadokite priests, and although there is a lacuna immediately before the word נֵזֶר, it appears to be in a cultic context because of the mention of the Holy of Holies.

A.10   *Nazirites*   The נֵזֶר of Nu 6 is usually defined according to context as either the period of special consecration to the Lord or to the hairgrowth specially consecrated to the Lord. It is possible, however, for the second definition to fit every context: 'consecrated hairgrowth', which is also a visible sign of the individual's consecration to God. It is not really necessary to postulate a more abstract definition of the word. The suggested emendation in Nu 6.2 would make good sense, as it would yield the meaning, 'when a man or woman makes a special vow to dedicate hairgrowth to the Lord' (אִישׁ אוֹ־אִשָּׁה כִּי יַפְלִא לִנְדֹּר נֶדֶר נֵזֶר לְהַזִּיר לִיהוה).

A.11   Later Jewish tradition appears to regard the two uses of נֵזֶר as related. In NumRabbah 10 the Nazirite's long hair is described as a crown, עֲטָרָה, but this could also be understood as a deliberate linking of the two uses in order to show that although long hair is normally seen as a disfigurement (especially in the light of mNaz 2.6, according to which the Nazirite's hair was not allowed to be combed!), its dedication to God makes it something glorious.

Art and Archaeology

From the point of view of archaeological artefacts, possible examples of this type of headgear would be the figured gold strips and the circular floral emblem found in sites to the south of Gaza, the former resembling the royal נֵזֶר and the latter the priestly נֵזֶר / צִיץ. (See Galling 1977:288, figure 75 [22–24].) The figured strips date from the fourteenth/thirteenth centuries and the floral emblem from the tenth/ninth centuries BCE. The same strips and other similar headbands can be found in Maxwell-Hyslop (1971:226), and Plates 202, 203.

7. Conclusion

It is hazardous to attempt a complete synthesis of the significances of נֵזֶר in case the meaning developed over time, but nonetheless it may be helpful to see if there is a basic meaning behind the word in its different occurrences.

On the synchronic level, an underlying sense common to all occurrences of נֵזֶר could be *a visible sign that the wearer had been consecrated to God*; a sign on the head marking out the bearer as being in a special relationship to the Deity. However, it is clear from the contexts in which it is found that there are three different objects denoted by the term נֵזֶר, two of which may be related in that they are some kind of ornament worn on the head, while the third refers to consecrated, uncut hair. Lv 21.12 is exceptional in appearing to refer to an abstract concept of consecration, unless this consecration is thought of as represented by the golden, priestly נֵזֶר, i.e. the '*diadem* of the anointing oil of his God'.

The two types of נֵזֶר certainly have elements in common in AH: *visible mark, sign of consecration to the Lord, connection with the head, vulnerability to defilement.* The biblical writers imply a common semantic background even when the word clearly denotes different objects. The influence of the Priestly circle on some passages should also be borne in mind: even the parallels 2Kg 11.12, 2Ch 23.11 involve the placing of the נֵזֶר on the king by a priest.

From an historical point of view it is harder to trace back with certainty the development of two such different meanings, 'diadem' and 'consecrated hair', from a common root, especially given the problems of the relationship between נדר and נֵזֶר.

BIBLIOGRAPHY

Albright, W.F. 1942. A votive stele erected by Ben-Hadad I of Damascus to the god Melcarth. *BASOR* 87:23–29.

Barth, J. 1894. *Die Nominalbildung in den semitischen Sprachen.* Leipzig.

Berlinerblau, J. 1996. *The Vow and the 'Popular Religious Groups' of Ancient Israel: A Philological and Sociological Inquiry.* JSOTSS 210. Sheffield.

Blau, J. 1977. 'Weak' phonetic change and the Hebrew *šin. Hebrew Annual Review* 1:81–110.

Boyd, J.L. 1986. The etymological relationship between NDR and NZR reconsidered. *UF* 17:61–75.

Caquot, A., and P. de Robert. 1994. Commentary on *Samuel* (CAT).

Cartledge, T.W. 1992. *Vows in the Hebrew Bible and the Ancient Near East.* JSOTSS 147; Sheffield.

Caspari, D.W. 1926. Commentary on *Samuel* (KAT).

Cogan, M., and H. Tadmor. 1988. Commentary on *Kings* (AB).

Dahood, M. 1968. Commentary on *Psalms* II (AB).

———. 1970. Commentary on *Psalms* (AB).

Dorival, G. 1995. L'originalité du livre grec des Nombres. 89–107 in *VIII Congress of the International Organization for Septuagint and Cognate Studies, Paris 1992,* ed. L. Greenspoon and O. Munnich. SBLSCS 4. Atlanta, GA.

Dunand, M. 1939. Stèle araméenne dédiée à Melqart. *Bullétin du Musée de Beyrouth* 3:65–76.

———. 1942. A propos de la stèle de Melqart du Musée d'Alep. *Bullétin du Musée de Beyrouth* 6:41–45.

Elliger, K. 1966. Commentary on *Leviticus.*(HzAT).

Fronzaroli, P. 1965. Studi sul lessico comune semitico IV. *Atti della Accademia Nazionale dei Lincei. Rendiconti* series VIII/ 20:246–61.

Galling, K. [2]1977. Article 'Schmuck' in *BRL*[2], 282–89.

Gemser, B. 1937. Commentary on *Proverbs* (HzAT).

Gibson, J.C.L. 1975. *Textbook of Syrian Semitic Inscriptions* II. *Aramaic Inscriptions including inscriptions in the dialect of Zenjirli.* Oxford.

Ginsberg, H.L. 1945. Psalms and inscriptions of petition and acknowledgment. 159–71 in *Louis Ginzberg Jubilee Volume* AAJR. New York.

Görg, M. 1976. Die Kopfbedeckung des Hohepriesters. *BN* 3:24–26.

———. 1977. 'Weiteres zu nzr ('Diadem') *BN* 4:7–8.

Keller, C.A. 1976. Article נדר in *TH* II:39–43.

Kühlewein, J. 1976. Article נזיר in *TH* II:50–53.

Leslau, W. 1956. *Etudes descriptive et comparative du Gafat*. Paris.

Levi della Vida, G. 1943. Some notes on the stele of Ben-Hadad. *BASOR* 90:30–32.

Levine, B.A. 1993. Commentary on *Numbers*.(AB).

Licht, Y.Sh. 1962. Article כתר ועטרה in *EM* IV:399–408.

Maxwell-Hyslop, K. 1971. *Western Asiatic Jewellery c. 3,000–612 B.C.* London.

Milgrom, J. 1991. Commentary on *Leviticus*.1-16 (AB).

Mayer, G. 1986. Article נזר in *TWAT* V:329–34.

Priebatsch, H.Y. 1980. Spiranten und Aspiratae in Ugarit, AT und Hellas. *UF* 12:317–33.

Plöger, O. 1983. Commentary on *Proverbs* (BK).

Rabin, Ch. 1970. La correspondance *d* hébreu — *d̲* arabe. 290–97 in *Mélanges Marcel Cohen: études de linguistique, ethnographie et sciences connexes offertes par ses amis et ses élèves à l'occasion de son 80ème anniversaire* ed. D. Cohen. The Hague/Paris.

Scott, R.B.Y. 1965. Commentary on *Proverbs* and *Ecclesiastes* (AB).

Winton Thomas, D. 1953. A consideration of some unusual ways of expressing the superlative in Hebrew. *VT* 3:209–24.

Alison Salvesen
University of Oxford

נָקַב II

Introduction

Grammatical Type: vb, qal.
Occurrences: Total 3x OT (Lv 24.11, 16a, 16b), 0x Sir, 0x Qum, 0x inscr.
Text doubtful: none.
Qere/Ketiv: none.

1. Root and Comparative Material

A.1 The root of נָקַב II is disputed. It may be the same vb as נָקַב I, "to pierce", which may also have the meaning "to name" (e.g. Nu 1.17, Is 62.2), and *HAL* places the three occurrences of נָקַב in Lv 24 mentioned above under the same entry as it (679). Alternatively, the root may be a by-form of קָבַב (BDB:666), which is often thought (e.g. Ringgren 1977:1138) itself to be derived from the vb נָקַב I (see קָבַב, section 1. Root and Comparative Material).

A.2 Cognates in other languages will depend on from which of the above the word is derived.

B.1 If the impf form in Lv 24.11 thought to be of נָקַב II is actually derived from קָבַב (Bertholet 1901:85), it could be understood as a case of impf doubling, common in Arm (GK:§ 67 *g*). This derivation would not explain, however, the ptc (נֹקֵב) and inf (נָקְבוֹ) forms in Lv 24.16. Bertholet sees a play on the roots קָבַב and נָקַב as explaining the inf in 16b, but there is no evidence to confirm this word-play.

2. Formal Characteristics

A.1 Pe-Nun, triliteral root.

B.1 [nil]

3. Syntagmatics

A.1 The direct object of נָקַב is שֵׁם [of the Lord] (Lv 24.11, 16a, 16b).

B.1 [nil]

4. Versions

a. LXX: ἐπονομάζω (Lv 24.11), ὀνομάζω (Lv 24.16a, 16b)
b. Pesh: *prš* (Lv 24.11, 16a, 16b)
c. Targum:

> TgO – פרש (Lv 24.11, 16a, 16b)
> TgPsJ – פרש וחרף (Lv 24.11, 16a), חרף (Lv 24.16b)
> TgNeo – פרש וגדפין (Lv 24.11, 16a, 16b)
> TgNeoMg – חרף (Lv 24.11), בזה (24.16a)

TgFrg (P, V & N) – חרף (Lv 24.11)
d. Vulgate: *blasphemare* (Lv 24.11, 16a, 16b)

A.1 The LXX understands the lexeme to mean uttering the name of God, with its translation of "to name", whilst the Vg renders the result of uttering the name, that is "to blaspheme". One codex of the LXX contains the reading λοιδορέω, "to rebuke, revile", in Lv 24.16, the vb chosen by Sym to render קלל in 24.16 (Field 1875:vol. 1, 210). In that same codex we also find at Lv 19.14 לא־תקלל translated by the doublet οὐ καταράσῃ, οὐ λοιδορήσεις.

A.2 The Pesh continues the tradition that the lexeme means "to utter", using a vb (פרש) cognate to the Arm of TgO.

A.3 The Tgs reflect a combination of the interpretations of the LXX and Vg. They avoid using the word "curse" in relation to God and hence use other renderings for נקב. This can also be seen in the way TgO in this passage renders קלל by the aphel of רגז, "to provoke", TgPsJ by רגז (in 24.11, 14) or חרף, "to blaspheme" (in 24.15), TgNeo by חרף, and TgFrg by בזי, "to despise". Likewise, the word קדם ("before") is inserted in verse 15 to avoid speaking of provoking God but rather to speak of provocation before God (cf. Tg to Nm 15). TgO understands נקב in the same way as Pesh and renders it as פרש.

A.4 TgNeo ("and pronounced with blasphemies") and PsJ ("spoke and blasphemed") in each instance appear to try to give the sense of "to curse" to נקב, while at the same time maintaining the sense of "to utter", by translating the vb as "to pronounce with blasphemies". NeoMg at Lv 24.16a translates "the name of the Lord" by "the name of the Memra of the Lord", which Hayward has shown refers in NeoMg to the pronounced tetragrammaton with its proper vowels (Hayward 1981:100–101). This may also be seen in the Test. of Moses 8.5 (Le Déaut 1979:491). Likewise, PsJ on 24.16b has the blasphemy made against "the distinguishing name" (שמא דמייחד), meaning the tetragrammaton.

A.5 The preference of TgNeoMg for בזה rather than חרף at Lv 24.16 is explicable by the association of curse words with בזה. It may be significant, for example, that the verb קבב in Sir 41.7 is in parallelism with the phrase היה בוז. קלל in particular develops in semantic range to include "to scorn, despise" (Kister 1983:129), such that the TgFrg (V) glosses ומקלל (Ex 21.17) as ודי מבזי. The vb קלל in Sir 3.11, 16 would similarly be best translated as "to demean". In Ml 1-2 the curse by God of his priests is related to their contempt. Priestly contempt of the divine name (בוזי שמי, Ml 1.6) leads to contempt for the priestly offering (נבזה, Ml 1.12) and finally the priests themselves (נבזים, Ml 2.9). It is also of interest that the Geez translation of Ml 3.9 uses the vb *taʿawwara*, "to be neglected, despised", where the Heb has אָרַר (see Muraoka 1993:24). In addition, the Tigre vb *qebba*, possibly cognate with קבב, has the meaning "to despise" (Leslau:46).

B.1 Commentators on the Tg (e.g. Grossfeld 1988:55; Hayward in McNamara 1994:97) conclude that the primary meaning evinced by the Tg for נקב is "to pronounce". This does not seem to be warranted by the evidence, where, in the cases of TgNeo, NfMg, Frg and PsJ and in the Vg, "blaspheming" has as much prominence as "pronouncing". Indeed, the evidence suggests that perhaps the meaning "pronounced" was later added to avoid direct blasphemy of God. For, in TgNeo to Lv 24.15 the vb קלֵּל, "to curse", is rendered also by the expression "pronounces the name of God in blasphemy".

5. Lexical/Semantic Field(s)

A.1 [see אָרַר]

A.2 In Lv 24 there seems to be an association with the verb קלֵּל, which appears a number of times in the account. It follows the phrase containing נָקַב in 24.11, and reappears in 24.14 and 15 immediately before verse 16, which has the two references to נָקַב. It can then be found again in 24.23.

B.1 [nil]

6. Exegesis

A.1 It is unclear whether we have in the three cases of Lv 24 froms derived from the verb נָקַב, "to pierce" or from a root belonging to the same semantic field as קָבַב or even as a secondary formation of קָבַב. The lexica accordingly differ in their understanding of the lexeme. BDB (866), for example, see it as an alternative form of קָבַב, and hence render it as "curse". Zorell (530), in view of its context, translates נָקַב as "*blasphemavit*", whilst Alonso Schoekel (484) combines both cursing and blaspheming in his rendering "maldecir, blasfemar". *HAL* (679) sees נָקַב in Lv 24 as an instance of the meaning "bezeichnen" for נָקַב I, and translates it as "lästern", expounding that it is "ungünstig: auszeichnen durch magische Durchbohrung".

A.2 The presence of the verb קלֵּל without an object in Lv 24.11 raises questions over the correct rendering of נָקַב, and over the redaction of the verse. Brichto (1963:145–146) is uncomfortable with the repetition of thought in the verses if נָקַב is understood to be a derivative of קָבַב. As the denotation of נָקַב is nowhere else in doubt, he takes it in Lv to mean "to specify", deriving from נָקַב I (see Root and Comparative Material **A.1**). The contrast drawn in verses 15 and 16 is between one who curses in general, and one who does so by actually specifying the name of the Lord. Likewise, Hartley suggests (unconvincingly) that since the object of נָקַב is שֵׁם, it is probably a weaker term than קלֵּל, meaning "to name" or "to designate" rather than "to curse" (1992:408).

A.3 Weingreen (1972:118–123) suggests that verse 16 clarifies that it refers to uttering the divine name, rather than to blaspheming, by the presence of the inf נָקְבוֹ (although see Root and Comparative Material **B.1**). He cites TgO and m.Sanh VII 5 in support of this interpretation, although the rabbinic (see below) and versional evidence is more ambiguous than he suggests.

A.4 The Talmud debates from which of the two roots the lexeme in Lv 24.16 is derived (bSanh 56a), although the Mishna appears to suggest that it indicates the pronouncing of the name, and hence from the root נָקַב (mSanh VII 5: יפרשׁ השׁם). Likewise, TgO understands it in this sense (see Versions **A.3**). The Talmudic passage shows awareness of three meanings of נָקַב: to blaspheme, to pierce (here considered as piercing a hole in parchment containing the divine name) and to name.

A.5 The Mekhilta de R. Ishmael (Nezikin 5:98–105) presupposes that the lexeme in Lv 24.16 means to curse. The verse is quoted as a proof-text in a discussion of cursing (קִלֵּל) by means of the tetragrammaton. The same is true of Mekhilta de R. Simeon b. Yohai p. 173, and pSanh VII 5.

A.6 Philo assumes that verses 15 and 16 refer to pronouncing the Name, saying that if anyone does not even blaspheme the Lord (οὐ λέγω βλασφημήσειεν εἰς ... κύριον), but only utters the name (φθέγξασθαι τοὔνομα), he should suffer the death penalty (De vita Mosis II 206–208).

B.1 Morgenstern detects a development in the law reflected in the wording of Lv 24. His argument begins with the fictitious narrative of the man of mixed parentage, which ought to have concluded with a generalized ruling to govern all subsequent cases of blasphemy. Instead, it leads on to the case of blaspheming by the pronouncing of the divine name. This, for Morgenstern, can only be an interpolation from the time of the middle post-exilic period, when God's transcendence had led to even his name being too august to pronounce. The second law of the Decalogue (i.e., the third in the more familiar numbering) was, hence, reinterpreted so that even pronouncing the name was equivalent to blasphemy (Morgenstern 1931-32:27–28). He proceeds to argue that נָקַב is properly derived from קָבַב, and with a reinterpretation of the verb as if it is derived from נָקַב I, "to name", and the insertion of the words אֶת־הַשֵּׁם, a change from blasphemy to pronouncing the divine name was effected (ibid.:29). This is speculation that cannot be substantiated. He further adds that the original wording in verse 16 was probably מקלל יהוה. If, however, he wishes the verb to be קִלֵּל, on the basis of the Decalogue, then he must account for the choice in verse 11 of the derivative from קָבַב, which led, in his opinion, to the reinterpretation.

B.2 Sifra (ʾEmor XIV: 19 p. 104B) concentrates its discussion on the use of the very divine name rather than cursing with a euphemism. As the emphasis is on the use of the divine name, it is unclear whether it understands נָקַב in the sense of articulating or cursing.

7. Conclusion

There are two possible interpretations of the meaning of נָקַב II: "to curse" or "to utter". The etymology plays a factor in its interpretation, but it cannot be proved whether it is a by-form of קָבַב or the same lexeme as נָקַב I. The redaction of Lv 24 is also important. If וַיְקַלֵּל in Lv 24.11 is seen as a later addition, then נָקַב would seem to mean "to curse", but if it is original, then to avoid repetition of cursing, it could mean "to utter". The text in its present form suggests that the uttering of the name is a form of cursing, and scholars tend to favour the meaning of נָקַב as uttering. In this they are supported by the majority of the versions and rabbinic evidence. We should not, however, be misled by later caution regarding blaspheming of the divine name, as perhaps Hartley has been (1992:408). The vb may have had this denotation (as Zorell:530; Alonso Schoekel:484). It is possible, indeed, that the vb means both "to curse" and "to utter", its meaning changing according to the context, time and redaction of the passage.

BIBLIOGRAPHY

Bertholet, A. 1901. Commentary on *Leviticus* (KHC). Tübingen/Leipzig.

Brichto, H.C. 1963. *The Problem of "Curse" in the Hebrew Bible*. *JBL* monograph series, XIII; Philadelphia.

Field, F. 1875. *Origenis Hexaplorum quae supersunt: sive Veterum interpretum Graecorum in totum Vetus Testamentum fragmenta*. Oxford.

Grossfeld, B. 1988. *The Targum Onqelos to Leviticus and the Targum Onqelos to Numbers, translated, with apparatus* (The Aramaic Bible, 8). Edinburgh.

Hartley, J.E. 1992. Commentary on *Leviticus* (WBC, 4). Dallas.

Hayward, C.T.R. 1981. *Divine Name and Presence: The Memra*. Totowa.

Kister, M. 1983. בשולי ספר בן־סירא [In the Margins of the Book of Ben Sira]. *Leš* 47:125–146.

Le Déaut, R. 1979. *Targum du Pentateuque. Traduction des deux recensions palestiniennes complétes avec introduction, parallèles, notes et index par Roger le Déaut, avec le collaboration de Jacques Robert, tome 2: Exode et Lévitique* (Sources Chrétiennes, 256). Paris.

McNamara, M. 1994. *Targum Neofiti I: Leviticus, translated, with Appendix by M. McNamara; introduction and notes by R. Hayward. Targum Pseudo-Jonathan: Leviticus, translated, with notes by M. Maher* (The Aramaic Bible, 3). Edinburgh.

Morgenstern, J.A. 1931-32. The Book of the Covenant, Part III – the Ḥuqqim. *HUCA* 8–9:1–149.

Muraoka, T. 1993. *A Greek-English Lexicon of the Septuagint (Twelve Prophets)*. Leuven.

Ringgren, H. 1977. Article קבב in *TWAT* VI:1138–1139.

Weingreen, J. 1972. The case of the blasphemer (Leviticus XXIV 10ff). *VT* 22:118–23.

James K. Aitken
University of Cambridge

עֲטָרָה

Introduction

Grammatical type: n f.

Occurrences: 23 occurrences BH (2Sm 12.30//1Ch 20.2, Is 28.1,3,5; 62.3, Jr 13.18, Ezk 16.12; 21.31; 23.42, Zc 6.11,14; Ps 21.4; Prv 4.9; 12.4; 14.24; 16.31; 17.6, Jb 19.9; 31.36, Lm 5.16, Ct 3.11, Est 8.15); 3 occurrences Sir (6.31 [A]; 45.12 [B]; 50:12 [B]); 3 occurrences Q (1QSb 4.3, 11QT 17.1; 40.11). No occurrences Ep.

Text doubtful:

A.1 Zc 6.11 עֲטָרוֹת is pl in form but described as placed on the head of a single individual: v.14 הָעֲטָרוֹת is pointed as pl abs but with sg vb. LXX and Pesh versions both have sg nouns, also Tg in v.11 (the occurrence in v.14 receives a theological translation).

a) Lipiński (1970:34–35) believes it to be an archaic or archaising form, cf. חָכְמוֹת used of Wisdom in Pr 1.20; 9.1. Similarly, Rudolph (1976:128) denies that the pl is to express size (cf Tg, 'a great crown') or that it is a collective to express a stepped crown like a papal tiara, but that it is a sg ending וֹת- as possibly also in Jb 31.36, cf. Hos 10.5 לְעֶגְוֹת. See Rignell (1950:223), Beuken (1967:275 n1).

b) Lipiński (1970:34–35) makes the alternative suggestion that the defective spelling in v.14 could represent an alternative form, cf. עֲצֶרֶת/עֲצָרָה, תִּפְאֶרֶת/תִּפְאָרָה, and v.11 may have been given a mistaken plene pl form later.

c) Amsler (1981:108f.) follows Beyse (1972:77) in understanding עֲטָרוֹת 6.11 as pl, and correcting the verb of v.14 to pl, with the result that both Joshua and Zerubbabel are crowned. Myers and Myers (1987:349-53) argue similarly that two crowns were made, since v13 suggests that both Zerubbabel and Joshua were crowned, and for that reason they read both forms as pl.

A.2 Sir 45.12: Skehan and di Lella (1987:510) emend to עטרת פז מעל מצנפתו with the Greek text, 'on his turban the diadem of gold'.

A.3 11QT 17:1: Yadin (1983:72) reconstructs [עֲ as abs. sg, Qimron (1996:27) as pl. Yadin defines the meaning as 'wreath', cf. mBikk. 3.3, jBikk. 3.3, 65c.

1. Root and Comparative Material

A.1 There is a cognate vb עטר 'to surround, encircle', qal, in BH: Ps 5.13 (surrounding with favour as with a large shield), 1Sm 23.26 (Saul's men surrounding David), though in neither case is there the implication that the action forms a complete circle. There are pi and hiph forms which may be denomv (עטר 'to crown') and refer to some sort of honorific or symbolic action (pi Ps 65.12; 8.6; 103.4; hiph Is 23.8).

The noun occurs as the PN of the wife of Jerahmeel (1Ch 2.26), presumably with the same sense as the noun (Stamm 1967:327f). pSanh II 20b says that

Jerahmeel married a gentile woman in order to be crowned through her [royal ancestry].

In the plural it is found as the name of a number of places (Nu 32.3,34,35, Josh 16.2,5; 18.13; 1Ch 2.54) perhaps referring to a ring of fencing (Elliger 1962:144, 'enclosure': *HAL* 698 'cattle pens': Kellermann 1989:30 'Kronsteine').

A.2 RH 'wreath, crown', often of flowers or vegetation, and further figurative or derived senses are found (Jastrow 1064–65). There are few royal nuances. Architectural references, e.g. 'crenellations' (Yadin 1983:171), show up in 11QT 17.1 and RH (mOhol. 14.1, mMidd. 3.8, mKelim 5.3), and also some anatomical ones (bYeb 55b, bNid 47a, tNid 6.4).

The verb עטר also exists in RH in the qal, pi, meaning 'wreathe, adorn', and in the hith and nith 'be crowned' or 'be surrounded, protected', though the latter seems to be based on the exegesis of Pr 12.4 אֵשֶׁת חַיִל עֲטֶרֶת בַּעְלָהּ and 17.6 עֲטֶרֶת זְקֵנִים בְּנֵי בָנִים, via Ps 65.12; 8.6; 103.4.

A.3 Ph and Neo-Pun ʿṭrt 'crown', often in architectural sense, e.g. Neo-Pun brʾš ʿṭr, 'au sommet du fronton' (Ferron 1966:77 line 6): see Kellermann 1989:22.

A.4 Arm/Syr: JArm ᶜᵃṭartā 'a crown', ᶜᵃṭar pe pass ptc 'distinguished', pa, ithpa, with similar meaning to RH, 'adorn, surround' (Jastrow 1065). The fact that the noun and verb in this sense occur only in JArm, and nowhere else, including Syr, strongly suggests that they are loans from AH. The native Arm root ᶜᵃṭar means 'to smoke' etc.

A.5 Akk eṭru 'headband' (*HAL* 698), possibly idru or itru, iṭru, 'a strap or band' (CAD 7:10), are considered likely cognates.

B.1 An Ug cognate has been suggested. The meaning of tlm k ʿṭrṭrt (*KTU*² 1.16 III 11) is uncertain, but Caquot (1974:561 note n) suggests 'like a crown of rows'. However, it seems likely that Caquot based his translation on knowledge of the AH word, and there is no independent confirmation of the existence of a cognate to עֲטָרָה in Ug.

B.2 The suggested cognate Akk eṭēru 'spare, rescue' is rejected by Kellermann (1989:22).

2. Formal characteristics

A.1 a) *qatal-h* (?; see BL:463 *u″*)

b) Root עטר

c) Pē Guttural

d) I Guttural: II Emphatic: III Guttural

B.1 F. of inf. of form *qăṭāl*? — 'a surrounding'? See GK § 84 *f* and n. 2: Barth 1894:87 *qăṭălat*: an AH transitive abstract noun.

3. Syntagmatics

A.1 An עֲטָרָה is generally the direct *object* of a verb:

a) Various verbs describe the placing of the עֲטָרָה on the head: נתן qal Ezk 16.12 (בְּרֹאשׁ), Ezk 23.42 (עַל), Pr 4.9 (לְ), 11QT 17.1; שׂית (לְ) qal Ps 21.4. עֲטָרָה is the presumed obj of שׂים Zc 6.11.

b) לקח qal 2Sm 12.30//1Ch 20.2; רום hiph Ezk 21.31; סור hiph Jb 19.9: all denote separation from the head (מֵעַל רֹאשׁ, 2Sm 12.30//1Ch 20.2).

c) An עֲטָרָה is created with the verbs עשׂה qal Zc 6.11; ענד qal Jb 31.36.

d) It can be the object of the denominative pi עטר Ct 3.11 (in a relative clause); in apposition to the obj. Sir 6.31.

A.2 It can be the *predicate* of ברכות עולם 1QSb 4.3; of the Lord Is 28.5, of Zion Is 62.3: with the vb 'to be' understood in Pr 12.4; 14.24; 16.31; 17.6, Sir 50.12 + סביב לו.

A.3 It may be the *subject* of ירד qal if understood as being in parallellism with מַרְאֲשׁוֹתֵיכֶם Jr 13.18; of נפל qal Lm 5.16; of היה ל Zc 6.14; and of רמס niph Is 28.3.

(For emendation of Jr 13.18, see summary in Holladay 1986:408: a) reading 'from your head' in Gk and Vg, Volz 1922:153; b) Duhm [1901:124] 'from the head/head-pieces'; c) on the basis of the alternative m and f pl forms of *rašt* 'head' in Ug, Dahood [1961:462] revocalizes as מֵרָאֲשׁוֹתֵיכֶם 'from your heads', f pl form.)

A.4 It can be addressed directly (Is 28.1 הוֹי), perhaps because it represents the wearer.

A.5 It is governed by the *preposition* בְּ when worn by a person (Ct 3.11), and possibly proleptically in list of royal garments (Est 8.15). It occurs without a preposition in the list in Sir 45.12. In phr with סביב Sir 50.12.

A.6 As *nomen regens*

i) it is often followed by the material or elements of which it consists: זָהָב (Est 8.15), פַּז (Ps 21.4, Sir 45.12), בנים (Sir 50.12),

ii) or the nomen rectum can function in an adjectival sense, 'glorious' etc. (Is 28.1,3 גֵּאוּת, Is 28.5 צְבִי; תִּפְאֶרֶת Is 62.3, Ezk 16.12, Pr 4.9, Jr 13.18, Pr 16.31, Ezk 23.42, Sir 6.31),

iii) or the nomen rectum can denote the wearer or possessor, either in a literal or metaphorical sense (מלכם 2Sm 12.30//1Ch 20.2: for vocalisation as 'their king' or 'Milcom', see Exegesis A below): רֹאשׁ Jb 19.9, Lm 5.16, בַּעְלָהּ Pr 12.4, חֲכָמִים Pr 14.4; 17.6.

4. Versions

LXX:

A.1 στέφανος 'crown' 2Sm 12.30, Is 28.1 (and οἱ λ´, Sym),3,5; 62.3, Jr 13.18, Ezk 16.12; 21.31(26) (= Sym *coronam*); 23.42; Zc 6.11,14: Ps 21(20).4; Pr 4.9; 12.4 (= Sym *klila*); 14.24; 16.31; 17.6, Jb 19.9; 31.36, Est 8.15, Lm 5.16, Ct 3.11, 1Ch 20.2, Sir 6.31; 45.12; 50.12.

A.2 κίδαρις 'diadem' Aq Sym Is 62.3.

Tg:

A.1 כְּלִילָא 'crown, wreath' 2Sm 12.30, Is 28.5 (// כִּתְרָא); 62.3 (// כִּתְרָא), Jr 13.18, Lm 5.16, 1Ch 20.2, Est (Sperber) 8.15, Ct 3.11 (+ כלל vb), Ps 21.4, Pr 4.9; 12.4; 14.24; 16.31; 17.6, Jb 19.9; 31.36.

A.2 כִּתְרָא 'crown' Is 28.1,3: Ezk 21.31; 23.42.

A.3 תֻּשְׁבְּחָא 'glory' Zc 6.14.

B.1 Tg מַלְאַךְ שְׁלִיחַ 'a messenger sent (from before Me)' Ezk 16.12 is a theological interpretation.

Pesh:

A.1 *klilā* 'crown' 2Sm 12.30, Ps 21.4, Pr 4.9; 12.4; 14.24; 16.31; 17.6; Is 28.1,3,5; 62.3, Jr 13.18, Ezk 16.12; 21.(26)31; 23.42; Zc 6.11,14; (sg for MT pl), Jb 19.9; 31.36, Lm 5.16, Ct 3.11, Est 8.15.

A.2 *tāgā* 'diadem' 1Ch 20.2.

Vg:

A.1 *diadema* 'diadem' 2Sm 12.30, Ct 3.11 (+ *coronavit* '(she) crowned' for verb).

A.2 *corona* 'crown' Is 28.1,3,5; 62.3, Jr 13.18, Ezk 16.12; 21.(26)31; 23.42; Zc 6.11,14; Ps 21.4; Prv 12.4; 14.24; 16.31; 17.6, Jb 19.9; 31.36, Est 8.15, Lm 5.16, 1Ch 20.2.

A.3 *honor* Prv 4.9.

5. Lexical and Semantic Field

A.1 Used in parallel to מִצְנֶפֶת Ezk 21.31, תִּפְאֶרֶת Prv 17.6, שִׂכְרֵי אֶפְרַיִם, Is 28.1,3, צִיץ נֹבֵל and צְבִי תִפְאַרְתּוֹ Is 28.1, צְפִירַת תִּפְאָרָה Is 28.5.

A.2 Often acts as *nomen regens* of גֵּאוּת Is 28.1,3; of צְבִי Is 28.5; of תִּפְאֶרֶת Is 62.3, Jr 13.18, Ezk 16.12.

6. Exegesis

A.1 An עֲטָרָה is usually connected with the *head*, e.g. Jb 19.9, Lm 5.16, 1QSb 4.3. (In these occurrences it is used figuratively.) The עֲטָרָה may be on someone's head (2Sm 12.30 //1Ch 20.2): one can place it on someone's head (Zc 6.11, Ezk 16.12, Ps 21.4, perhaps 11QT 17.1), or remove it from another's head (2Sm 12.30 //1 Ch 20.2; Jb 19.9).

A.2 However, it can also be held in the *hand*, Is 62.3 בְּיַד יהוה (Brettler 1989:182f), or trampled, Is 28.3.

A.3 a) An עֲטָרָה can be very heavy and made of gold (2Sm 12.30 //1Ch 20.2) or of gold and silver (Zc 6.11), and contain a precious stone (2Sm 12.30 //1Ch 20.2). Crowns can be manufactured of metal (Zc 6.11); or bound, ענד, presumably indicating a garland (Jb 31.36: e.g. Dhorme 1926:428, ET 470; Duhm 1963:425, 427; Gordis 1978:355). Often in the construct followed by the material of which it is made: gold (Est 8.15), fine gold (Ps 21.4, Sir 45.12b).

b) In Is 28.1–5 עֲטָרָה probably refers to a floral garland, because of the allusions to flowers: צִיץ נֹבֵל, צִיצַת נֹבֵל. Asen (1996:73–87) perceives some similarities to pagan *marzēaḥ* banquets in the Ancient Near East. He suggests that flowers were a luxury item in Ancient Near East, and that therefore the garlands of Is 28.1–5 are indicative of sybaritic living.

A.4 Wearers of an עֲטָרָה include:

a) *kings*: Jr 13.18. As for 2Sm 12.30, if the weight of the crown described there—a talent of gold—is to be accepted, it would be unwearable by a human: perhaps the phrase וַתְּהִי עַל רֹאשׁ דָּוִד refers to the precious stone, אֶבֶן יְקָרָה, in the crown, as the wording of 1Ch 20.2 suggests (see Slotki [1952:112], following rabbinic tradition; Smith 1912:327; Schulz 1920:139–40; McCarter 1984:II,311).

However, Stoebe (1994:313f) rejects this interpretation. Kraus (1973:31ff) thinks that the צִיץ and therefore the עֲטָרָה in Is 28.1,3 allude to the king's fillet, the prophetic message being aimed at the monarch who is out of control and unable to protect his people. But this interpetation depends on the king's wearing of a נֵזֶר which is similar to that of the high priest's decorated with a floral motif or צִיץ. Another royal wearer would be the נָשִׂיא (Ezk 21.31), referring apparently to Zedekiah, and the גְּבִירָה, probably the queen mother in Jr 13.18.

b) an idol?: 2Sm 12.30//1Ch 20.2: S.R. Driver (1913:294) suggested that since there has been no mention of a king of the Ammonites or the people themselves (the supposed referent of the m pl possessive suffix of מַלְכָּם), and in view of the LXX doublet translation. Μελχὸλ τοῦ βασιλέως αὐτῶν (variant readings Μελχόμ, Μολχόμ etc.) along with the enormous weight of the crown, the crown actually belonged to the god Milcom mentioned in 1Kg 11.5,33: see Smith (1912:327), Schulz (1920:139–40), McCarter (1984:II,311). However, Stoebe (1994:313–14) thinks that the understanding of מלכם as Milcom comes later, and that the vocalization of MT is original. (See below, on *Art*, for Ammonite crowns.)

c) *revellers*: the drunkards of Ephraim, Is 28.1,3.

e) *women*, a 'crown of glory' as a mark of a lover's or husband's favour, Ezk 16.12; 23.42.

f) bridegrooms? Solomon is described as having been crowned with an עֲטָרָה by his mother in Ct 3.11, 'on the day of his wedding, when his heart rejoiced'.

g) *high priest* - Joshua, Zc 6.11. It has perturbed scholars that Joshua seems to be granted quasi-royal status by being given a crown and possibly also a throne, but it may be that the wearing of an עֲטָרָה was not confined to the king alone (Rose 1997:29–42).

h) Mordecai, a commoner honoured by the Persian king and raised to high rank (Est 8.15).

A.5 Those bestowing crowns: God Ezk 16.12, Ps 21.4; Zechariah (at the Lord's behest) Zc 6.11; Wisdom Pr 4.9; סָבָאִים Ezk 23.42 Qere; Solomon's mother Ct 3.11; priests? — 11QT 17.1.

A.6 Used metaphorically, עֲטָרָה is a *mark of distinction*:
A noble wife is said to be the עֲטָרָה of her husband (בַּעְלָהּ Pr 12.4): wealth is the עֲטָרָה of the wise (חֲכָמִים, Pr 14.24); grandchildren of the elderly (זְקֵנִים, Pr 17.6): similarly, wisdom is a crown of glory (Sir 6.31). Jb 31.36, 'I would bind it [the indictment of Job's adversary] on me as garlands/a crown'; 1QSb 4.3 'eternal blessings are the עֲטָרָה of your head'. Sir 50.12(B) appears to describe a *circle* of sons, but the honorific aspect of עֲטָרָה may also be present.

A.7 References to the *removal* of a crown are often figurative and denote loss of status, e.g. Jb 19.9, Lm 5.16, Jr 13.18. However, Terrien (1963:145) takes Jb 19.9 more literally to refer to Job's original princely rank.

A.8 Sometimes a *nomen rectum* functions in adjectival sense for עֲטָרָה:
גֵּאוּת Is 28.1,3: צְבִי Is 28.5: תִּפְאֶרֶת Is 62.3, Jr 13.18 (+ כֶם-), Ezk 16.12; 23.42, Pr 4.9; 16.31: perhaps these are garlands of honour, and such expressions are not used of metal crowns?

Art and archaeology

A.1 There are many representations of royal and divine figures wearing headdresses marking their high status, but it is hard to say what exactly could be considered an עֲטָרָה by a writer in AH. Roughly contemporaneous with the biblical period in Israel are the pictures of Assyrian royal headresses (*ANEP* 441–454), Aramæan regal caps (*ANEP* 455, 460), Persian crowns (*ANEP* 462), and there are many depictions from the same period of Syrian, Assyrian and Babylonian gods and goddesses in special headgear (*ANEP* 529, 531–536, 538). This is in sharp contrast to the absence of literary references to any sort of crown for Yahweh, except for the עֲטֶרֶת תִּפְאֶרֶת held in his hand (Is 62.3).

A.2 Several Ammonite plaques and busts depicting heads wearing crowns have been found. They date from the Late Bronze Age to the Iron II Period, and usually have the Egyptian Atef crown, the white crown of upper Egypt with ostrich plumes on each side or a reed crown bound at the top and flanked by ostrich feathers. A clay plaque found near Amman is identified by Abou Assaf (1980:76–79, 85) as the deity Milkom, partly on the basis of 2Sm 12.30//1Ch 20.2. Younker (1989:378) equates Milkom with Ba'al Hammon and Canaanite El, and onomastic data (Israel 1991:333-34; Herr 1989:369–70 and 1992:187–200) have led Daviau and Dion (1994:164) to argue that it was El who was the god of the Ammonites, that Milkom may have been an epithet for him as head of the pantheon, and that the Amman plaque of a crowned deity depicts El.

8. Conclusion

A.1 עֲטָרָה is not an unequivocal emblem of monarchy, given that it is worn not only by the king but by commoners and women, unlike נֵזֶר. Even a gold עֲטָרָה is not restricted to the king or royal family, since both Mordecai and Joshua are given them, though in these contexts significant honour must be indicated. Ezk 21.31, where the word is coupled with מִצְנֶפֶת, does seem to point to עֲטָרָה being a sign of kingship, but even that passage seems to have more to do with utter humiliation than with loss of kingship *per se*.

A.2 Altogether, the word is used in non-royal contexts more frequently than royal, especially to indicate ceremony and/or rejoicing. In Ct 3.11 it is likely that the עֲטָרָה, with which Solomon was crowned by his mother, was part of his marriage celebrations, not part of royal insignia. עֲטָרָה is a symbol of distinction or rejoicing, but not connected with the cult of Yahweh, though it may be a feature of an Ammonite idol.

A.3 An עֲטָרָה can be made of flowers if a wreath, or of precious metal if a crown, and can contain gems. It has many similarities with the Greek word στέφανος, which also means a crown or a wreath, and connotes victory and celebration.

A.4 Both the meanings 'garland' and 'crown' are frequently used in a figurative sense, and in this way עֲטָרָה differs from the other words for royal headdresses, נֵזֶר and כֶּתֶר.

BIBLIOGRAPHY

Abou Assaf, A. 1980. Untersuchingen zur Ammonitischen Rundbildkunst. *UF* 12:7–102.

Amsler, S. 1981. Commentary on *Zecharias* 1-8 (CAT).

Asen, B.A. 1996. The garlands of Ephraim: Is 28.1–6 and the *marzēaḥ*. *JSOTSS* 71:73–87.

Beuken, W.A.M. 1967. *Haggai–Sacharja 1–8. Studien zur Überlieferungsgeschichte der frühnachexilischen Prophetie*. Studia Semitica Neerlandica 10; Assen.

Beyse, K.-M. 1972. *šerubbabel und die Königserwartungen der Propheten Haggai und Sacharja. Eine historische und traditionsgeschichtliche Untersuchung*. Arbeiten zur Theologie 1. Reihe; Heft 58; Stuttgart.

Brettler, M.Z. 1989. *God is King. Understanding an Israelite Metaphor*. JSOTSS 76. Sheffield.

Caquot, A., M. Sznycer, A. Herdner. 1974. *Textes ougaritiques*. I. *Mythes et Légendes*. Paris.

Dahood, M. 1961. Two textual notes on Jeremiah. *CBQ* 23:462–64.

Daviau, P.M. and P.E. Dion. 1994. El the god of the Ammonites? The Atef-crowned head from Tell Jawa, Jordan. *ZDPV* 110:158–67.

Dhorme, E. 1926. *Le Livre de Job*. Paris. ET 1967, *Commentary on the Book of Job*. London.

Driver, S.R. ²1913. *Notes on the Hebrew Text and the Topography of the Books of Samuel*. Oxford.

Duhm, B. 1901. Commentary on *Jeremiah* (KHC).

_____, 1963. Commentary on *Job* (KAT).

Ferron, J. 1966. L'épitaphe de Milkpillès à Carthage. *Studi Magrebini* 1:67–80.

Gordis, R. 1978. *The Book of Job. A Commentary, New Translation and Special Studies*. New York.

Greenberg, M. 1983. Commentary on *Ezekiel* 1–20 (AB).

Guillaume, A. 1961–62. Hebrew and Arabic lexicography. A comparative study. *AbrN* 3:1–10.

Herr, L.G. 1989. The inscribed seal impression. 369–74 in *The Madaba Plains Project. The 1984 Season at Tell el-'Umeiri and Vicinity, and Subsequent Studies*, I, ed. L.T.Geraty. Berrien Springs, MI.

_____. 1992. Epigraphic finds from Tell El-'Umeiri during the 1989 season. *Andrews University Seminary Studies* 30:187–200.

Holladay, W. 1986, 1989. Commentary on *Jeremiah*. 2 vols. (Herm).

Israel, F. 1991. Note ammonite II. La religione dei Ammoniti attraverso le fonti epigrafiche. *Studi e materiali di storia delle religioni* 57:307–37.

Kellermann, D. A. 1989. Article עטר, עטרה in *TWAT* VI:21–31.

Kraus, H.-J. ⁵1978. Commentary on *Psalms*. (BK). ET 1988, *Psalms 1–59* . Minneapolis.

_____. 1973. *hōj* als profetische Leachenklage über das eigene Volk. *ZAW* 85:15–46.

Lipiński, E. 1970. Recherches sur le livre de Zacharie. *VT* 20:25–55

McCarter, K. 1984. Commentary on *II Samuel* (AB).

Meyers, C. L. and E. M. Meyers. 1987. Commentary on *Haggai, Zechariah*

1–8 (AB).

Mitchell, H.G. et al. 1912. Commentary on *Haggai, Zechariah, Malachi, Jonah.* (ICC).

Pope, M. H. 1977. Commentary on *Song of Song* (AB).

Procksch, O. 1930. *Jesaia I* (KAT).

Qimron, E. 1996. *The Temple Scroll. A Critical Edition with Extensive Reconstructions.* Beer Sheva.

Rignell, L.G. 1950. *Die Nachtgesichte des Sacharja.* Lund.

Rose, W. 1997. Zerubbabel and Zemah—Messianic expectations in the early post-exilic period. Doctoral thesis, Oxford.

Rudolph, W. 1976. Commentary on *Zechariah* (KAT).

Skehan, P. and A. di Lella. 1987. Commentary on *Ben Sira* (AB).

Slotki, I.W. 1952. *Chronicles* (Soncino).

Smith, H.P. 1912. Commentary on *Samuel* (ICC).

Stamm, J.J. 1967. Hebräische Frauennamen. 301–39 in *Hebräische Wortforschung* (= FS Baumgartner) ed. B. Hartman et al. VTS 16; Leiden. Repr. 97–136 in *Beiträge zur hebräischen und altorientalischen Namenkunde.* OBO 30; Göttingen 1980.

Stoebe, H.J. 1994. Commentary on *2 Samuel* (KAT).

Terrien, S. 1963. Commentary on *Job* (CAT).

Toy, C.H. 1899. Commentary on *Proverbs* (ICC). Repr. [5]1959.

Volz, P. 1922. Commentary on *Jeremiah* (KAT).

Yadin, Y. 1983. *The Temple Scroll* II. Jerusalem.

Younker, R.W. 1989. Historical background and motifs of a royal seal impression. 375–80 in *The Madaba Plains Project. The 1984 Season at tell el-'Umeiri and Vicinity, and Subsequent Studies,* I, ed. L.T.Geraty. Berrien Springs, MI.

Zimmerli, W. 1969. Commentary on *Ezekiel* I (BK). ET 1979, *Ezekiel I 1–24* (Herm).

Alison Salvesen
University of Oxford

קָבַב

Introduction
Grammatical Type: vb.
Occurrences: Total 14x OT, 1x Sir (41.7), 0x Qum, 0x inscr.
Text doubtful:
A.1 [nil].

B.1 In Jb 5.3 אֲקוֹב is rendered by the LXX with the vb ἐβρώθη ("was consumed") and by the Pesh with ʾbd, ("to perish"), which has led to proposals for emendation, e.g. יִקַּב, "was cursed [by God]" (Cheyne; see Driver & Gray 1921:Part 2, 27–28). In view of the vb being followed by the adverb פִּתְאֹם, "suddenly", a description of the resultant state (as in the LXX) might fit the context better, but this is not beyond doubt (see Versions **A.6**). Perhaps אקוב was misread as אבד, as may be inferred from the Pesh.

B.2 Greenfield suggests that both Jb 5.3 and Pr 24.24 have suffered from mispointing (1990:158) and should be from קָבַב and not נָקַב. Hence, at Jb 5.3, for example, אֲקוֹב, which could be from either קָבַב or נָקַב, should be vocalized as אָקוֹב.
Qere/Ketiv: none.

1. Root and Comparative Material
A.1 The root קבב appears in BH only as a vb and only in the qal conjugation. It is often thought to be from the same derivation as the root of the vb נָקַב I (e.g. Ringgren 1977:1138; see **B.1**). It is not to be found in RH, although there may exist a denominative of קָבַב (see **B.2**).

A.2 The form qbʾ is attested once in Ug (*KTU*[2] 1.161:3), where it means "to summon" (Healey 1978:84, 86). Its direct object in that text is qbṣ, "assembly". That it is a possible cognate with Akk qabû "to speak, proclaim" is noted by Healey (1978:86) and it is compared with Heb קָבַב by Rouillard (1985:83).

A.3 There are four possible instances of a cognate root in the Deir ʿAlla texts (Hoftijzer & van der Kooij 1976). In II 17 we find the expression wmlqb, although the reading of the b is very uncertain. Hoftijzer has interpreted in this expression the w as a conjunction, the m as the "neutral" interrogative pronoun, the l as the preposition and qb as an inf cstr of qbb (Hoftijzer & van der Kooij 1976:247). He, therefore, translates it as "it will be impossible to curse anymore (i.e. for you)", noting for comparison nominal clauses in BH in which ל + inf cstr is the subject and the "neutral" interrogative pronoun is predicate (e.g. 2Kg 4.13, 14, Is 5.4, Ps 50.16). If the two words at the beginning of IX a3 (lqb. nqb) are to be taken as belonging to the same root, then it is probable that these are forms of qbb (Hoftijzer & van der Kooij 1976:262). lqb will be the inf abs with l as the negation (cf. Gn 3.4, Am 9.8, Ps 49.8) and nqb will be either the impf 1p pl (of e.g. peʿal or niph) or the niph perf 3p s. Finally, qbt at X a3 may be from this root, either as a verbal or a nominal form (Hoftijzer & van der Kooij 1976:263), but it is the only word extant on the line such that little can be established from the context. Hoftijzer (ibid.:263) does note, however, the possibility that it could be the cstr of a nominal form *qbh* (= "dome, vault, women's room"). All other reconstructions of this verb elsewhere are too tenuous to be considered. For a bibliography of alternative interpretations of the readings, see *DNWSI*:978.

A.4 The Phoen qal s *qb* and the substantive *qbt* (s or pl?) appear in the phrase: *wqb ... qbt ᵓdrt*, "and M. cursed a mighty curse" (Mosca & Russell 1987:15). This inscription is dated, on palaeographical grounds solely, to c. 625–600 BCE (ibid.:4).

The qal *qbt* is also attested in Pun (*CIS* i 4945.5): *wᵓš yrgz tmtnt z wqbt tnt pnbᶜl*, "And whosoever will disturb this gift, may Tanit Pane Ba'al curse him (reading *qabbatu*)". Mosca describes this form as the f s ptc (Mosca & Russell 1987:15), but Greenfield proposes that it is perfect (1990:157, n. 6). Greenfield also notes that the discovery of the Phoen forms dispels any doubt on the Pun case. They are, however, the only attestations in these languages.

A.5 In the Mari documents a prophetess has the title *qabbatum* or *qamatum* (Dossin & Finet 1978:122, no. 80.6). Dossin & Finet transcribe the text with the word *qamatum*, denoting the important status of the prophetess (ibid.:122), and they note that the alternative reading *qabbatum* (preferred by *AHw*:886) would be a hapax legomenon (ibid.:267 n). Malamat (1987:38), however, suggests that the title *qabbatum* is derived from the Akk *qabû* ("to speak, proclaim", see **A.6**) and that it may be linked with the Heb קָבַב.

A.6 The Akk vb *qabû*, "to speak, proclaim", is used in a wide range of contexts (CAD 13:22–42; *AHw*:889–90). There are various derivatives from it, including the n *qabû* I (CAD 13:18–21; *AHw*:889) "speech, statement" and *qabiānu* "speaker of a particular utterance" (CAD 13:3; *AHw*:888).

A.7 The vb in Tigre *qebba* (not *qabba*, as given in *HAL*:992) has the meaning of "to despise" (Leslau 1958:46). Leslau makes comparison with Tigri *qabebe* and the possible cognate in Amh, *aš-qabbebe*, "to mock at, be haughty".

A.8 There is an Arb conjugated form *qabiba*, "to be thin, slight", that may be cognate with Heb קָבַב (Scharbert 1958:14).

B.1 קָבַב is sometimes said to be a verbal form derived from the vb נָקַב (e.g. *HAL*:992). Barthélemy & Rickenbacher place the occurrence of יקב in Sir 41.7 under the root bqn (1973:270), perhaps for the same reason. Scharbert is probably correct to reject any etymological connection between קָבַב and נָקַב (1958:14). Rouillard, however, speculates that there may have been a "contamination" of one by the other, and that it is not impossible that traces of this derivational and semantic contamination can be found in Nu 22–24. She notes that in order to curse someone, one "pronounces" (נָקַב) their name distinctly and thus there is a direct connection between cursing and the concrete act of uttering the name (1985:83). The text, as she observes, however, does not provide enough details as to whether such an act of pronouncing was involved, and she expresses doubt over her own suggestion (1985:85).

In view of the lack of a certain etymological connection between קָבַב and

נָקַב, Rouillard discusses instead the connection between קָבַב and Akk *qabû* (1985:83). As *qabû* signifies "tout simplement «parler»", for her קָבַב denotes pronouncing a curse (cf. Zohar 111 § 198b). She concludes that קָבַב is more "concrete" than אָרַר, but with the sense "toute sa force est dans sa bouche" (1985:85). Rouillard is perhaps inferring too much from the etymology here, as there is rarely a direct equivalence of meaning between Akk and Heb words. Furthermore, *qabû* is widely attested in Akk in a range of uses that perhaps suggest that the lexeme has a more varied meaning than simply that of "to speak".

B.2 Mosca compares the appearance of a form in Phoen (see **A.4**) to the post-biblical Heb *qabbāh* (Mosca & Russell 1987:15), but Greenfield notes that no such form actually exists in post-biblical Heb (Greenfield 1990:157, n. 6). Nevertheless, although it appears that no such verbal form exists, a denominative קבה is found at bSanh 92a, where in reference to Pr 11.26 (יִקְּבָהוּ) it said אין קבה אלא קללה (Jastrow:1307). Hoftijzer also notes the nominal form as a tentative comparison to *qbt* in the Deir ʿAlla texts (Hoftijzer & van der Kooij 1976:263). In bSot 41b the form קוב appears. Quotations of Nu 22.11 in RH obviously include the impv form קָבָה (e.g. NumR 20.9).

2. Formal Characteristics

A.1 Double ʿAyin vb.

A.2 The two cases of the impv form קָבָה־לִּי in Nu 22.11,17 are not the expected form קָבָּה־לִּי*. The form קָבָה־לִּי is intended to avoid two instances of gemination one after another (JM:§ 82 *l*). In the same way we find at Nu 22.6 and 23.7 the impv אָרָה־לִּי.

A.3 The form קָבְנוֹ־לִי in Nu 23.13 has an epenthetic נ (JM:§ 82 *l*), a feature common in Ug (*UT*: § 6.16, 17). BHS has in the apparatus the note "וְקָבֶנּוּ =", suggesting the impv קֹב with an energic nun and the 3ms obj suf.

B.1 Malamat suggests that the form קַבֹּה (Nu 23.8) is irregular and perhaps derives from a root *qbh (Malamat 1987:38).

3. Syntagmatics

A.1 In the two instances where a subject is specifiec for קָבַב , in one case it is אֵל "God" (Nu 23.8) and in the other it is לְאֹם "people" (Pr 11.26).

A.2 The direct object of the vb קָבַב may be a people (עַם Nu 22.17), the enemy (אֹיֵב, Nu 23.11, 24.10), the one who withholds grain (מֹנֵעַ בָּר, Pr 11.26), those who curse the day (אֹרְרֵי־יוֹם, Jb 3.8), a habitation (נָוֶה, Jb 5.3), or one's son (יֶלֶד, Sir 41.7). It may be marked either with אֵת (plus suf, Nu 22.11) or without it (e.g. Nu 23.11, 24.10, Jb 5.3).

A.3 The impv קָבָה־לִּי is sometimes preceded by the impv לְכָה (Nu 22.11, 17). The action of the vb may be performed from a place (מִשָּׁם, Nu 23.13, 27).

A.4 When the curse is uttered on behalf of someone, this is indicated by l plus suffix (Nu 22.11, 17, 23.13, 27).

A.5 The action of קָבַב is contrasted with that of בָּרַךְ in the piel (Nu 23.11, 24.10).

B.1 [nil]

4. Versions

a. LXX: ἀραόμαι (Nu 22.11, 23.8aα, 8aβ); καταράομαι (Nu 23.8aβ [Vaticanus], 23.13, 25aβ, 27, 24.10, Jb 3.8); ἐπικαταράομαι (Nu 22.17); μέμφομαι (Sir 41.7); κατάρασις (Nu 23.11: εἰς κατάρασιν = לְקֹב); κατάρα (Nu 23.25aβ: κατάραις = inf abs); εἰμὶ ἐπικατάρατος (Pr 24.24); βιβρώσκω (Jb 5.3 [Aq = καταράομαι]); ὑπολείπω (Pr 11.26).

b. Pesh: *lwṭ* (Nu 22.11, 17, 23.8 (2x), 11, 13, 25 (2x), 27, 24.10, Jb 3.8, Pr 24.24, Sir 41.7); *ʾbd* (Jb 5.3); *šbq* (Pr 11.26).

c. Targum:

לוט – TgO, TgNeo, TgPsJ (Nu 22.11, 17, 23.8aα, 11, 13, 25 [2x], 27, 24.10);

סני – TgNeo (Nu 23.8aβ);

ברך – TgO, TgPsJ, TgFrg (P, V, N) – (Nu 23.8aβ);

לוט – (Jb 3.8, Jb 5.3, Pr 24.24);

שבק – (Pr 11.26).

d. Vulgate: *maledico* (Nu 22.11, 17, 23.8 [2x], 11, 13, 25 [1x], 27, 24.10, Jb 3.8, 5.3, Pr 11.26, 24.24); *queror de* (Sir 41.7).

A.1 The LXX in Nu 22–24 does not distinguish between קָבַב, זָעַם and אָרַר, although it does not translate consistently. καταράομαι is chosen for both קָבַב (23.13, 25, 27, 24.10), אָרַר (22.6b [2x], 12, 24.9 [2x]) and זָעַם (23.8 [2x]), but then ἀράομαι is also used to render both קָבַב (22.11, 23.8aa, 8ab) and אָרַר (22.6a, 23.7). ἐπικαταράομαι is used to render both קָבַב (22.17) and זָעַם (23.7). קָבַב is also translated in this narrative by the substantives κατάρασις (23.11) and κατάρα (23.25). Rouillard (1985:82, n. 61) does speculate whether the LXX translator did impart to קָבַב a stronger sense than to אָרַר in view of the relative proportions of their translation equivalents. אָרַר is rendered twice by ἀράομαι and only twice by καταράομαι, whilst קָבַב is rendered three times (Rouillard says twice, see **A.2**) by ἀράομαι, but five times (Rouillard says six) with the prefixes κατα (not ἐπι, as Rouillard says) or ἐπικατα. Proportionally, therefore, the simple verb ἀράομαι seems to be associated more with אָרַר, although Rouillard herself suggests that perhaps the assonance of אָרַר/ἀράομαι is at work here (1985:82, n. 61).

Dorival also observes that when Balaam reports the words of Balak to God, he uses the same verb, ἀράομαι, as Balak (in contrast to the alternation in the Heb between קָבַב and אָרַר). In this way the LXX presents Balaam as a faithful reporter in a manner that the Heb fails to do (1994:104–05).

A.2 At Nu 23.8ab Vaticanus, which is preferred here in Rahlfs' edition of the LXX, translates קָבַב by καταράομαι, whilst the other MSS have the simple form ἀράομαι. Since the first of the two occurrence of קָבַב in the verse is rendered by ἀράομαι, and then the two occurrences of זָעַם are rendered by καταράομαι, it seems probable that the LXX translated the two Heb pairs by two Gr pairs (Wevers 1982:125; Dorival 1994:435). Therefore, the LXX would have two simple forms (ἀράομαι) followed by two compound forms (καταράομαι). See, however, Rouillard's interpretation in **A.3** below.

A.3 Rouillard (1985:81–82, n. 61) wonders whether the LXX should be considered in Nu 22–24 almost as a text in its own right, displaying translation features not reflective of the Heb Vorlage. She notes how there is in the LXX a progression of the forms of ἀράομαι with prefixes in Nu 23.7–8: δεῦρο ἄρασαί ... καὶ δεῦρο ἐπικατάρασαί ... τί ἀράσωμαι ὃν μὴ καταρᾶται κύριος. This is not a systematic feature of the translation.

A.4 The Vg does not distinguish between קָבַב and אָרַר, rendering them both uniformly as *maledicere*. It translates זָעַם, however, as *detestare*.

A.5 The LXX (ὑπολείπω), Pesh (*šbq*) and Tg (שׁבק) to Pr 11.26 all read the vb "to abandon", suggesting a misreading of שׁבב for קבב.

A.6 In Jb 5.3 the LXX (βιβρώσκω, "to consume") and Pesh (*ʾbd*, "to perish") both read a passive vb with a meaning denoting destruction or removal. This has led to various suggestions for emendation of the Heb אֶקּוֹב, and these suggestions have been catalogued by Driver and Gray 1921:Part 2, 27–28. The Versions give warrant to those who are uncomfortable with the meaning "to curse" alongside the adverb פִּתְאֹם, "suddenly" (Driver & Gray 1921:Part 1, 50), although the objection to this meaning is not strong. The slightest change from the MT would be the suggestion of Cheyne to emend to the passive וַיֻּקַּב, "and was cursed [by God]". Even this may not be necessary if the LXX and Pesh misread אקוב as אבד, as may be implied by the Pesh's choice of *ʾbd*. It should be noted, indeed, that Aq here reads κατηρασάμην, "I cursed", and that the Vg (*maledicere*) and Tg (לוט) likewise reflect the MT.

A.7 In TgNeo (Nu 23.8aβ) the word as it appears in the text, מסגי, "he multiplies", has two small supralinear strokes written by the scribe to indicate that it is not the correct reading. It is the verb from the end of verse 8 (translating לֹא זָעַם) in TgNeo and TgPsJ, and has presumably been duplicated earlier in the verse. In TgNeo to 23.7 and 8 זָעַם is translated by זער "to diminish" and this may have influenced a copyist here where לֹא קַבֹּה could have been understood in this light as "he does not diminish", i.e. "he multiplies". The other Targumim render the negative לֹא קַבֹּה by the positive מברך, "he blesses".

5. Lexical/Semantic Field(s)

A.1 [see אָרַר]

A.2 קָבַב occurs almost exclusively in EBH, being found in Nu 22–24 and the earlier portions of Jb (chapters 3 and 5) and Pr (chapters 11 and 24). The one exception is its appearance in LBH at Sir 41.7. The majority of its occurrences are in the Balaam-Balak narrative of Nu 22–24 (22.11, 17, 23.8 [2x], 11, 13, 25 [2x], 27, 24.10).

A.3 קָבַב occurs in parallelism with זָעַם (Nu 23.8 [2x], Pr 24.24), בָּרַךְ in the piel (Nu 23.25) or the n בְּרָכָה (Pr 11.26), as well as the phrase היה בוז, "to become a disgrace" (Sir 41.7). It is also collocated with אָרַר (Jb 3.8).

A.4 It may be significant that outside of the Balaam-Balak narrative קָבַב only appears in sapiential literature (Jb, Pr, Sir).

6. Exegesis

A.1 Scharbert (1958:14), who is followed in this by Brichto (1963:200), notes that the relative rarity of the word renders it difficult to determine its denotation. They do observe that its frequent occurrence in the Balaam-Balak narrative in Nu implies the meaning "to curse".

A.2 Greenfield, observing that קָבַב occurs almost entirely in the Balaam pericope (Nu 22–24), "a repository of dialect words", suggests that the form *qb* in Ph and Pun indicates the dialectical usage in BH (1990:157–158). Ph had its own word, which was then adopted into BH in some instances.

A.3 In the Balaam-Balak narrative the vb אָרַר occurs six times (22.6 [3x], 12, 23.7, 24.9), whilst קָבַב appears ten times (22.11, 17, 23.8 [2x], 11, 13, 25 [2x], 27, 24.10). Balak speaks using the vb אָרַר (22.6; cf. also 22.12 when God speaks), but when Balaam cites him (Nu 22.11) and when Balak responds (Nu 22.17), they use the verb קָבַב, suggesting that קָבַב is a substitute for אָרַר (Rouillard 1985:81). The next instances are in Balaam's oracle, where Balaam first quotes the words of Balak with the verb אָרַר (Nu 23.7 citing 22.6), and then responds with his own question using the verb קָבַב (23.8). This might suggest that קָבַב was a word used by Balaam from his own dialect (see A.2), and that Balak uses the standard word אָרַר, except at Nu 22.17 where he uses קָבַב under the influence perhaps of Balaam. Nevertheless, the reverse happens in chapter 24 when Balaam speaks of those who curse being cursed (אָרַר, 24.9 [2x]) and Balak responds that he had ordered him to curse (קָבַב) his enemies (24.10). Also the five other cases of קָבַב in this passage are in the mouth of Balak (23.11, 13, 25 [2x], 27). Therefore, the author may have chosen both אָרַר and קָבַב to use as stylistic variants, although the predominance of קָבַב rather than other synonyms of אָרַר indicates that this lexeme was particularly favoured, probably because it was associated with the dialect of Balaam (cf. the appearance of the cognate in the Deir ʿAlla texts). The only other lexeme from the semantic field of "curse" to be found in the narrative is זָעַם in 23.7 and 23.8 (2x), in the first instance in parallelism with אָרַר and in the second with קָבַב. The synonymity of קָבַב with אָרַר is also suggested by the LXX (See Versions A.1).

A.4 There seems to be a synonymity of קָבַב with זָעַם, which is found in parallelism with קָבַב at Pr 24.24, as well as in Nu 23.7 and 23.8 (2x).

A.5 In Sir 41.7 קָבַב seems to mean little more than "to chastise, reproach", portraying the action of a wicked father. It is in parallelism with היה בוז, which also suggests this. This reflects a general tendency with words for "curse" to come to be used of castigation. קִלֵּל in particular develops in semantic range to include "to scorn, despise" (Kister 1983:129), such that the TgFrg (V) glosses ומקלל (Ex 21.17) as ודי מבזי. The vb קִלֵּל in Sir 3.11, 16 would similarly be best translated as "to demean". It is of interest for Sir 41.7 that TgNeoMg renders נָקַב II, a verb possibly cognate to קָבַב, by בזה at Lv 24.16. In Ml 1-2 the curse by God of his priests is also related to their "contempt". Priestly contempt of the divine name (בוזי שמי, Ml 1.6) leads to contempt for the priestly offering (נבזה, Ml 1.12) and finally the priests themselves (נבזים, Ml 2.9). Further parallels may be noted in some cognates. The Geez translation of Ml 3.9 uses the vb *taʿawwara*, "to be neglected, despised", where the Heb has אָרַר (see Muraoka 1993:24). In addition, the Tigre vb *qebba*, possibly cognate with קָבַב, has the meaning "to despise" (Leslau:46).

B.1 Rouillard suggests that the appearance of the lexeme in Job and of its cognate in Deir ʿAlla indicates that it is a dialect word different from the dialect of Jerusalem, and certainly more southern (1985:86). Whilst she may well be correct that קָבַב is a dialectal lexeme (see A.2), two occurrences in Jb is not sufficient to demonstrate its southern origin. We still must account for its appearances in Pr and, more difficult still, in Sir. Also the existence of cognates in Phoen, Pun, Ug and Akk, and not only in Deir ʿAlla, indicates its widespread use. The fact, however, that it is used primarily in the Balaam-Balak narrative does suggest that it could have been associated originally with a Transjordanian dialect.

7. Conclusion

The vb קָבַב, in view of the lexemes that are found in parallelism with it, and the contexts in which it is found, has the meaning "to curse". We are unable to determine the precise nature of the act of cursing, and any suggestion that it is more of a "concrete" act than in the case of other lexemes in the field in terms of the manner of its utterance cannot be substantiated. It seems probable that קָבַב is originally a dialectal word, but that by the time of LBH the lexeme has been integrated with the Classical Hebrew vocabulary (Sir 41.7). In Sir it is clear that the meaning of the lexeme, as with many others in the field, had changed to that of "to reproach, chastise". Perhaps קָבַב began as a dialectal word for "to curse" and over time came to be used in Heb with the changed meaning, especially in poetic or sapiential literature. Its parallelism with זָעַם in Pr 24.24 may suggest this.

BIBLIOGRAPHY

Barthélemy, D. & O. Rickenbacher. 1973. *Konkordanz zum hebräischen Sirach mit syrisch–hebräischen Index*. Göttingen.
Brichto, H.C. 1963. *The Problem of "Curse" in the Hebrew Bible*. *JBL* monograph series, XIII; Philadelphia.
Dorival, G. 1994. *La Bible d'Alexandrie: Les Nombres*. Paris.
Dossin, G. & A. Finet. 1978. *Correspondance Féminine: Transcrite et traduite* (Archives royales de Mari, X). Paris.
Driver, S.R. & and G.B. Gray. 1921. Commentary on *Job* (ICC). Edinburgh.
Greenfield, J.C. 1990. Some Phoenician words. *Semitica* 38:155–158.
Healey, J.F. 1978. Ritual text *KTU²* 1.161—translation and notes. *UF* 10:83–91.
Hoftijzer, J. & G. van der Kooij. 1976. *Aramaic Texts from Deir 'Alla*. Leiden.
Kister, M. 1983. In the margins of the Book of Ben Sira [in Hebrew]. *Leš* 47:125–146.
Malamat, A. 1987. A forerunner of Biblical prophecy: The Mari documents. In P.D. Miller, P.D. Hanson and S.D. McBride (eds). *Ancient Israelite Religion: Essays in honor of Frank Moore Cross*. Philadelphia:33–52.
Mosca, P.G. & J. Russell. 1987. A Phoenician inscription from Cebel Ires Daği in Rough Cilicia. *Epigraphica Anatolica* 9:1–28.
Ringgren, H. 1977. Article קבב in *TWAT* VI:1138–1139.
Rouillard, H. 1985. *La Péricope de Balaam (Nombres 22–24): La Prose et les «Oracles»* (Études Bibliques, ns 4). Paris.

Scharbert, J. 1958. "Fluchen" und "Segnen" im Alten Testament. *Bib* 39:1–26.
Wevers, J.W. 1982. *Text History of the Greek Numbers* (Abhandlungen der Akademie der Wissenschaften). Göttingen.

James K. Aitken
University of Cambridge

שֵׁבֶט

Introduction

Grammatical type: n m. However, Delitzsch (1885:388–89) considered that it may be common gender.

Occurrences: a total of 190 occurrences in BH, with approx. 46 occurrences having the meaning of 'stick' or 'sceptre' as opposed to 'tribe', depending on classication. In Sir 2 occurrences have this sense, and Q has 4 occurrences.

Qere/Kethiv: none.

A.1 Even-Shoshan (1983:1104–05) divides this lexeme into three main groups, a) 'stick', b) 'sceptre' and c) 'tribe'. Naturally here we are most interested in b), but since it is difficult to distinguish all cases of a) from those of b), these will be considered together: those which represent rulership and authority and those which are used in a more neutral sense. Some cases of c) will also be considered, since scholars have debated whether some instances of שֵׁבֶט traditionally taken as 'tribe' should be considered as equivalent to, or as forms of, שֵׁפֶט. The semantic relation of c) to a) and b) also needs some discussion.

A.2 The following classification into 'stick' and 'sceptre' is according to Even Shoshan, since BDB does not list all occurrences, and its classification is more complex. An alternative grouping will be suggested in *Exegesis*.

a) 'stick': Ex 21.20, Lv 27.32, Jdg 5.14, 2Sm 7.14; 18.14; 23.21//1Ch 11.23, Is 9.3; 10.5, 15, 24; 11.4; 14.29; 28.27; 30.31, Ezk 21.15, 18, Mc 4.14; 7.14, Ps 2.9; 23.4; 89.33; 125.3, Pr 10.13; 13.24; 22.8, 15; 23.13, 14; 26.3; 29.15; Jb 9.34; 21.9, Lm 3.1.

b) 'sceptre': Gn 49.10, Nu 24.17, Is 14.5, Ezk 19.11, 14, Am 1.5, 8; Zc 10.11, Ps 45.7^2.

A.3 Jb 37.13 and Ezk 20.37 are classified by Even Shoshan as 'tribe', but BDB, some versions and some scholars would place them with 'stick'. Sir 32.23 שבט זדון could be classified with b), and Sir 37.18 ארבעה שבטים יפריחו with a). The occurrences in Q of שֵׁבֶט in a non-tribal sense are biblical quotations or allusions, though CD 7.19f identifies the שֵׁבֶט of Nu 24.17 as the prince of the whole congregation, and thus with b), and 1QSb 5.23–27 would fall into category a). (1QM 11.6f, 4QTest 12, CD 7.19f = Nu 24.17: 1QSb 5.23–27 cf. Is 11.4).

Text doubtful

2Sm 7.7: A good deal has been written on this verse, most of it suggesting that שֵׁבְטֵי 'tribes' should be emended to *שֹׁפְטֵי, 'judges'. Some of the emendations or interpretations suggested bring the occurrence into the realm of 'stick' or 'sceptre', hence its inclusion here. Bibliography on the subject up until 1982 is recorded by Begg (1982), who covers a similar problem in Dt 29.9. In both cases he argues for retention of MT, but in the sense 'leaders', the tribes being understood as collective leaders. The main alternatives are those of Dahood (1963) *שֹׁבְטֵי, 'judges', due to a dialectal interchange of /b/ and /p/ found in Ug too: Falk (1966) *שֹׁבְטֵי 'judges': de Robert (1971) שִׁבְטֵי 'tribes' (i.e. the plain sense of MT): Reid (1975) *שֹׁבְטֵי 'staff bearers', a denominative qal act ptc from שׁבט (cf. the Akk denominative vb šabāṭu , though this means 'to strike'): Gevirtz (1980) *שֹׁבְטֵי 'judges', following Dahood but preserving the vocalisation of MT. More recently Murray (1987) has made a different emendation, adding *מִכֹּל before שִׁבְטֵי, on the ground that this is a very common construction which makes excellent sense in the context, but which may well have fallen out due to haplography.

2Sm 18.14: The plural use of שֵׁבֶט, the apparent support of Tg and LXX and the fact that Joab appears to pierce Absalom's heart with the sticks, lead many to emend MT to *שְׁלָחִים, e.g. Wellhausen (1871:202), Smith (1899:359), Nowack (1902:222), Budde (1902:284), S.R. Driver (²1913:330), Caspari (1926:622). Otherwise one has to redefine the sense of MT שְׁבָטִים to mean a sharpened staff, arrows (cf. Tg and LXX), a spear (Schulz 1920:284), 'a bunch of stout sticks' (McCarter 1984:401, 406–7) or Hertzberg's interpretation 'darts' (1960:292; ET 359). Fokkelman (1981:I,247–48) and McCarter (1984:406–7), following G.R. Driver (1962:129–34), suggest another possibility if the reading of MT is retained: Joab struck Absalom with the sticks to dislodge him from the tree before leaving him to the mercy of his men. Hertzberg (1960:292; ET 359) suggests that Joab's action is not intended to be lethal in itself but symbolic, giving licence to Joab's men to kill the king's son, and starting the flow of blood that marks Absalom for death.

Gn 49.10: Joüon (1912) emends שֵׁבֶט to *שֹׁפֵט, on the ground that a human figure is implied by the parallel מְחֹקֵק. Cross and Freedman (1975:82 n.31) suggest the same emendation, or that of Albright, šēpeṭ (cf. Ug ṭpṭ), because of מְחֹקֵק and the parallel pairs in Jdg 5.14, Is 33.22, 2Sm 7.7 // 1Ch 17.16. They regard the error as having arisen by oral or graphic confusion between פ and ב. Dahood (1963:43 n.1) vocalises the consonantal form as *שֹׁבֵט, a dialectal form of שֹׁפֵט, and cites 2Sm 7.7 and 1Ch 17.6 in support. Kutscher (1968:274) observes that שׁבט and מְחֹקֵק occur in early biblical poetry but not שֹׁפֵט, suggesting that שֵׁבֶט could sometimes refer to a person in authority. Brettler (1989:80, 183 n.11) understands שֵׁבֶט to mean 'king' through metonymy, understood thus by all the Targumim to the verse, and rejects emendation of MT.

1. Root and Comparative Material

A.1 A native Sem root, cf. Akk šabbiṭu 'stick', šabāṭu 'smite, slay', šibṭu 'rod, sceptre', and related month name in Bab sābāṭu = שְׁבָט ; Eth vb šbṭ 'strike'; Sab sbṭm, 'rod, blow'; Arm šibṭā /Syr šabṭā, 'rod, staff: tribe' (the latter meaning due to Heb influence), Syr pael verb šabbeṭ 'beat out, hammer': loanword in Eg New Kingdom šbd, 'sign of power, weapon, defence', also Eg Dem šbtē, pl hier. š-b-dỉ-y, Copt šbōt (HAL 1291; BDB 986; Hassan 1979; Lewy 1895:122: cf. Gk σπάθη). The Ug personal name ṭbṭ is probably from the root ṭpṭ 'judge', by phonetic interchange of the bilabials.

A.2 Mayer Modena (1987) notes that of the semantically related words מַקֵּל, מִשְׁעֶנֶת, מַטֶּה and שֵׁבֶט שֵׁבֶט probably has a Sem base, < * šibṭu, cf. Arm šibṭa, SArb sbṭ, Akk šibṭu, whereas מַקֵּל may have an Indo-Mediterranean origin, cf. Basque makhila, Lat baculus, Ebla ma-ga-lu-um, Akk mak/qilu. מַטֶּה is not from *nṭy with m instrumental prefix, as stated in Ges and KB, in view of Ug mṭ, 'staff', Ebla ma-ṭa-um, 'little stick', which may also have Indo-Med. origins. But see also the sections on etymology given by Simian-Yofre (1984:818) and André (1984:1129).

A.3 Caquot (1956: 36) observes that שֵׁבֶט occurs 8 times in Pss, and מַטֶּה only once, in Ps 110.2. Since שֵׁבֶט has no Ug cognate, but Ug mṭ exists, he suggests that מַטֶּה in Ps 110.2 is influenced by Can.

A.4 In view of their similarity and occasional semantic overlap, Falk (1966) proposed that the roots שבט and שפט were connected etymologically. However, Loewenstamm (1968) demonstrated that שבט is derived from PS *šbṭ, whereas שפט must come from PS *ṯbṭ. Gevirtz (1980) follows Loewenstamm, but on the basis of the commonly found interchange of the voiced and voiceless bilabial plosives /b/ and /p/ in AH, Ug, Pun, and Arm also noted by Dahood (1963:43 n.1) he posits the existence of two homonymous roots, שבט I and שבט II, the first from PS *šbṭ, 'staff', and the second from PS*ṯbṭ, 'judge', by later phonetic interchange. This would explain the passages where שְׁבָטִים appears to mean 'judges, rulers' rather than 'tribes', e.g. 2Sm 7.7 (// שֹׁפְטֵי 1Ch 17.6), Dt 33.5 (// רָאשֵׁי), Jdg 20.2 (// פִּנּוֹת), Dt 29.9 רָאשֵׁיכֶם שִׁבְטֵיכֶם זִקְנֵיכֶם וְשֹׁטְרֵיכֶם, the Versions of Gn 49.10 for שֵׁבֶט // מְחֹקֵק. In these passages emendation is often proposed, but Gevirtz's suggestion would render this unnecessary.

2. Formal Characteristics
    A.1 n. m.
    A.2 Segholate, qiṭl.

3. Syntagmatics
    A.1 Pl.: 2 Sm 18.14, Ezk 19.11.
    A.2 *Subject* of: סור qal Gn 49.10, Zc 10.11; נוח qal Ps 125.3; כלה qal Pr 22.8,

קום qal Nu 24.17,

פרח hiph Sir 32.23,

נוף hiph Is 10.15,

שבר niph Is 14.29,

נחם pi Ps 23.4,

רחק hiph Pr 22.15,

נתן qal Pr 29.15,

מחץ qal Nu 24.17.

    A.3 *Object* of שבר qal Is 14.5; חתת hiph Is 9.3; ירש hiph Sir 32.23; סור hiph Jb 9.34,

לקח qal 2Sm 18.14,

תקע qal 2Sm 18.14,

חשׂך qal Pr 13.24.

    A.4 *Ptc/adj*: נכה hiph Is 14.29; מאס qal (f!) Ezk 21.15,18 (disputed readings).

    A.5 *Nomen regens* of מֹשְׁלִים Is 14.5, Ezk 19.11, cf. Ezk 19.14 לִמְשׁוֹל

        סֹפֵר Jdg 5.14

        הַנֹּגֵשׂ Is 9.3

        הָרֶשַׁע Ps 125.3; זָדוֹן Sir 32.23

        אֱלוֹהַּ Jb 21.9

        מִצְרַיִם Zc 10.11; אֲנָשִׁים 2Sm 7.14

        מִישֹׁר Ps 45.7; מוּסָר Pr 22.15

        מַלְכוּת Ps 45.7

        אַף Is 10.5; פֶּה Is 11.4; עֶבְרָה Pr 22.8, Lm 3.1

        אֵמָה Jb 9.34; פַּחַד Jb 21.9

    A.6 *Nomen rectum* of תּוֹמֵךְ Am 1.5, 8

    A.7 In *parallelism* with: (synonymous) מְחֹקֵק Gn 49.10, cf. Jdg 5.14; כּוֹכָב Nu 24.17

        מַטֶּה Is 14.5 (cf. Ezk 19.11,14), Sir 32.23B, Is 9.3, 10.5, 15, 24; 28.27

        עֹל Is 9.3; מִשְׁעֶנֶת Ps 23.4; מֶתֶג Pr 26.3; שׁוֹט Pr 26.3

        נְגָעִים Ps 89.33

        מוּסָר Pr 13.24; תּוֹכַחַת Pr 29.15

        antithetical: חָכְמָה Pr 10.13

    A.8 With -בְּ: Lm 3.1

    With -בְּ instrumenti: 2Sm 23.21//1Ch 11.23

    governed by נכה hiph Ex 21.20, Is 10.24, 11.4, 30.31, Mc 4.14; 7.14, Pr 23.13,14

        by משׁך qal Jdg 5.14

        by יכח hiph 2Sm 7.14, פקד qal Ps 89.33

        by חבט niph Is 28.27

        by רעע qal or רעה qal Ps 2.9

    With תַּחַת: Lv 27.32, Ezk 20.37.

4. Versions

    LXX:

    A.1

    ῥάβδος 'rod' Ex 21.20, Lv 27.32, Jdg 5.14 (B text, Sym, Thd), 2Sm 7.14; 23.21//1Ch 11.23, Is 9.3; 10.5,15,24 (and Sym), (Is 11.4 Aq, Sym, Thd; 14.29 Sym, Thd), (Ezk 21.15[10] Sym in Syh, Thd), (Am 1.5 Sym in Syh, 1.8 'the Rest'), Mc 4.14; 7.14, Ps 2.9; 23(22).4; 45(44).7[2], 89(88).33; 125(124).3 (Sym in Syh); Pr 10.13 (and Thd); 22.15; 23.13, 14; 26.3 (and Sym and Quinta in Syh), Jb 9.34; Lm 3.1.

    σκῆπτρον 'sceptre' Jdg 5.14 (A text); Zc 10.11; (Aq Gn 49.10, Is 14.29, Am 1.5, Ps 45(44).7[2]); (Sym Nu 24.17, Ezk 19.14).

    βακτηρία 'staff' Pr 13.24 (Is 10.24; 14.5; 28.27 Sym).

    βέλος 'dart' 2Sm 18.14.

    ἀκίς 'dart, arrow' (Luc 2Sm 18.14).

    πληγή 'blow' Is 30.31; Pr 29.15.

    μάστιξ 'whip' Jb 21.9.

    παιδεία 'instruction' Jb 37.13 ('Thd').

    φυλή 'tribe' (as if שֵׁבֶט [c]) Ezk 19.11,14; 21.18; Am 1.5,8.

B.1 Theological or contextual rendering: ἄρχων 'ruler' Gn 49.10; ἐξουσία 'authority' Gn 49.10 (Sym); ἄνθρωπος 'man' Nu 24.17 (see Lust 1995); λόγος 'word' Is 11.4(5); ζυγόν 'yoke' Is 14.5, 29.

B.2 Omitted in Is 28.27, which has a loose translation style and uses ῥάβδος for מַטֶּה earlier in the verse: in the difficult verse Ezk 21.15; in Pr 22.8 (LXX Pr tends to be free).

Vg:
A.1
virga 'stick' Ex 21.20, Lv 27.32, Nu 24.17, 2Sm 7.14; 23.21//1Ch 11.23, Ps 2.9; 23(22).4; 89(88).33; 125(124).3, Pr 10.13; 13.24; 22.8, 15; 23.13, 14; 26.3; 29.15; 10.5, 15, 24; 11.4; 14.5, 29; 30.31, Lm 3.1, Mc 4.14(5.1); 7.14, Jb 9.34; 21.9.
sceptrum 'sceptre' Gn 49.10, Ps 44(45).7(2x), Is 9.3(4), Ezk 19.11, 14, Am 1.5,8, Zc 10.11.
baculus 'staff' Is 28.27 (synonymous with מַטֶּה, *virga*, cf. Is 10.5,15,24, 14.5, 28.27, where *baculus* renders מַטֶּה)
lancea 'spear' 2Sm 18.14
Sceptrum may indicate a ruler's sceptre, but is not used in all instances where שֵׁבֶט appears to be a symbol of rule, e.g. Nu 24.17, Is 14.5, versus Is 9.3.

B.1 Omitted in the loose translation of Jdg 5.14, and the difficult Ezk 21.15, 18.

Tg:
A.1
שַׁרְבִיטָא 'stick' Ex 21.20 TgNeo, TgPsJ; Lv 27.32 TgNeo, TgFrg, TgPsJ.
חוּטְרָא 'staff' Lv 27.32 TgO; 2Sm 23.21//1Ch 11.23, Is 10.15, Mc 4.14, Lm 3.1.
מַלְקוּת 'lashing' 2Sm 7.14.
מַחְבּוֹטָא 'flail' (?) Is 28.27
גֻּסִּין 'javelins' 2Sm 18.14.
שֻׁלְטוֹן 'ruler' Is 9.3, 14.29, doublet Gn 49.10 TgFrg.
שׁוּלְטָן 'authority' Gn 49.10 TgO; Ex 21.20(!), Is 10.5, 24; 14.5; 30.31, Am 1.5, 8, Zc 10.11.

B.1
קֻלְמַס 'pen' (!) Jdg 5.14.
מֵימְרָא 'word' (cf. LXX ad loc.) Is 11.4, Mc 7.14 (with שִׁבְטָא 'tribe' inserted afterwards for צֵאן).
שִׁבְטָא 'tribe' Ezk 21.15,18 (as part of paraphrase to explain these difficult verses): in doublet translation—Nu 24.17 TgPsJ ('messiah and powerful tribe').
(מַלְכִין) 'kings' Ezk 19.11,14 (as part of paraphrase, 'kings powerful/heroic enough to subdue a kingdom'): Gn 49.10 TgNeo, 440, 264; 'kings and rulers' 110, Z, TgPsJ.
(פָּרוֹק וְשַׁלִּיט) 'saviour and ruler' Nu 24.17 TgNeo, TgFrg.
(מְשִׁיחָא) 'Messiah' doublet Nu 24.17 TgPsJ.

Pesh:
A.1

šabṭā 'rod' Gn 49.10, 2Sm 7.14; 18.14, Jb 9.34; 21.9, Ps 2.9; 23.4; 45.7(6)[2]; 89.33(31); 125.3, Pr 10.13; 13.24; 22.8; 22.15; 23.14; 29.15, Is 9.3(4); 10.5, 15, 24; 11.4; 14.5, 29; 30.31, Lm 3.1, Ezk 19.11,14, Am 1.5,8, Mc 4.14(5.1); 7.14.

rišā 'head, leader' Nu 24.17 (contextual).

ḥuṭrā 'staff' (usual trn for מַטֶּה) Ex 21.20, Lv 27.32, 2Sm 23.21//1Ch 11.23.

qanyā 'reed, pen' Jdg 5.14 (contextual: 'those who write with the pen of a scribe': cf. Tg).

zeqṭā 'goad' Pr 26.3 (repeated from first half of verse?), Is 28.27 (!).

šulṭānā 'rule' Zc 10.11 (contextual).

šarbṭā 'tribe' Ezk 21.15,18.

B.1 Omitted in the otherwise literal Pr 23.13.

5. Lexical/Semantic Field

A.1 Lexemes with the similar meaning 'staff, rod' etc. include מַטֶּה, מַקֵּל, מִשְׁעֶנֶת. See Power (1928:437–38).

A.2 For שֵׁבֶט the sphere of meaning is divided up in various ways by the different authorities. BDB 986–87 has the system 1a) rod staff; b) shaft (to explain the odd occurrence at 2Sm 18.14); c) shepherd's implement; d) truncheon, sceptre: 2) tribe. Zobel (1993: 966–69) has a different division, 1) rod, stick, thus weapon (of wood); 2) agricultural implements: a) threshing flail; b) shepherd's staff; c) instrument of chastisement/education d) sign of leadership: 3) tribe etc. Exegetes disagree on the exact classification of some occurrences of שֵׁבֶט, and these will be discussed in *Exegesis* below. It is also difficult to be certain how the meaning 'tribe' developed from 'stick', a problem that also exists for the semantically similar Eng word 'club', which can refer to a thick stick or to an association of people with a common purpose (*Oxford English Dictionary* [1971: 534]).

A.3 Brenner (1979: 80) maps the respective semantic fields of מַטֶּה and שֵׁבֶט: both mean firstly 'branch, stick or weapon', secondly a symbol of authority, and thirdly a group of people bound together by family relationship, ethnicity, comradeship and religion. The difference between the words is that only שֵׁבֶט can mean 'leader, ruler, king or judge' by itself (ibid. 108). (It is precisely this last point that is under dispute when scholars wish to emend שֵׁבֶט Gn 49.10 to *שֹׁפֵט or see it as a denominv ptc from שֵׁבֶט.)

A.4 Stoebe (1966:2234), and similarly Fohrer (1964:946), describe the development of שֵׁבֶט and מַטֶּה as originally denoting a shepherd's staff used as a weapon and means of control (Lv 27.32, Mc 7.14, Ps 23.4), then representing both the authority of the leader of a tribe (Gn 38.18, Jdg 5.14, hence the meaning 'sceptre' for שֵׁבֶט) and the group that he heads. Mendenhall, however (1973:184f), sees the connection between שֵׁבֶט 'staff' and שֵׁבֶט 'tribe' as the baton of authority governing the group. But Lemaire (1986:26) explains the link between שֵׁבֶט 'stick' and שֵׁבֶט 'tribe' as arising through the latter being a 'branch' of Israel.

6. Exegesis
Most occurrences of שֵׁבֶט fall into one of the following 4 categories, and in fact several could be considered as having overtones of a second category e.g.

    A. Agricultural/pastoral implement

    B. Rod for punishment or chastisement

    C. Weapon

    D. Symbol of power (not necessarily of a monarch, but of any leader of a group).

The exception to this grouping would be Sir 37.18, which refers to living branches, but there may be hints of D in the verse in that the tongue is said to rule over these four שְׁבָטִים.

A. Agricultural/pastoral implement
Lv 27.32 , Is 9.3; 10.15 (both with overtones of B?), Is 28.27, Mc 7.14, Ps 23.4, Pr 26.3 A/B.

Lv 27.32 describes the procedure for selecting every tenth beast of a herd or flock for the Lord: the animals pass under the herder's staff (Elliger 1966: 392).

Ps 23.4: Against those who denied that Israelite shepherds carried two separate implements, Power (1928:435–36) draws attention to early 20th century accounts of shepherds in modern Palestine, who were reported as carrying two sticks, one a club with a bulbous end and often studded with iron nails, and the other a long staff. He identifies these as respectively the שֵׁבֶט and the מִשְׁעֶנֶת of this verse. Thus Dalman (*AuS* VI: 238) defines שֵׁבֶט here as a weapon designed for striking, and מִשְׁעֶנֶת as a longer, supporting staff for walking along rocky paths. Dahood (1966:147) interprets the verb יְנַחֲמֻנִי as 'they lead me', נחה plus enclitic Mem, not 'they comfort me', נחם, an old suggestion rejected by Power (1928:439) as incompatible with Ancient Near Eastern pastoral practice.

Is 9.3: Dalman (*AuS* II: 120) identifies שֵׁבֶט here as a primitive substitute for an ox goad. Gray (1912:170) extends the metaphor of a driven animal through the verse, to give the series 'yoke', 'bars', 'stick of his driver', instead of taking the last as a taskmaster's rod. But the metaphor refers to the end of Israel's oppression to foreign rule, so שֵׁבֶט may have echoes of D. as well.

Is 10.15: From the parallels with axe and saw, it is clear that שֵׁבֶט is an implement, but the metaphor refers to Assyria's arrogance in acting as the rod, שֵׁבֶט, of the Lord's anger (Is 10.5), so שֵׁבֶט has overtones of B (Gray 1912: 199).

Is 28.27: Usually translated 'flail', but like מַטֶּה, שֵׁבֶט is not a specialised technical term and is only defined by its context here. Also Dalman (*AuS* III: 93, 114).

B. Rod of chastisement/punishment
This sense is particularly prominent in Proverbs (Pr 10.13, 13.24, 22.8,15, 23.13,14, 26.3 (also A), 29.15) to which there are parallels in Ahiqar (*ANET* 428b). It is also present in most of the occurrences of שֵׁבֶט in First Isaiah: Is 9.3 (also A: but cf. Wildberger 1972: 375, 'ruler's staff'); 10.5, 15 (also A), 24; 11.4 and 1QSb 5.23–27; 14.29; 30.31. Other instances are at Ex 21.20, 2Sm

7.14, Mc 4.14, Ps 89.33, Jb 9.34; 21.9, Lm 3.1. Sir 32.23 may belong with B or possibly with D. Is 14.5, Zc 10.11 and Ps 125.3 belong with D, but may have overtones of B. Often it is God who chastises and punishes, sometimes using a hostile nation to accomplish this (Gray 1912:196, 204).

C. Weapon

B often shades into C, depending on the degree of force and hostility expressed. Included here are only those occurrences where a military and lethal intent is expressed.

2Sm 18.14: See *Text doubtful.*

2Sm 23.21//1Ch 11.23: Here the stick carried by Benaiah seems to be a weapon (a club? — Fohrer *BHH* II:946), but from the heroic mismatch between him and the Egyptian, and the way in which he kills the Egyptian with his own spear, a שֵׁבֶט is evidently a less powerful weapon in combat than a spear.

D. Symbol of Authority

D also shades into B when it expresses the authority to chastise, e.g. Is 9.3, 10.15, perhaps Ps 125.3, Is 14.5, Nu 24.17, Zc 10.11. However, in Gn 49.10, Jdg 5.14, Ezk 19.11, 14, Am 1.5, 8, Ps 45.7[2] שֵׁבֶט is a more static symbol of leadership.

Gn 49.10: שֵׁבֶט here is often emended to שֹׁבֵט or שֹׁפֵט (see *Text doubtful*), on the ground that the parallel מְחֹקֵק implies a human figure. Such emendation is not accepted by all scholars. Indeed, 'between his feet' seems to have a literal application, referring to a long staff resting between a ruler's feet on the ground, as well as a possible allusion to Judah's pre-eminent progeny. Against Skinner (1930:519-20), it is clear from the section of *Syntagmatics* that שבט can be treated almost as an animate being, being the subject of several active verbs, cf. Nu 24.17. However, as Westermann (1982:261) points out, it cannot refer to a Judaean king but to the staff of the commander of a tribe.

Nu 24.17: This would be a good example of שֵׁבֶט of category D. It certainly symbolises both power and the human possessor of power, and the verb מחץ also suggests an element of meaning D. Zobel (1993:968–69) takes it to indicate the rise of David, and Gray (1903: 369) as part of the royal insignia. However, Ehrlich (1909:202) argued for the sense 'comet' for שֵׁבֶט, a meaning known from the Talmud (כוכבא דשביט), and supported both by the parallelism of כּוֹכָב and the use of the vb דרך. He has been followed by Gemser (1925:301-302), and Hempel (1950:276 n. 3), against Albright (1944:219, 225) who understands it as 'tribes'.

Jdg 5.14: שֵׁבֶט here is not always regarded as indicating a sceptre, but the parallel מְחֹקְקִים is similar to that found in Gn 49.10. The problem seems to be that the word סֹפֵר does not normally indicate someone with supreme authority. Thus Moore (1898:153) compares it to שֹׁטֵר and translates the parallel phrases as 'truncheon-bearers//muster-master's staff'. However, Rudolph (1947:201), followed by Lindars (1995:255), suggested punctuating as *סְפָר 'bronze', cf. Akk *siparru,* or alternatively as *סַפָּר, 'sapphire'. In contrast, Tsevat (1952–53:107), followed by Soggin (1981:89), pointed to the Akk vb *šapāru,* 'to rule', for evidence that סָפַר can refer to a ruler.

Ps 2.9: There is general agreement that this is a royal psalm, and that therefore שֵׁבֶט here is likely to represent a royal sceptre. However, it is unclear whether Ps 2.9 depicts the king with his rod of iron shattering the nations (= MT תְּרֹעֵם, from the Arm root רעע) or shepherding them (= LXX, *תִּרְעֵם, from the AH root רעה). Either pointing of the consonantal text is possible: see Soggin (1970:195). Kleber (1943) argues that MT reflected an ancient Sum and Eg ceremony of breaking pots, but Wilhelmi (1977) prefers the understanding of LXX, on the ground that the reference is to the king's judicial function. Though this latter interpretation does not fit very well with the rather violent imagery of v.9b, it might fit in with the ideas of v.10 where chastisement and discipline are the keynotes, rather than destruction. Emerton (1978:502-03) suggests translating the verb as 'thou mayest break them', indicating the potential power of the king towards rebellious subjects.

Thus, depending on the interpretation of תרעם, שֵׁבֶט in Ps 2.9 may have overtones of either A or C. However, Tsevat (1952–53:107) denies that the iron staff is an emblem of sovereignty: it is 'merely the tool for smashing the nations'.

Though some have identified the 'iron sceptre' with some maces bearing iron heads found in the Ancient Near East, Lemaire (1986:30) disputes this identification, on the ground that there is no proof that such maces are royal. Instead he notes types of the 8th century found at Nimrud, Samos, Zenjirli and Byblos which consist an iron rod inserted into a bronze sceptre, making a formidable mace. These seem to be typical of Aramaean or Aramaized areas, and appear to be royal in that they are inscribed with the owners' names. Sawyer (1983) takes the description 'rod of iron' less literally, noting the violent and foreign overtones that the noun בַּרְזֶל has in BH. Ps 2.9 is one of the few references to iron in BH that are associated with Yahweh and Israel. Singer (1980:188) speaks of the general ambivalence in BH towards iron as a symbol, but sees its significance in Ps 2.9 as repesenting the absolute and irrestistible power of the Messiah over iniquity.

Caquot (1956:36) has argued that the מַטֵּה עֹז in Ps 110.2 is equivalent to the שֵׁבֶט בַּרְזֶל in Ps 2.9, both symbols of power and sovereignty.

Ps 45.7: The phrase שֵׁבֶט מִישֹׁר occurs in Ps 45.7b, and is understood as 'sceptre of justice'. Olivier (1979) indicates similar phrases and their contexts in the Ancient Near East, e.g. Akk ḫaṭṭu išartu 'just sceptre', which denotes the divine mandate to rule and which is used with the verbs reʾû 'to shepherd' and rapāšu 'to enlarge': Ug ḫṭ mṭpṭk, Arm ḫṭr mšpṭh 'sceptre of judgement'. He suggests that therefore שֵׁבֶט מִישֹׁר is a metaphor for just rule, influenced by the Neo-Assyrian court as is the rest of the psalm.

Ps 125.3: Dahood (1970:215) understands in the sense of D, in taking it as 'sceptre of the wicked', referring to the rule of the wicked. Others take it as the scourge or punishment of the wicked (B), which will not come to pass for the righteous.

Ezk 19.11,14: Here שֵׁבֶט fits well into the metaphor of a vine, with its double meaning of 'stick' and 'sceptre'. Zimmerli (1969:I,429–30: ET I,397–98) and Greenberg (1983:353) understand 'rulers' sceptres' as an allusion to the many members of the royal dynasty. However, the form שִׁבְטֵי may be a pl of majesty (GK § 124). Ehrlich (1909:72) emends to sg, following LXX.

Ezk 21.15,18: These verses are so obscure that it is hard to determine whether שֵׁבֶט refers to a tribe, a sceptre (van den Born 1954:135f, Caquot 1956:37 n.2) or a rod of discipline (Bewer 1951:197f; 1953:161-62): in fact Zimmerli (1969:I,470–71;ET I,426–29) refrains from translating what he considers to be independent glosses on the main text. Caquot (1956:37 n. 2) has no difficulty with the verse, however, and believes that שֵׁבֶט represents the king, who laughs at all other trees, i.e. other sovereigns. Allen (1989) takes note of the textual difficulties, such as the f ptc with the m noun. He explains Ezk 21.15b, 18a as arising from the incorporation of marginal glosses referring to the downfall of Zedekiah into the main text: the king is seen as 'the rejected sceptre'. This explanation involves reading *נִמְאָסֶת for מֹאֶסֶת in both cases, and taking נָשִׂיא as a misreading of the abbreviation for *נְשִׂיא יִשְׂרָאֵל in v.15, giving 'the ruler of Israel, the rejected sceptre' (15b), and 'what if also the rejected sceptre will not continue?' (18a). The f ptc is due to זֹאת in v. 32b to which the gloss refers. Van den Born (1954:135-36) considered that the use of שֵׁבֶט alluded to Gn 49.10.

Zc 10.11: Meyers and Meyers (1993:226-27) note the parallel with גָּאוֹן, referring to the political or economic power of a nation or city.

Am 1.5, 8: This is a clear example of D, though it is unclear exactly what sort of rank the תֹּמֵךְ שֵׁבֶט holds (Andersen and Freedman 1989:254).

Brettler (1989:80) notes that although God has a sceptre, שֵׁבֶט never occurs in contexts to do with God's kingship, for instance the enthronement psalms or Is 6.1. So it may indicate a weapon executing divine punishment rather than symbolising royal authority (Is 10.5,26, 30.31; Ps 110.2; Jb 9.34, 21.9; Lm 3.1). But God is also described as having a שֵׁבֶט in his role as a shepherd (cf. Zobel 1993: 971-72), which may of course be a sub-metaphor of kingship (Mc 7.14; Ps 23.4). The idea of the Lord bearing a staff of authority is conveyed by the participle מְחֹקֵק, not by the noun שֵׁבֶט plus verb: Is 33.22 כִּי יהוה שֹׁפְטֵנוּ יהוה מְחֹקְקֵנוּ יהוה מַלְכֵּנוּ הוּא יוֹשִׁיעֵנוּ. Since there is a close connection between royal justice and שֵׁבֶט, it is surprising that the Lord is never described as having a sceptre of justice.

7. Art and Archaeology

A.1 Since there are various functions attached to the noun שֵׁבֶט, there are a number of possible artefacts to consider in art and archaeology: weapons such as maces and clubs, staffs for defence, rods for punishing or disciplining, sceptres.

A.2 In the Ancient Near East a club was generally a stick with a bulbous end sometimes made separately from the shaft. Warclubs existed in Palestine before 1500 BCE. Most ancient examples have a stone for the head, though this is sometimes made of bronze or lead, and one found SW of Gaza has an iron head, cf. Ps 2.9 (Bonnet 1926, Fohrer BHH II:946), though Lemaire (1986) disputes this interpretation (see above in Exegesis). Keel has a number of illustrations of kings wielding maces or scimitars over a cowering enemy. Most are Eg (figures 395–399), but figures 400 a–c are from Palestine, and figure 401 from Samaria.

A.3 Bonnet (1986) observes how, in the historical period in Eg and Bab, clubs became symbols of the cult or of kingship rather than weapons. Against this, van Buren (1956) sees the origin of the Sumerian and Assyrian sceptre in the fertility symbol of a green leafy bough which kings or gods bear in ancient art, later replaced by a sceptre with a floral motif in precious stones and metals at the tip. The sceptre symbolised the granting of regal power by the gods to a monarch and was described in the Sumerian kinglist as having descended from heaven.

A.4 Lurker (1973:299) describes the sceptre of Eg gods and kings as a crook, which was originally a shepherd's staff. Its sign in writing meant 'to rule'. This gives a rather different picture from that of Bonnet's development from club to sceptre.

A.5 Roeder/Thomsen/Unger (1929:523–27) give examples of sceptres in Ancient Near Eastern art and archaeology. In Eg tomb pictures Syrians carry a sceptre with a bulbous end, and possibly a staff with golden rings, and in the annals of Thutmosis II Syrian princes have a sceptre decorated with gold. A more ornate sceptre came from the sack of Megiddo and was decorated with gold and gems. In Mesopotamia there were several different words for sceptres and clubs, depending on the material from which they were made. A *šibṭu* or *šabbiṭu* referred to a sceptre made from a reed, a *ḫuṭaru* (cf. AH חֹטֶר) meant a sceptre made of wood. In the stele of Shalmaneser III the Assyrian king has a sceptre in the form of a long thin staff. However, sceptres are not mentioned in connection with Israel in the monarchic period: they belong to foreigners (Am 1.5 Aramaeans; Am 1.8 Philistines; Est 5.2 etc. Persians; and one could add Is 14.5, Zc 10.11). שֵׁבֶט, מְחֹקֵק, מִשְׁעֶנֶת, מַטֶּה are symbols of Israelite military leadership in BH.

A.6 There are various rods, batons and clubs carried by many of the royal and divine figures from Egypt, Mesopotamia and Syria in *ANEP* 379–572. These can sometimes be identified as sceptres, i.e. emblems of sovereignty: see the commentaries on the individual illustrations.

8. Conclusion

A.1 שֵׁבֶט (in the non-tribal sense) occurs primarily with verbs of striking, but can itself be broken. It implies a rigid instrument used for hitting. What is struck by a שֵׁבֶט can be inanimate as in Is 28.27, or living, either animals or people. Generally the striking takes place as an act of violence, punishment or chastisement. However, it is not always easy to discern to which category an occurrence of שֵׁבֶט belongs. Being at base a prosaic word like Eng 'stick', when שֵׁבֶט occurs in parallel with another word, this second word often has a more poetic or specialised meaning which can clarify the sense in which שֵׁבֶט is being used.

A.2 Although שֵׁבֶט often appears as a concrete instrument in AH, it frequently functions as the subject in the sentence. Since it can take on animate qualities in this way, it is not surprising that it is sometimes personified by the Versions.

שֵׁבֶט can be used symbolically for the power to rule, punish, fight, comfort or chastise, and so can stand for a ruler, as in Gn 49.10.

A.3 As for functioning as a symbol of royalty, the only convincing connection of שֵׁבֶט with the monarchy is at Ps 45.7, a composition which may be influenced by the Assyrian court. Ps 45.7 is also the only place where שֵׁבֶט occurs both in connection with the Israelite monarchy and seemingly in the sense of a modern sceptre, an ornamental baton held by the monarch as a token of royal power. In Ps 2.9 שֵׁבֶט is not a mere emblem but a shepherd's rod or a weapon. The four occurrences in Ezk may allude to monarchical rule in Israel, though there are unresolved textual difficulties in Ezk 21.15, 18 that hinder interpretation. In other cases where שֵׁבֶט is a sign of rulership, the ruler is not indisputably both Israelite and royal (Is 14.5, Am 1.5, 8, Zc 10.11, perhaps Sir 32.23: Gn 49.10, Nu 24.17, Jdg 5.14).

BIBLIOGRAPHY

Albright, W.F. 1944. The oracles of Balaam. *JBL* 63:207–33.

Allen, L.C. 1989. The rejected sceptre in Ezekiel XXI 15b, 18a. *VT* 39:67–71.

Andersen, F.I., and D.N. Freedman. 1989. Commentary on *Amos* (AB 24A).

André, G. 1984. Article מַקֵּל in *TWAT* IV:1129–31.

Begg, C. 1982. The reading *šbṭy(km)* in Deut 29,9 and 2 Sam 7,7. *ETL* 58:87–105.

Bewer, J.A. 1951. Beiträge zur Exegese des Buches Ezechiel. *ZAW* 63:193–201.

_____. 1953. Textual and exegetical notes on the Book of Ezekiel. *JBL* 72:158–68.

Bonnet, H. 1926. Chapter Schlagstock und Keule in *Die Waffen der Völker des Alten Orients* 1–16. Leipzig.

van den Born, A. 1954. *Ezechiël* . Roermond.

Brenner, A. 1979–80. על מטה ושבט וסיווגן הסמנטי [*Maṭṭeh* and *šebeṭ* semantically] *Leš* 44:100–108.

Brettler, M.Z. 1989. *God is King. Understanding an Israelite Metaphor.* JSOTSS 76. Sheffield.

Budde, K. 1902. Commentary on *Samuel.* (KHC).

van Buren, E.D. 1956. The sceptre, its origin and significance. *Revue d'assyrologie et d'archéologie* 50:101–103.

Caquot, A. 1956. Remarques sur le Psaume CX. *Semitica* 6:33–52.

Caspari, D.W. 1926. Commentary on *Samuel* (KAT VII).

Cross, F.M. and Freedman, D.N. 1975. *Studies in Ancient Yahwistic Poetry.* SBLDS. Missoula, MT.

Dahood, M. 1963. *Proverbs and North West Semitic Philology.* Rome.

_____. 1966. Commentary on *Psalms* I (AB).

_____. 1970. Commentary on *Psalms* III (AB).

Dalman, G. *AuS = Arbeit und Sitte in Palästina II: Der Ackerbau, III:Von der Ernte zum Mehl, VI: Zeltleben, Vieh- und Milchwirtschaft, Jagd, Fischfang* (Gütersloh 1932, 1933, 1939, repr. Hildesheim 1964).

Delitzsch, F. 1885. Assyriologische Notizen zum Alten Testament IV. Das Schwertheid Ezech. 21, 13–22. *ZK* 2:385–98.

Driver, G.R. 1962. Plurima mortis imago, 133–34 in *Studies and Essays in Honour of Abraham A. Neumann,* eds. M. Ben-Horin, B.D. Weinryb, S. Zeitlin. Leiden.

Driver, S.R. [2]1913. *Notes on the Hebrew Text and Topography of the Books of Samuel.* Oxford.

Ehrlich, A.B. 1909. *Randglossen zur hebräischen Bibel* II. Leipzig, repr. Hildesheim 1968.

Eidelberg, Sh. 1968. עוד על שופט ושבט. *Leš* 32:275–76.

Elliger, K. 1966. Commentary on *Leviticus* (HAT I/4).

Emerton, J.A. 1978. The translation of the verbs in the imperfect in Psalm II,9. *JTS* 29:499–503.

Falk, Z.W. 1966. שופט ושבט. *Leš* 30:243–47.

Fohrer, G. 1964. Article 'Keule' in *BHH* II:946.

Fokkelman, J.P. 1981. *Narrative Art and Poetry in the Books of Samuel.* I–II. Assen.

Gemser, B. 1925. Der Stern aus Jakob (Num. 24.17) *ZAW* NF 2:301f.

Gevirtz, S. 1980. On Hebrew *šēbeṭ* 'judge'. 61–66 in *The Bible World. Essays in Honour of C.H.Gordon* ed. G. Rendsburg et al. New York.

Gottwald, N.K. 1979. *The Tribes of Yahweh,* esp. 245–56. New York.

Gray, G.B. 1903. Commentary on *Numbers* (ICC).

_____. 1912. *Isaiah* (ICC).

Greenberg, M. 1983. Commentary on *Ezekiel 1–20* (AB).

Hassan, A. 1979. Die Wörter *šbd* und *m'wd. Mitteilungen des deutschen Instituts Kairo* 35:119–24.

Hempel, J. 1950. Rev. of C.H. Gordon, *Ugaritic Handbook,* in *ZAW* 62:275f.

Hertzberg, H.W. [2]1960. Commentary on *Samuel* (ATD). ET 1964 *I and II Samuel.* (OTL).

Joüon, P. 1912. Notes de critique textuelle (suite). *Mélanges de l'Université S. Joseph* 5:452.

Keel, O. 1972. *Die Welt der altorientalischen Bildsymbolik.* Neukirchen-Vluyn: ET 1978 *The Symbolism of the Biblical World. Ancient Near Eastern Iconography and the Book of Psalms.* New York.

Kleber, W. 1943. Ps 2:9 and an ancient oriental ceremony. *CBQ* 5:66.

Kutscher, Y. 1968. בשולי מאמרו של פרופ' ליונשטם. [A marginal note to S.E. Loewenstamm's article] *Leš* 32:274.

Lemaire, A. 1986. 'Avec un sceptre de fer'. Ps II,9 et l'archéologie. *BN* 32:25–30.

Lewy, H. 1895. *Die semitischer Fremdwörter in griechischen.* Berlin.

Lindars, B. 1995. *Judges 1–5* . Edinburgh.

Loewenstamm, S.E. 1968. שופט ושבט. *Leš* 32:272–74.

Lurker, M. 1973. Article 'Stab' in *Wörterbuch biblischer Bilder und Symbole* 299–301. Munich.

Lust, J. 1995. The Greek version of Balaam's third and fourth oracles. The ἄνθρωπος in Num 24:7 and 17. Messianism and lexicography. 233–57 in *VIII Congress of the International Organization for Septuagint and Cognate Studies, Paris 1992,* ed. L. Greenspoon and O. Munnich. SBLSCS 41. Atlanta GA.

Mayer Modena, M.L. 1987. 'A proposito di alcune denominiazioni del 'bastone' in ebraico biblico' *Annali della facoltà di filosofia e lettere dell'università statale die Milano* 40:25–30.

McCarter, K. 1984. Commentary on *2 Samuel* (AB).

Mendenhall, G.E. 1973.*The Tenth Generation.* Baltimore/London.

Meyers and Meyers, C.L. and E.M. 1993. Commentary on *Zechariah* 9–14 (AB).

Moore, G.F. 1898. Commentary on *Judges* (ICC).

Murray, D. 1987. Once again *ʾt ʾḥd šbṭy yśrʾl* in II Samuel 7:7. *RB* 94:389–96.

Nowack, W. 1902. Commentary on *Samuel* (HKAT I,4).

Olivier, J.P.J. 1979. The sceptre of justice and Ps 45:7b. *JNWSL* 7:45–54.

Pedersen, J. 1926. *Israel: its Life and Culture I-II,* esp. 29–46. London-Copenhagen.

Power, E. 1928. The shepherd's two rods in modern Palestine and in some passages of the Old Testament. *Bib* 9:434–42.

Reid, P.V. 1975. *šbṭy* in 2 Samuel 7:7. *CBQ* 37:17–20.

Robert, P. de. 1971. Juges ou tribus en 2 Samuel vii 7. *VT* 21:116–18.

Roeder, Thomsen, Unger, 1929. Article 'Zepter' in *Reallexicon der Vorgeschichte* 14:523–27.

Rudolph, W. 1947. Textkritische Anmerkungen zum Richterbuch, 199–212 in *Festschrift Otto Eissfeldt zum 60. Geburtstage,* ed. J. Fück. Halle an der Saale.

Sasson, J.M. 1972. A note on *šarbiṭ. VT* 22:111.

Sawyer, J.F.A. 1983. The meaning of *barzel* in the biblical expressions 'chariots of iron', 'yoke of iron', etc. 129–34 in *Midian, Moab and Edom,* ed. J.F.A. Sawyer and D.J.A. Clines. JSOTSS 24. Sheffield.

Schulz, A. 1920. Commentary *Samuel.*(EHAT).

Schunk, K.D. Article 'Stamm 1. AT' in *BHH* III:1851f.

Simian-Yofre, H. and H.-J. Fabry. 1984. Article מַטֶּה in *TWAT* IV:818–26.

Singer, K.H. 1980. *Die metalle Gold, Silber, Kupfer and Eisen im AT ind ihre Symbolik* 120–26, 185–88. Forschung zur Bibel 43. Würzburg.

Skinner, J. ²1930. Commentary on *Genesis* (ICC).

Smith, H.P. 1899. Commentary on *Samuel* (ICC).

Soggin, J.A. 1970. Zum zweiten Psalm. 191–207 in *Wort-Gebot-Glaube, Walter Eichrodt zum 80. Geburtstag,* ed. H.J. Stoebe. Abhandlungen zur Theologie des Alten und Neuen Testaments 59. Zürich.

———. 1981. *Judges* . London.

Stoebe, H.J. 1966. Article 'Zepter' in *BHH* III:2234.

———. 1994. commentary on *2 Samuel.*(KAT).

Toombs, L.E. 1962. Article 'Scepter' in *IDB* IV:234–5.

Tsevat, M. 1952–53. Some biblical notes. *HUCA* 24:107–14.

Wellhausen, J. 1871. *Der Text der Bücher Samuelis.* Göttingen.

Westermann, C. 1982. Commentary on *Genesis* 37–50 (BK).

Wildberger, H. 1972–92. Commentary on *Isaiah* (BK).

Wilhelmi, G. 1977. Der Hirt mit dem eisernen Szepter: Űberlegungen zu Ps ii,9. *VT* 27:196–204.

Zimmerli, W. 1969. Commentary on *Ezekiel* (BK) = ET 1979 *Ezekiel* I 1-24 (Herm).

Zobel, H.-J. 1993. Article שֵׁבֶט in *TWAT* VII:966–74.

Alison Salvesen
University of Oxford

APPENDIX

Translation equivalents of frequent lexemes in versions

דֶּרֶךְ

LXX

ἁμάρτημα (Ho 10.13 [Vaticanus]);
ἅρμα (?Ho 10.13 [pl for s]);
ἁμαρτία (1Kg 22.53);
ἀνάπαυμα (?Jb 3.23);
ἀνομία (Ezk 20.30 [pl for s]);
ἀσεβής (?Jb 8.19);
ἀτραπός (Sir 5.9 [or the translation of שביל in MS C]);
βλέπω ἀπέναντι (Ezk 42.7);
βλέπω εἰς (Pr 16.25b);
βλέπω κατά (Ezk 40.32, 47.2b);
βλέπω πρός (Ezk 40.24αβ, 42.15b);
γῆ (Jr 2.18 [2x, Alexandrinus], Jb 38.19);
γνῶσις (?Pr 9.6);
δίκαιος (?Pr 16.9 [=16.1, pl for s]);
δικαίωμα (Jb 34.27);
δίοδος (Pr 7.8 [pl for s]);
ἑαυτός (?Nu 24.25= דרכו);
ἐγγίζειν (Gn 48.7a);
τὸ κατ᾽ ἐθισμόν (Gn 31.35);
ἔννοια (Pr 23.19 [pl for s]);
ἔξοδος (Ezk 16.25 [Alexandrinus]);
ἐπί (Ezk 21.2, 42.4);
ἐπιβαίνω (?Sir 51.15);
ἔργον (Jb 34.21, 36.23 [pl for s], Pr 16.2, Sir 10.6 [pl for s], 26, 32.22 [=32.23, s for pl]);
ἔρημος (Sir 8.16);
ἔρχομαι εἰς (Pr 14.12b);
εὐοδόω (Gn 24.27 [= בַּדֶּרֶךְ נחה]);
ζωή (Ps 36.7 [Vaticanus, Sinaiticus]);
ἡμέρα (Ezk 28.15);
θεός (?Am 8.14);
ἴχνος (Pr 30.19αα [pl for s]);
καθήκω (Gn 19.31);
κακία (1Kg 13.33; Jr 15.7);
καρδία (Ps 37.14 [=36.14]);
κατά (Ezk 40.6, 10, 22, 24αα, 42.1αα, 12b, 43.1, 4b, 46.9);
καταβαίνω (Ezk 47.15);

κατάβασις (Ezk 48.1);
καταδιώκω (La 3.11);
κατέναντι (Ezk 40.10, 42.1αβ);
καθ᾽ ὁδόν (Ezk 42.15a);
κατὰ τὴν ὁδόν (Ezk 43.2, 4a, 44.1, 3 [2x], 4, 46.2, 8a, 9 [4x], 47.2αα);
λαλέω (?Jb 13.15);
τὸ λιθῶδες (Sir 32.20b [MS B: נֶגֶף]);
νόσος (?Jb 24.23);
νοῦς (?Pr 31.3 [s for pl]);
ὁδοποιεῖν (Is 62.10 [Heb: פַּנּוּ דֶרֶךְ]);
ὁδός (Gn 3.24, 6.12, 16.7, 18.19 [pl for s], 19.2, 24.21, 40, 42, 48, 56, 28.20, 30.36, 31.23, 32.2, 33.16, 35.3, 19, 38.16, 21, 42.25, 38, 45.21, 23, 24, 48.7b, 49.17, Ex 3.18, 4.24, 5.3, 8.23, 13.17, 18, 21, 18.8, 20 [pl for s], 23.20, 32.8, 33.3, Lv 26.22, Nu 9.10, 13, 10.33 [2x], 11.31 [2x], 14.25, 20.17, 21.1, 4 [2x], 22, 33, 22.23 [3x], 31, 32, 34, 33.8, Dt 1.2, 19, 22, 31, 33 [2x], 40, 2.1, 8, 27 [1x; Heb 2x], 3.1, 5.33, 6.7, 8.2, 6, 9.12, 16, 10.12, 11.19, 22, 28, 30, 13.6, 14.24, 17.16, 19.3, 6, 9, 22.4, 6, 23.5, 24.9, 25.17, 18, 26.17, 27.18, 28.7 [2x], 9, 25 [2x], 29, 68, 30.16, 31.29, 32.4, Josh 1.8 [pl for s], 2.7, 16, 22 [pl for s], 3.4 [2x], 5.4, 7, 9.11, 13, 10.10, 12.3, 22.5, 23.14, 24.17, Jdg 2.17, 19, 22, 4.9, 8.11, 9.25, 37, 17.8, 18.5, 6, 26, 19.9, 27, 20.42, 1Sm 1.18, 4.13, 6.9, 6.12 [2x], 8.3 [s as Ketiv], 5 [s for pl], 9.6, 8, 12.23, 13.17, 18 [2x], 15.2, 18, 20, 17.52, 18.14 [pl for s], 21.6, 24.4, 8, 20, 25.12, 26.3, 25, 28.22, 30.2, 2Sm 2.24, 4.7, 11.10, 13.30, 34, 15.2, 23, 16.13, 18.23, 22.22, 31, 33, 1Kg 1.49, 2.2, 3, 4, 3.14, 8.25 [pl for s], 32, 36, 39, 44 [2x], 48, 58, 11.29, 33, 38, 13.9, 10 [2x], 12 [2x], 17, 24 [2x], 25, 26, 28, 15.26, 34, 16.2, 19, 26, 18.6 [2x], 7, 43, 19.4, 7, 15, 20.38, 22.43, 53 [2x], 2Kg 2.23, 3.8 [2x], 9, 20, 6.19, 7.15, 8.18, 27, 9.27, 10.12, 11.16, 19, 16.3, 17.13, 19.28, 33, 21.21, 22, 22.2, 25.4 [2x], Is 2.3 [s for pl], 8.11, 23, 10.24, 26, 15.5, 30.11, 21, 35.8 [2x? for Heb 3x], 37.29, 34, 40.3, 14, 27, 42.16, 24, 43.16, 19, 45.13, 48.15, 17, 49.9, 11, 51.10, 53.6, 55.7 [s for pl], 8 [2x], 9 [s for pl], 9, 56.11, 57.14 [pl for s], 14, 17 [pl for s], 18, 58.2, 59.8, 63.17 [s for pl], 64.4, 65.2, 66.3, Jr 2.18 [2x], 23bα [pl for s], 23bβ, 33a [pl for s], 33b, 36 [pl for s], 3.2, 13, 21 [pl for s], 4.11, 18 [pl for s], 5.4, 5, 6.16 [2x], 25 [pl for s], 27, 7.3, 5, 23 [pl for s], 10.2 [pl for s], 23, 12.1, 12.16 [s for pl], 16.17, 17.10 [pl as Qere], 18.11 [1x for 2x], 15 [2x], 21.8 [2x], 22.21, 23.12, 25.5, 26.3 [=LXX 33.3], 26.13 [=33.13], 28.11 [=35.11], 31.9 [=38.9], 31.21 [=38.21], 32.19 [=39.19], 19 [s for pl], 39, 35.15 [=42.15], 36.3 [=43.3], 7, 42.3 [=49.3], 48.19 [=31.19], 50.5 [=27.5], 52.7 [2x], Ezk 3.18 [pl for s], 19, 7.3 [=7.7], 4 [=8, s for pl], 8 [=5], 9 [=6], 27 [pl for s], 9.2, 10 [pl for s], 11.21, 13.22, 14.22 [pl for s], 23 [pl for s], 16.25, 27, 31, 43 [pl for s], 47 [2x], 61 [s for pl], 18.25 [2x], 25 bβ [s for pl], 29 [2x], 29b [s for pl], 30 [s for pl], 20.43, 44, 21.24 [2x], 25, 26 [2x], 22.31 [pl for s], 23.13, 31, 24.14, 33.8, 9 [2x], 11 [2x], 17 [2x], 20 [2x], 36.17 [2x], 19, 31, 32, 46.8b, 47.2b, Ho 2.8, 4.9, 6.9, 9.8, 12.3, 13.7, 14.10, Jl 2.7, Am 2.7, 4.10, Jn 3.8, 10 [pl for s], Mc 4.2 [s for pl], Nah 1.3, 2.2, Hg 1.5, 7, Zc 1.4, 6, 3.7, Ml 2.8, 9, 3.1, Ps 1.1, 6 [2x], 2.12, 5.9, 10.5 [=9.26, pl as Qere], 18.22 [=17.22], 31, 33, 25.4 [=24.4], 8, 9, 12, 27.11 [=26.11], 32.8 [=31.8], 35.6 [=34.6], 36.5 [=35.5], 37.5 [=36.5], 7, 23, 34, 39.2 [=38.2], 49.14 [=48.14], 50.23 [=49.23], 51.15 [=50.15], 67.3 [=66.3], 77.14

[=76.14], 20, 80.13 [=79.13], 81.14 [=80.14], 85.14 [=84.14], 86.11 [=85.11], 89.42 [=88.42], 91.11 [=90.11], 95.10 [=94.10], 101.2 [=100.2], 6, 102.24 [=101.24], 103.7 [=102.7], 107.4 [=106.4], 7, 17, 40, 110.7 [=109.7], 119.1 [=118.1], 3, 5, 14, 26, 27, 29, 30, 32, 33, 37, 59, 168, 128.1 [=127.1], 138.5 [=137.5], 139.3 [=138.3], 24 [2x], 143.8 [=142.8], 145.17 [=144.17], 146.9 [=145.9], Jb 4.6 [s for pl], 12.24, 17.9, 19.12, 21.14, 29, 31, 22.3 [s for pl], 28, 23.10, 11 [pl for s], 24.4, 26.14 [s as Ketiv], 28.23, 26, 31.4 [s for pl], 7, 38.25, Pr 1.15, 31, 2.8, 12, 13, 3.6, 3.17 [2x], 23 [pl for s], 31, 4.11 [pl for s], 14 [pl for s], 19 [pl for s], 26, 5.8, 21, 6.6, 23, 7.19, 25, 27, 8.13 [pl for s], 22 [pl for s], 10.9, 11.5 [pl for s], 20 [pl for s], 12.15 [pl for s], 26, 28 [pl for s], 13.15 [pl for s], 14.2, 8 [pl for s], 12a, 14, 15.9 [pl for s], 19 [pl for s], 16.7 [s for pl], 17 [pl for s], 25a [pl for s], 29 [pl for s], 31 [pl for s], 19.3 [pl for s], 16, 20.24 [pl for s], 21.8 [pl for s], 16, 29 [pl as Ketiv], 22.5 [pl for s], 23.26, 26.13, 28.10, 29.27, 30.19aβ [pl for s], 19bβ [pl for s], 20, Ru 1.7, Ec 10.3, 11.5, 9, 12.5, La 1.4, 12, 2.15, 3.9, 40 [s for pl], Ezr 8.21, 22, 31, Neh 9.12, 19 [2x], 2Ch 6.16, 23 [pl for s], 27, 30, 31, 34 [2x], 38, 7.14, 11.17 [pl for s], 17.3, 6 [s for pl], 18.23, 20.32, 21.6, 12bα [s for pl], 12bβ, 21.13 [pl for s], 22.3 [s for pl], 27.6, 28.2, 34.2, Sir 11.14 [=11.15], 14.21, 16.20, 32.20a, 21 [1x, Heb doublet], 33.11, 37.9, 48.22);

ὁδὸς δικαιοσύνης (Jb 24.13 [s for pl]);
ὁδοιπόρος (Sir 42.3);
ὁδὸς πονηρά (Ezk 18.23 [s for pl]);
ὁδὸς σκολιός (Pr 28.18);
ὁμοιόομαι (Sir 13.1 [= לִמֹּד דרך]);
πάρειμι [ἰέναι] (Pr 9.15 [= עֹבְרֵי דָרֶךְ]);
πάροδος (Gn 38.14);
περίπατος κατά (Ezk 42.11aα);
περίπατος (Ezk 42.12 aβ);
πλάσμα (Jb 40.19 [s for pl]);
πόθεν (Jb 38.24 [= אֵי־זֶה הַדֶּרֶךְ]);
πολυοδία (Is 57.10 [pl for s; Heb רֹב דֶּרֶךְ]);
πούς (Is 58.13);
πρᾶξις (2Ch 13.22, 27.7, 28.26);
πρός (Ezk 8.5 [2x], 40.20, 27 [2x], 44 [2x], 45, 46, 41.11, 12, 42.10, 11aβ, 12aα);
σεαυτόν (?Ex 33.13 [= דְּרָכֶךְ]);
συμβουλεύω (Sir 37.7 [= יוֹעֵץ דרך]);
τὰ μετὰ ταῦτα (?Sir 3.31);
ταραχή (?Sir 11.34c [pl for s]);
τελευτή (?Sir 46.20 [s for pl]);
τρίβος (Is 3.12, Pr 2.20 [pl for s], 30.19bα [pl for s]);
φόβος (?Pr 10.29);
ὡς (?Ezk 42.12aγ).

No translation equivalent: Nu 22.22, 26, Josh 5.5, 8.15, Jdg 5.10, Jr 2.17, 18.11, 23.22, Jb 6.18, Pr 13.6, 21.2, 28.6.
    Unclear: 1Kg 18.27, Pr 8.2.

Large omission in text: Jr 39.4 [2x], Jb 24.18, Pr 8.32, 22.6, Sir 7.17 (doublet), 11.34a.

<u>Pesh</u>

ʾurḥaʾ (Gn 3.24, 6.12, 16.7, 18.19 [pl for s], 19.2, 31, 24.21, 27, 40, 42, 48, 56, 28.20, 32.2, 33.16, 35.3, 19, 38.16, 42.25, 38, 45.21, 23, 24, 48.7 [2x], 49.17, Ex 3.18, 4.24, 13.17, 18, 21, 18.8, 20, 23.20, 32.8, 33.13, Lv 26.22, Nu 9.10, 13, 14.25, 20.17, 21.1, 4 [2x], 22, 22.22, 23 [3x], 26, 31, 32, 34, Dt 1.22, 33 [2x], 40, 2.1, 8, 27 [2x], 3.1, 5.33, 6.7, 8.2, 6, 9.12, 16, 10.12, 11.19, 22, 28, 30, 13.6, 14.24, 17.16, 19.3, 6, 9, 22.4, 6, 23.5, 24.9, 25.17, 26.17, 27.18, 28.7 [2x], 9, 25 [2x], 29, 68, 30.16, 31.29, 32.4, Josh 2.7, 16, 22, 3.4 [2x], 5.4, 5, 8.15, 9.11, 13, 10.10, 12.3, 23.14, 24.17, Jdg 2.17, 19 [pl for s], 22, 4.9, 5.10 [pl for s], 8.11, 9.25, 37, 17.8, 18.5, 6, 26, 19.27, 20.42, 1Sm 1.18, 4.13, 6.9, 6.12aα, 8.3 [pl as Qere], 5, 9.6, 8, 12.23, 13.17, 18 [2x], 15.2, 18, 20, 17.52, 18.14 [pl for s], 21.6, 24.4, 8, 20, 25.12, 26.3, 25, 28.22, 30.2, 2Sm 2.24, 4.7, 11.10, 13.30, 34, 15.23, 16.13, 18.23, 22.22, 31, 33, 1Kg 1.49, 2.2, 3, 4, 3.14, 8.25 [pl for s], 32, 36, 39, 44 [2x], 48, 58, 11.29, 33, 38, 13.9, 10 [2x], 12 [2x], 17, 24 [2x], 25, 26, 28, 33, 15.26, 34 [pl for s], 16.2 [pl for s], 19 [pl for s], 26, 18.6 [2x], 7, 27, 43, 19.7, 15, 20.38, 22.43, 53 [3x, pl for s], 2Kg 2.23, 3.8 [2x], 20, 6.19, 7.15, 8.18, 27, 9.27, 10.12, 11.16, 19, 16.3, 17.13, 19.28, 33, 21.21, 22, 22.2, 25.4 [2x], Is 2.3, 3.12, 8.11, 23, 10.24, 26, 15.5, 30.11, 21, 35.8 [2x for Heb 3x], 37.29, 34, 40.3, 14, 27 [pl for s], 42.16, 24, 43.16, 19, 45.13, 48.15, 17, 49.9, 11 [pl for s], 51.10, 55.7 [s for pl], 8 [2x], 9 [2x?], 56.11 [pl for s], 57.10 [pl for s], 14 [2x], 17, 18, 58.2, 13 [s for pl], 59.8, 62.10, 63.17 [s for pl], 64.4, 65.2, 66.3, Jr 2.17, 18 [2x], 23bα [pl for s], 23bβ, 33a [pl for s], 33b, 36 [pl for s], 3.2, 13, 21 [pl for s], 4.11, 18 [pl for s], 5.4, 5, 6.16 [2x], 25, 27 [pl for s], 7.3, 5, 23, 10.2, 23 [pl for s], 12.1, 12.16, 15.7, 16.17, 17.10 [pl as Qere], 18.11 [2x], 15 [2x], 21.8 [2x], 22.21, 23.12 [pl for s], 22 [pl for s], 25.5, 26.3, 26.13, 28.11, 31.9 [pl for s], 32.19 [2x], 35.15, 36.3, 7, 39.4 [2x], 42.3, 48.19, 50.5 [pl for s], 52.7 [2x], Ezk 3.18, 19, 7.3, 4, 8, 9, 27, 8.5 [2x], 9.2, 10, 11.21, 13.22 [pl for s], 14.22 [pl for s], 23 [pl for s], 16.25, 27 [pl for s], 31 [pl for s], 43 [pl for s], 47 [2x], 61, 18.23 [s for pl], 25 [2x], 25bα [pl for s], 29 [2x], 29a [pl for s], 30, 20.30, 43, 44, 21.2, 24 [2x], 25, 26 [2x], 22.31 [pl for s], 23.13, 31 [pl for s], 24.14, 28.15, 33.8, 9b, 11bβ, 17a, 17b [pl for s], 20 [2x], 36.17bα [pl for s], 17bβ, 19 [pl for s], 31, 32, 42.11 [2x], 12 [4x], 43.2, 4a, 44.3bα, 47.15, 48.1, Ho 2.8 [pl for s], 4.9, 6.9, 9.8, 10.13 [pl for s], 12.3, 13.7, 14.10, Jl 2.7 [s for pl], Am 2.7, 4.10, 8.14, Jn 3.8, 10 [pl for s], Mc 4.2 Nah 1.3, 2.2, Hg 1.5, 7, Zc 1.4, 6, 3.7, Ml 2.8, 9, 3.1, Ps 1.6 [2x], 2.12, 5.9, 10.5 [pl as Qere], 18.22, 31, 33, 25.4, 8, 9, 12, 27.11, 32.8, 35.6, 36.5, 37.5, 7, 14 [pl for s], 23, 34, 39.2 [s for pl], 50.23, 51.15 [s for pl], 67.3 [pl for s], 77.14, 20, 80.13, 81.14, 86.11, 89.42, 91.11, 95.10, 101.2, 6, 103.7, 107.4, 7, 17, 40, 110.7, 119.1, 3, 5, 14, 26, 27, 29, 30, 32, 33, 37 [pl for s], 59, 168, 138.5, 139.3, 24 [2x], 143.8, 145.17, 146.9, Jb 4.6 [s for pl], 6.18 [pl for s], 8.19 [pl for s], 12.24, 17.9, 19.12 [pl for s], 21.14, 29, 31, 22.3, 28, 23.10, 11 [pl for s], 24.4, 13, 18, 23, 26.14 [pl as Qere], 28.23 [pl for s], 26, 29.25 [pl for s], 31.4, 7, 34.21, 27, 36.23 [pl for s], 38.19, 24, Pr 1.15, 31 [pl for s], 2.8 [pl for s], 12 [pl for s], 13 [s for pl], 20, 3.6, 3.17 [2x], 23 [pl for s], 31, 4.11 [pl for s], 14, 19 [pl for s], 26 [pl for s], 5.8, 21, 6.6, 23, 7.19, 25, 27, 8.13, 32, 9.6, 15, 10.9, 29, 11.5, 20, 12.15, 26, 28, 13.6, 15, 14.2 [s for pl], 8, 12 [2x], 14, 15.9, 19 [pl for s], 16.2, 7, 9 [pl for s], 17, 25a, 29, 31, 19.3, 16, 20.24, 21.2 [pl for s], 8, 16, 29 [pl as Ketiv], 22.5, 6, 23.26, 26.13, 28.6, 10, 18, 29.27, 30.19 [4x], 20, 31.3, Ec 10.3, 11.5, 9, 12.5 [pl for s], La 1.4, 12, 2.15, 3.9, 11, 40, Ezr 8.21, 22, 31, Neh 9.12, 19 [2x], 2Ch 6.16, 23, 27, 30, 31, 34 [2x], 38, 7.14, 13.22, 17.3, 6, 20.32 [pl for s], 21.6 [pl for s], 12 [2x], 13, 22.3, 27.6, 7, 28.2, 26, 34.2, Sir 3.31, 10.6, 11.14, 34a, 13.1, 14.21, 16.20, 32.20a, 21c, 37.9, 46.20, 48.22);

> *ʾarʿaʾ* (Nu 21.33, Dt 1.19, 31, Ps 85.14, 102.24, Sir 33.11);

> *ʾat̲raʾ* (Sir 8.16);

> *b* (Ezk 46.8 [2x], Ezk 46.9 [4x], 47.2aα);

> *b + ʾurḥaʾ* (Ezk 40.27a, 32);

> *brit̲aʾ* (Jb 40.19; Pr 8.22);

> *d* (Ezk 40.24aβ, 42.1aβ);

> *drk* (Sir 51.15);

> *hlak̲t̲aʾ* (Ezk 42.4);

> *ḥarbaʾ* (Dt 25.18);

> *ḥek̲maʾ* (?Pr 8.2);

> *keʾpaʾ* (Sir 32.20 [MS B: ogn]);

> *l* (Ezk 40.6, 22, 44 [2x?], 45, 46, 41.11, 15aβ, 43.1, 4b, 46.9);

> *l + ʾorḥaʾ* (Ezk 40.24aα, 42.1aα, 15aα, 44.1, 4);

> *maʿlanaʾ* (Ezk 42.10, 46.2?);

> *men* (Ezk 40.10, 20, 47.2aβ);

> *merd̲aʾ* (Gn 30.36, 31.23, Ex 5.3, 8.23, Nu 10.33 [2x], 11.31 [2x], 33.8, Dt 1.2, 1Kg 19.4, 2Kg 3.9);

> *set̲raʾ* (Is 53.6);

> *ʿbad̲aʾ* (Sir 10.26, 32.22);

> *ʿawlaʾ* (Ezk 33.11bα);

> *pālšat̲ ʾurḥaʾ* (Gn 38.14 [pl for s], 21 [pl for s]);

> *ruḥaʾ* (Jr 32.39);

> *reʿyanaʾ* (Ps 1.1);

> *šbilaʾ* (Ps 49.14, 128.1, Pr 7.8, Pr 16.25b, Sir 5.9 [or the translation of שביל in MS C]);

> *šappir* (?Sir 37.7);

> *t̲humaʾ* (1Sm 6.12aβ);

> *tarʿaʾ* (2Sm 15.2);

> *tarʿit̲aʾ* (Pr 23.19);

> feminine pronominal suffix (Ezk 44.3bβ).

No translation equivalent: Josh 1.8, 5.7, 22.5, Jdg 19.9, Jr 31.21, Ezk 33.9a, 40.27b, 41.12, 47.2b, Ru 1.7, 2Ch 11.17.

Large omission in text: Ezk 42.7 (haplography), Jb 38.25, Sir 7.17 (doublet not in MS C), 11.34c, 32.21a (doublet not in MSS E, F), 42.3.

Targum

The Pentateuch (TgO, Neo and PsJ):

אׁרְחָ(ׁי)א (Gn 3.24 [O], 6.12 [Neo has pl for s], 16.7, 18.19, 19.2, 31, 24.21, 27, 40, 42, 48, 56, 28.20, 30.36 [Neo], 31.23 [Neo], 35, 32.2, 33.16, 35.3, 19,

38.14 [O, Neo], 16, 21, 42.25, 38, 45.21, 23, 24, 48.7 [2x], 49.17 [O], Ex 3.18
[Neo?], 4.24, 8.23 [Neo], 13.17, 18, 21, 18.8, 20, 23.20 [O, PsJ], 32.8, 33.3, 13
[Neo has pl for s], Lv 26.22, Nu 9.10, 13, 10.33a [Neo], 11.31aα [Neo], 14.25,
20.17, 21.1, 4a [O, Neo], 4b, 22, 33, 22.22 [O, Neo], 23aα [O, Neo], 23aβ, 23b
[O, Neo], 26, 31 [O, Neo], 32, 34, 24.25 [O, PsJ], Dt 1.2 [O, PsJ], 19, 22, 31,
33 [2x], 40, 2.1, 8a [O, Neo], 8b, 27aα, 27aβ [O, Neo], 3.1, 5.33, 6.7, 8.2, 6,
9.12, 16, 10.12, 11.19, 22, 28 [O, NeoMg, PsJ], 30, 13.6, 14.24, 17.16, 19.3, 6,
9, 22.4, 6 [O, Neo], 23.5, 24.9, 25.17, 18, 26.17, 27.18, 28.7 [2x], 9, 25 [2x],
29, 68, 30.16, 31.29, 32.4);

אֻ(ו)רְחָא כְּבִישׁ (Dt 2.27aβ [PsJ]);

אֻ(ו)רְחָא מֵהֲלַךְ (Ex 5.3 [Neo], Nu 33.8 [Neo], Dt 1.2 [Neo]);

אֻ(י)סְרָטָא (PsJ: Nu 22.22, 23aα, 23b, 31, Dt 22.6);

אַרְעָא (Gn 49.17 [Neo], Ex 23.20 [Neo]);

מֵהֲלַךְ (Gn 30.36 [O, PsJ], 31.23 [O, PsJ], Ex 3.18 [O, PsJ], 5.3 [O, PsJ],
8.23 [O, PsJ], Nu 10.33a [O, PsJ], 33b [O, Neo, PsJ], 11.31aα [O, PsJ], 11.31aβ
[O, NeoMg], 21.4a [PsJ], 33.8 [O, PsJ]);

אֲתְרָא (Nu 24.25 [Neo]);

פָּרְשׁוּת אֻ(ו)רְחָא (PsJ: Gn 38.14, 49.17, Nu 24.25 [doublet]);

שְׁבִילֵי אֻ(ו)רְחָא (Gn 3.24 [PsJ]);

No translation equivalent: Gn 3.24 (Neo), Dt 2.8a (PsJ).

Prophets and Writings (TgPro and TgHag):

אֻ(ו)רְחָא (Josh 1.8 [pl for s], 2.7, 16, 22, 3.4 [2x], 5.4, 5, 7, 8.15, 9.11, 13,
10.10, 12.3, 22.5, 23.14, 24.17, Jdg 2.17, 19, 22 [pl for s], 4.9, 5.10 [pl for s],
8.11, 9.25, 37, 17.8, 18.5, 6, 26, 19.9, 27, 20.42, 1Sm 1.18, 4.13, 6.9, 6.12 [2x],
8.3 [pl as Qere], 5, 9.6, 8, 12.23, 13.17, 18 [2x], 15.2, 18, 20, 17.52, 18.14,
21.6, 24.4, 8, 20, 25.12, 26.3, 25, 28.22, 30.2, 2Sm 2.24, 4.7, 11.10, 13.30, 34,
15.2, 23, 16.13, 22.22, 31, 33, 1Kg 1.49, 2.2, 3, 4, 3.14, 8.25, 32, 36, 39, 44
[2x], 48, 58, 11.29, 33, 38, 13.9, 10 [2x], 12 [2x], 17, 24 [2x], 25, 26, 28, 33,
15.26, 34, 16.2, 19, 26, 18.6 [2x], 7, 27, 43, 19.7, 15, 20.38, 22.43, 53 [3x],
2Kg 2.23, 3.8 [2x], 20, 6.19, 7.15, 8.18, 27, 9.27, 10.12, 11.16, 19, 16.3, 17.13,
19.28, 33, 21.21, 22, 22.2, 25.4 [2x], Is 2.3, 3.12, 8.11, 10.24, 26, 30.11, 21,
35.8 [3x], 37.29, 34, 40.3, 14, 27, 42.16, 24, 43.16, 19, 45.13, 48.15, 17, 49.9,
11, 51.10, 53.6, 55.7, 8 [2x], 9 [2x], 56.11, 57.10 [pl for s], 14 [2x], 18, 58.2, 13
[s for pl], 59.8, 62.10, 63.17, 64.4, 65.2, 66.3, Jr 2.17, 23bα [pl for s], 23bβ, 33a
[pl for s], 33b, 36 [pl for s], 3.2, 13, 21 [pl for s], 4.11, 18 [pl for s], 5.4, 5, 6.16
[2x], 25, 27, 7.3 [s for pl], 5, 23, 10.2 [pl for s], 23, 12.1 [pl for s], 12.16, 15.17,
16.17, 17.10 [pl as Qere], 18.11 [2x], 15a, 15b [pl for s], 21.8 [2x], 22.21, 23.12
[pl for s], 22 [pl for s], 25.5, 26.3, 13, 28.11, 31.9, 21, 32.19 [2x], 39, 35.15,
36.3, 7, 39.4 [2x], 42.3, 48.19, 50.5, 52.7 [2x], Ezk 3.18, 19, 7.3, 4, 8, 9, 27,
9.2, 10, 11.21, 13.22, 14.22, 23, 27, 43, 47 [2x], 61, 18.25 [3x, all pl], 29 [3x,
all pl], 30, 20.30, 43, 44, 21.2, 24 [2x], 25, 26aβ, 22.31, 23.13, 31, 24.14, 28.15,
33.8, 9 [2x], 11 [2x], 17a, 17b [pl for s], 20a [pl for s], 20b, 36.17bα [pl for s],
17bβ, 19 [pl for s], 31, 32, 40.44bβ, 42.4, 7, 11aα, 12 [3x], 43.2, 44.3 [2x],
46.2, 8b, 47.2aγ, 15, 48.1, Ho 2.8 [pl for s], 4.9, 6.9, 9.8, 10.13 [pl for s], 12.3,
14.10, Jl 2.7 [s for pl], Am 4.10, Jn 3.8, 10 [pl for s], Mc 4.2, Nah 2.2 [pl for s],
Hg 1.5, 7, Zc 1.4, 6, 3.7, Ml 2.8, 9, 3.1, Ps 1.1 [pl for s], 6a, 6b [pl for s], 2.12,

5.9 [pl for s], 10.5 [pl as Qere], 18.22, 31 [pl for s], 33, 25.4, 8, 9, 12, 27.11 [pl for s], 32.8, 35.6 [pl for s], 36.5, 37.5 [pl for s], 7, 14 23 [pl for s], 34, 39.2 [s for pl], 49.14 [pl for s], 50.23, 51.15, 67.3, 77.14 [pl for s], 20, 80.13, 81.14, 85.14, 86.11 [pl for s], 89.42, 91.11, 95.10 [s for pl], 101.2, 6, 102.24, 103.7, 107.4, 7, 17, 40, 110.7, 119.1, 3, 5, 14, 26 [s for pl], 27, 29, 30, 32, 33, 59 [s for pl], 168, 128.1, 139.3, 24 [2x], 143.8, 145.17, 146.9, Jb 3.23, 4.6, 6.18, 8.19, 12.24, 13.15, 17.9, 19.12 [pl for s], 21.14, 29, 31, 22.3, 28, 23.10, 11 [pl for s], 24.4, 13, 23, 26.14 [pl as Qere], 28.23, 29.25, 31.4, 7, 34.21, 27, 36.23, 38.19, 24, 25, Pr 1.15, 31 [pl for s], 2.8 [pl for s], 12, 13, 20 [pl for s], 3.6, 3.17 [2x], 23 [pl for s], 31, 4.11 [pl for s], 14, 19, 26, 5.8, 21, 6.6, 23, 7.8, 19, 25, 27, 8.2, 13, 32, 9.6, 15, 10.9, 29, 11.5 [according to Díez Merino; Lagarde: אנון], 20 [MS Z; MS Ee 5.9: omits] 12.15, 26, 28, 13.6 [pl for s], 15, 14.2, 8, 12a, 12 [s for pl], 14, 15.9, 19, 16.2, 7, 9 [pl for s], 17, 25 [2x], 29, 31, 19.3 [pl for s], 16, 20.24 [pl for s], 21.2 [pl for s], 8, 16, 29 [s as Qere], 22.5, 6, 23.19, 26, 26.13, 28.6, 10, 18, 29.27 [pl for s], 30.19 [4x], 20, 31.3, Ru 1.7, Ec 10.3 [pl for s], 11.9, 12.5, La 1.4, 12, 2.15, 3.9 [s for pl], 11 [s for pl], 40 [s for pl], 2Ch 6.16 [pl for s], 23, 27, 30, 31, 34 [2x], 7.14, 11.17, 13.22, 17.3, 6, 20.32, 21.6, 12 [2x], 21.13, 22.3, 27.6, 7, 28.2, 26, 34.2);

ב + אֻ(וֹ)רְחָא (2Sm 18.23, Ezk 40.10, 24aα, 27 [2x], 32, 42.10, 15bα, 43.4a, 44.1, 4, 46.9 [5x], 47.2a [2x]);

ל + אֻ(וֹ)רְחָא (Ezk 8.5 [2x], 40.6, 20, 22, 24aβ, 44bα, 45, 46, 41.11, 12, 42.1 [= הַדֶּרֶךְ דֶּרֶךְ], 11aβ, 12aα, 15bβ, 43.1, 4b);

לְאַפֵּי אֹרְחָא (2Ch 6.38);

אֻ(וֹ)סְרָטָא (Jb 38.25);

בְּרִיתָא (?Pr 8.22);

גְּבוּרָה (?Is 8.23);

דבר (?Nah 1.3, Ps 119.37);

דִּין (?Am 2.7);

כְּבִישׁ (Ps 138.5);

מַהֲלַךְ (1Kg 19.4, 2Kg 3.9, Jb 28.26);

מֵוֹתִיה (Is 15.5);

נִימוֹסִי (Am 8.14);

פָּרְשׁוּת אֻ(וֹ)רְחָא (Ezk 16.25, 31, 21.26a);

שְׁבִילָא (Ho 13.7, Jb 24.18);

שָׁעֲתָא (?2Ch 18.23);

בָּתַר הַרְהוּר (Is 57.17);

No translation equivalent: Jr 2.18 (2x).
Large omission in text: Ru 1.7.

Vulgate

ad (Ezk 40.22, 43.4b);
ad viam (Ezk 40.46, 44.1, 47.2aβ);
ambulo (Pr 11.20);
bivium (Gn 38.21, Ezk 21.26a [=21.21a, for אִם הַדֶּרֶךְ]);
bivium itineris quod ducit (Gn 38.14);
consiliarius (Sir 37.7 [=8, for יועץ דרך]);
consuetudo (Gn 31.35);

contra (1Kg 18.43);

cor (?Ps 95.10 [=Vg 94.10]);

devius (Ps 107.40 [=106.40]);

directus (Jr 31.21);

duceo ad (Pr 14.12b, 16.25b);

ea (Josh 3.4bβ);

fines vitae (46.20);

frustra (Jb 12.24 [= לא דרך]);

gressus (Jb 6.18 [pl for s], Pr 19.3 [pl for s]);

ibo (Jb 29.25);

in directum (1Sm 6.12aα);

introitus (2Sm 15.2);

iter (Gn 24.21, 27, 48, 32.2 [=Vg 32.1], 33.16, 35.3, 45.21, 23, 48.7a, Ex 4.24, 18.8, Nu 9.13, 11.31, 21.4b, 22.23b, Dt 1.22, 33b, 3.1, 6.7, 8.2, 27.18, Jdg 17.8, 18.5, 26, 1Sm 13.18b, 24.8, 28.22, 30.2, 2Sm 2.24, 13.30, 34, 1Kg 13.10aβ, 24b, 18.27, Is 57.14 [see **A.3**], Jr 18.15b, Pr 12.26, 28, 13.15, 15.19, 28.6, Neh 9.19b, 2Ch 21.13);

lapis (32.20b);

mores (Gn 19.31);

opus (2Ch 27.7, 28.26, Sir 10.6, 26, 32.22 [=27]);

per viam (Ezk 42.12, 15a, 43.4a, 44.4, 46.2, 8a, 9 [4x]);

per viam quae ducit ad (Nu 21.4, Josh 2.7, 2Kg 25.4b);

per viam quae ducit (Josh 12.3, 1Sm 6.12aβ, Jr 52.7);

per (Nu 10.33b, 2Kg 3.8b, 46.9, 47.2aα);

posterus (?Sir 3.31 [=3.34]);

quae ducit ad (Dt 2.1);

quae respiciebat ad (Ezk 40.24aβ);

quae se offerebant vianti (1Sm 24.4);

semita (Nu 22.23c, Is 57.14? [see A.3], La 3.11);

spatium itineris (Gn 30.36);

superbia (?Sir 13.1);

terra (?Gn 42.38);

turbor (Sir 11.34c [=11.36b]);

via (Gn 3.24, 6.12, 16.7, 18.19, 19.2, 24.40, 42, 56, 28.20, 35.19, 42.25, 45.24, 48.7b, 49.17, Ex 3.18, 5.3, 8.27, 13.17, 18, 21, 18.20, 23.20, 32.8, 33.3, 13, Lv 26.22, Nu 9.10, 10.33a, 21.1, 22, 33, 22.22, 23a, 31, 32, 24.25, Dt 1.2, 19, 33a, 40, 2.8, 27 [1x for Heb 2x], 5.33, 8.6, 9.12, 16, 10.12, 11.19, 22, 28, 30, 13.6 [=Vg 13.5], 14.24, 17.16, 19.3, 6, 9, 22.4 , 6, 23.5 [=23.4], 24.9, 25.17, 26.17, 28.7bα, 9, 25a, 29, 68, 30.16, 31.29, 32.4, Josh 1.8, 2.16, 22, 3.4bα, 5.4, 7, 8.15, 9.11, 13, 10.10, 22.5, 23.14, 24.17, Jdg 2.17, 19, 22, 5.10, 8.11, 37, 18.6, 19.27, 20.42, 1Sm 1.18, 4.13, 6.9, 8.3 [pl as Qere], 5, 9.6, 8, 12.23, 13.17, 18a, 15.2, 18, 20, 17.52, 18.14, 21.6 [=Vg 21.5], 24.20, 25.12, 26.3, 25, 2Sm 4.7, 11.10, 15.23, 16.13, 18.23, 22.22, 31, 33, 1Kg 1.49, 2.2, 3, 4, 3.14, 8.25, 32, 36, 39, 44 [2x], 48, 58, 11.29, 33, 38, 13.9, 10aα, 12 [2x], 17, 24a, 25, 26, 28, 33, 15.26, 34, 16.2, 19, 26, 18.6 [2x], 7, 19.4, 7, 15, 20.38, 22.43, 53 [2x for Heb 3x], 2Kg 2.23, 3.8a, 9, 20, 6.19, 7.15, 8.18 [pl for s], 27 [pl for s], 9.27, 10.12, 11.16, 19, 16.3, 17.13, 19.28, 33, 21.21, 22, 22.2 [pl for s], 25.4a, Is 2.3,

3.12, 8.11, 23 [=Vg 9.1], 10.24, 26, 15.5, 30.11, 21, 35.8 [3x], 37.29, 34, 40.3, 14, 27, 42.16, 24, 43.16, 19, 45.13, 48.15, 17, 49.9, 11, 51.10, 53.6, 55.7, 8 [2x], 9 [2x], 56.11, 57.10, 14 [2x, see A.4], 17, 18, 58.2, 13, 59.8, 62.10, 63.17, 64.4 [=64.5], 65.2, 66.3, Jr 2.17, 18 [2x], 23 [pl for s], 23, 33[2x], 36 [pl for s], 3.2, 13, 21, 4.11 [2x for Heb 1x, pl for s], 18 [pl for s], 5.4, 5, 6.16 [2x], 25, 27, 7.3, 5, 23, 10.2 [pl for s], 23, 12.1, 12.16, 15.7, 16.17, 17.10 [s as Ketiv], 18.11 [2x], 15a, 21.8 [2x], 22.21, 23.12, 22, 25.5, 26.3, 26.13, 31.9, 32.19 [2x], 39, 35.15, 36.3, 7, 39.4 [2x], 42.3, 48.19, 50.5, 52.7a, Ezk 3.18, 19, 7.3, 4, 8, 9, 27, 8.5 [2x], 9.2, 10, 11.21, 13.22, 14.22, 23, 16.25, 27, 31, 43 [pl for s], 47 [2x], 61, 18.23, 25 [3x], 29 [3x], 30, 20.30, 43, 44, 21.2 [=20.46], 21.24 [=21.19, 2x], 25 [=20], 26b [=21b], 22.31, 23.13, 31, 24.14, 28.15, 33.8, 9a [pl for s], 9b, 11 [2x], 17 [2x], 20 [2x], 36.17bα [pl for s], 17bβ, 19 [pl for s], 31, 32, 40.6, 10, 20, 24aα, 27 [2x], 32, 44 [2x], 45, 42.4, 7, 10, 11 [2x], 12 [2x], 15b, 43.1, 2, 44.3, 46.8b, 47.2b, 15, 48.1, Ho 2.8 [=2.6], 4.9, 6.9, 9.8, 10.13 [pl for s], 12.3 [=12.2], 13.7, 14.10, Jl 2.7, Am 2.7, 4.10, 8.14, Jn 3.8, 10, Mc 4.2, Nah 1.3, 2.2 [=2.1], Hg 1.5, 7, Zc 1.4, 6, 3.7, Ml 2.8, 9, 3.1, Ps 1.1, 6a, 2.12, 5.9 [=5.8], 10.5 [=9.25, pl as Qere], 18.22 [=17.22], 31, 33, 25.4 [=24.4], 8, 9, 12, 27.11 [=26.11], 32.8 [=31.8], 35.6 [=34.6], 36.5 [=35.5], 37.5 [=36.5], 7, 14, 23, 34, 39.2 [=38.2], 49.14 [=48.14], 51.15 [=50.15], 67.3 [=66.3], 77.14 [=76.14], 20, 80.13 [=79.13], 81.14 [=80.14], 85.14 [=84.14], 86.11 [=85.11], 89.42 [=88.42], 91.11 [=90.11], 101.2 [=100.2], 6, 102.24 [=101.24], 103.7 [=102.7], 107.4 [=106.4], 7, 17, 110.7 [=109.7], 119.1 [=118.1], 3, 5, 14, 26, 27, 29, 30, 32, 33, 37, 59, 168, 128.1 [=127.1], 138.5 [=137.5], 139.3 [=138.4], 24 [2x], 143.8 [=142.8], 145.17 [=144.17], 146.9 [=145.9], Jb 3.23, 4.6, 8.19, 13.15, 17.9, 19.12, 21.14, 31, 22.3 [s for pl], 28, 23.10, 11, 24.4, 13, 18, 23, 26.14 [pl as Qere], 28.23, 26, 31.4, 7, 21, 27, 36.23 [pl for s], 38.19, 24, 25, 40.19 [=40.14], Pr 1.31 [pl for s], 2.8 [pl for s], 12, 13, 20, 3.6, 3.17 [2x], 23, 31, 4.11, 14, 19, 26, 5.8, 21, 6.6, 23, 7.8, 19, 25, 27, 8.2, 13, 22 [pl for s], 32, 9.6 [pl for s], 15, 10.9, 29, 11.5, 12.15, 13.6, 14.2 [s for pl], 8, 12a, 14, 15.9, 16.2, 7, 9, 17, 25a, 29, 31 [pl for s], 19.16, 20.24, 21.2, 8, 16, 29 [s as Qere], 22.5, 6, 23.19, 26, 26.13, 28.10, 18, 29.27, 30.19 [4x], 20, 31.3, Ru 1.7, Ec 10.3, 11.5, 9, 12.5, La 1.4, 12, 2.15, 3.9, 40, Ezr 8.21, 22, 31, Neh 9.12, 19a, 2Ch 6.16 [pl for s], 23, 27, 30, 31, 34 [2x], 38, 7.14, 11.17 [pl for s], 13.22, 17.3, 6, 18.23, 20.32, 21.6 [pl for s], 12 [2x], 22.3, 27.6, 28.2, 34.2, Sir 5.9 [or the translation of שביל in MS C], 14.21, [=14.23], 16.20 [=21], 32.20a [=25a], 33.11, 37.9 [=10], 48.22 [=25]);

    via respiciens ad (Ezk 42.1, 12);

    viator (Jb 21.29 [= עֹבְרֵי דֶרֶךְ], Sir 42.3 [pl for s]);

    vicus (Jdg 4.9).

    No translation equivalent: Gn 31.23, 38.16, Nu 11.31bβ, 22.26, 34, 33.8, Dt 25.18, 28.7bβ, 25b, Jdg 19.9, Pr 1.15, Sir 51.15.

    Large omission in text: Nu 14.25 (=Vg 14.26), 20.17 (=20.18), Josh 5.5, Jr 28.11, Sir 7.17 (doublet), 11.14, 34a, 32.21a, 21c.

    Unclear: Josh 9.25, Ps 50.23 (=49.23).

כִּסֵּא

LXX

θρόνος 'throne' Gn 41.40, Ex 11.5; 12.29; Dt 17.18 in some MSS; Jdg 3.20 A, B; 1Sm 2.8; 2Sm 3.10; 7.13,16; 14.9; 1Kg 1.13,17,20,24,27,30,35, 37², 46, 47²,48; 2.4,12,19², 24,33,45; 3.6; 5.19; (pl) 7.7 (LXX 7.44); 8.20,25; 9.5 (1st); 10.9,18,19²;16.11;22.10,19; 2Kg 10.3,30; 11.19;13.13;15.12; 25.28²-2nd in pl); Is 6.1; 9.6; 14.9,13; 16.5; 22.23; 66.1; Jr 1.15; 3.17; 13.13 (pl MS A); 14.21; 17.12,25;22.2,4,30; Jr 29.16 (sub *); 33.17,21 (both sub *); 36(LXX 43).30; 43(50).10; 49.38(LXX 25.18); 52.32²; Ezk 1.26²; 10.1; 26.16; 43.7; Jn 3.6; Hg 2.22 (pl); Zc 6.13 (1st); Ps 9.5,8; 45(44).7; 47(46).9; 89(88).5,15,30,37, 45; 93(92).2; 94(93).20; 97(96).2; 103(102).19; 122(121).5²; 132(131).11,12; Pr 20.8,28; 25.5; 29.14, Lm 5.19, Jb 26.9 (sub *); 36.7 (sub *), Neh 3.7 (LXX Esd 13.7, some MSS only), Est A 1.2 (2.2); A 3.1 (4.1), A 5.1 (6.4(6)): Est LXX 5.1 (xv.6(9)), 1Ch 17.12,14; 22.10; 28.5; 29.23, 2Ch 6.10,16; 7.18²; 9.8,17,18; 18.9,18; 23.20; Sir 10.14; 40.3; 47.11.

θρόνος ἀρχῆς 'throne of rule' Pr 16.12

ἀρχή 'rule' Dt 17.18

δίφρος 'seat' Dt 17.18 doublet MS A; 1Sm 1.9; 4.13,18; 2Kg 4.10; Pr 9.14.

ἐνθρονίζω 'to enthrone' Est LXX 1.2 (= יֹשֵׁב עַל כסא)

πρωτοβαθρέω 'seat someone in front of others' Est LXX 3.1 (=כסא שִׂים מֵעַל)

ἀνὴρ ἡγούμενος 'a ruling man, leader' 1Kg 9.5 (2nd) (= אִישׁ מֵעַל כִּסֵּא)

Peshitta

kursyā ('seat, throne') throughout: for the exception, see B.1 below.

Targum

כָּרְסְיָא ('seat, throne') Jdg 3.20; 1Sm 1.9; 2.8; 4.13,18; 2Sm 3.10; 7.13; 14.9, 1Kg 1.13, 47 (1st); 2.12,19,33; 3.6; 7.7; 10.18,19 9²; 16.11; 22.10,19, 2Kg 4.10; 11.19; 13.13; 25.28²; Is 6.1; 9.6; 14.9; 16.5; 22.23; 47.1; 66.1, Jr 1.15; 13.13; 14.21; 17.12,25; 22.2,4,30; 29.16; 33.21; 36.30; 43.10; 52.32², Ezk 1.26; 10.1; 26.16, Hg 2.22, Zc 6.13², Est 1.2 (Sperber: in midrashic expansion); 3.1; 5.1; 1Ch 22.10; 28.5; 2Ch 7.18; 9.17,18²; 23.20, Jb 26.9, Ps 9.5,8; 11.4; 47.9; 89.30,37; 93.2; 94.20; 97.2; 103.19; 122.5²; 132.11,12, Pr 9.14; 16.12; 20.8,28; 25.5; 29.14.

כָּרְסֵי מַלְכוּתָא ('seat of the kingdom, royal throne': the nomen rectum is sometimes supplied where it is absent in the Hebrew) O, N, C, PJ Gn 41.40; O, N, PJ Ex 11.5 and 12.29 and Dt 17.18; 1Sm 7.16; 14.9, 1Kg 1.17,20,24,27,30, 35,37,47 (2nd),48; 2.4,24,45; 5.19; 8.20; 9.5²; 10.9, 2Kg 10.3,30; 15.12; Is 14.13, Jr 33.17; 49.38; Jn 3.6, 1Ch 17.12,14; 29.23, 2Ch 6.10,16; 9.8, Jb 36.7, Ps 89.5,45.

כָּרְסֵי יְקָרָא ('throne of glory': theological rendering) Ezk 43.7, Lm 5.19, 2Ch 18.18, Ps 45.7; 89.15.

Vulgate

(unum) solium regni 'seat of rule' Gn 41.40; *solium regni* Dt 17.18;

solium 'seat' Ex 11.5; 12.29, 1Sm 2.8, 1Kg 1.13,18,20,30,35,37,46,48; 2.4,24; 5.19(5); 7.7; 16.11; 22.10,19, 2Kg 10.3; 13.13, Is 6.1; 9.6(7); 14.9,13; 16.5; 22.23; 47.1, Jr 1.15; 3.17; 14.21; 17.12,25; 22.2,30; 29.16; 36.30; 49.38, Ezk 10.1; 43.7, Jn 3.6, Hg 2.22(23), Zc 6.13, Ps 9.5,8; 93(92).2; Pr 16.12; 20.8, Lm 5.19, Jb 26.9; 36.7, 1Ch 17.14; 22.10; 29.23, 2Ch 9.17,18; 18.9,18; 23.20.

thronus 'throne' Jdg 3.20; 2Sm 3.10; 7.13,18; 14.9, 1Kg 1.24,27,47; 2.12, 19, 33,45; 3.6; 8.20,25; 9.5; 10.9,18,19; 2Kg 10.30; 11.19; 15.12; 25.28^2; 13.13; 22.4; 33.17,21; 43.10; 52.32^2, Ezk 1.26, Ps 45(44).7; 47(46).9; 89(88).5, 15,30,37(38),45; 97(96).2; 103(102).19; 132(131).11; Pr 20.28; 25.5; 29.14, Est 1.2; 3.1; 5.1, 1Ch 17.14; 28.5, 2Ch 6.10,16; 7.18; 9.8, Sir 11.5;

sella 'chair' 1Sm 1.9; 4.13,18, 2Kg 4.10, Pr 9.14;

sedes 'seat' Is 66.1, Ezk 26.16, Ps 94(93).20; 122(121).5^2; 132(131).11; Sir 10.14(17); 40.3; 47.11(13).

INDICES

INDEX OF PASSAGES DISCUSSED IN SOME DETAIL

INDEX OF SELECT NON-HEBREW WORDS

PRINTED ON PERMANENT PAPER • IMPRIME SUR PAPIER PERMANENT • GEDRUKT OP DUURZAAM PAPIER - ISO 9706

ORIENTALISTE, KLEIN DALENSTRAAT 42, B-3020 HERENT